C000083543

CONFESSIONS OF A SHOOTING FISHING MAN

When Laurence Catlow, a 45-year-old classics master at a Cumbrian boarding school, sees a beautiful pheasant in flight, he wants to reach for his gun.

In this diary of his sporting year, he asks himself, between days on the local rivers and shoots, why this is so.

His answers are surprising, controversial and convincing. They provide an articulate response to the anti-fieldsports arguments, and he presents them in an entertaining, frank and amusing manner.

During the year, Laurence's diary records his hopes of buying some precipitous shooting ground on the Pennines, his fishing days on the Eden, Wharfe and other rivers, the arrival of a second gundog and days spent together on shoots. All this activity is interspersed with Laurence's quest for his true motives in killing what he most loves. He looks at foxhunting, vegetarianism, man as a hunter, man as created in God's image and man as a creature doomed, himself, to die.

This diary is highly topical, thought-provoking and original. Yet its tone is also very human and it comes from the pen of a true nature-lover.

LAURENCE CATLOW teaches classics at Sedbergh School in Cumbria. He also writes for various magazines, including *Trout & Salmon* and *Shooting Times*. He fishes on the Wharfe, the Eden, Driffield Beck and on the small upland brook that runs through his land. With equal enthusiasm, he also shoots pheasant and wildfowl, accompanied by friends and his gundogs. Other pleasures include food, wine, ornithology, religion and the sport of fives.

CONFESSIONS
OF A SHOOTING
FISHING MAN

Also published by Merlin Unwin Books
7 Corve Street, Ludlow, Shropshire SY8 1DB, U.K.

PRIVATE THOUGHTS FROM A SMALL SHOOT
Laurence Catlow £17.99 Hb

ONCE A FLYFISHER
Laurence Catlow £17.99 Hb

THE FAR FROM COMPLEAT ANGLER
Tom Fort £16.99 Hb

BRIGHT WATERS
Compiled by Tom Fort £25.00 Hb

TROUT & SALMON FLIES OF WALES
Moc Morgan £20.00 Hb

TROUT & SALMON FLIES OF IRELAND
Peter O'Reilly £20.00 Hb

RIVERS OF IRELAND
a flyfisher's guide, 6th edition
Peter O' Reilly £20.00 Hb

TYING FLIES WITH CDC
Leon Links £20.00 Hb

A HISTORY OF FLYFISHING
Conrad Voss Bark £25.00 Hb/£12.95 Pb

AN ANGLER FOR ALL SEASONS
the best of H.T.Sheringham £16.95 Hb

BEGINNER'S GUIDE TO FLYTYING
Chris Mann & Terry Griffiths £7.99 Hb

FALLING IN AGAIN
tales of an incorrigible angler
Chris Yates £17.99 Hb

FISHERMAN'S BEDSIDE BOOK
Compiled by BB £18.95 Hb

SHOOTING MAN'S BEDSIDE BOOK
Compiled by BB £18.95 Hb

SHRIMP AND SPEY FLIES FOR SALMON
Chris Mann and Robert Gillespie £20.00 Hb

HOOK, LINE AND THINKER
angling and ethics
Alex Schwab £20.00 Hb

CONFESSIONS
OF A SHOOTING
FISHING MAN

Laurence Catlow

Merlin Unwin Books

First published in Great Britain by Merlin Unwin Books, 1996
Reprinted 1999
Reprinted 2004

Copyright © Laurence Catlow, 1996

All rights reserved. No part of this publication may be reproduced,
stored in a retrieval system, or transmitted in any form or by any
means, electronic, mechanical, photocopying, recording or
otherwise, without the prior permission of Merlin Unwin Books.

MERLIN UNWIN BOOKS
7 Corve Street, Ludlow
Shropshire SY8 1DB, U.K.
Tel 01584 877456
Fax 01584 877457
email: books@merlinunwin.co.uk
website: www.countrybooksdirect.com

British Library Cataloguing in Publication Data
A catalogue record for this book is available from the British Library

ISBN 1-873674-244

Cover artwork by Bryan Poole
Cover design by Think Graphic Design, Ludlow
Designed and typeset by Merlin Unwin Books, Ludlow, U.K.
Printed in Great Britain by Redwood Books, Trowbridge, U.K.

Author's Preface

This diary was written for my own pleasure, to celebrate my joy in the countryside that surrounds me and my delight to be out in it with a fishing rod or with a spaniel and a shot gun. It was written for my own pleasure and satisfaction; if it gives others pleasure, then it will give me all the more satisfaction.

It was written two years ago, at a time when I sensed that many shooters and hunting men, in spite of their passionate belief in the innocent and wholesome nature of their sporting pursuits, had acknowledged that the mood of the times was against them and that their days as hunters and shooters were drawing to a close. I was troubled by the way in which they seemed to accept the imminent death of fox-hunting, and the less imminent but hardly less certain end of shooting for sport, as part of the irresistible process by which urban men were imposing their values on the traditional pattern of rural life.

I was troubled too by the evasive and unconvincing nature of the arguments produced in defence of fieldsports by those who felt themselves qualified to speak up on their behalf. And, although as a fisherman I did not feel seriously concerned for the immediate future of angling, there was a nagging suspicion that, if killing foxes and pheasants should ever be declared immoral and illegal, some rudimentary regard for equity or for intellectual consistency must eventually persuade our law-givers to a similar pronouncement concerning the killing of trout. Perhaps this was an unfounded suspicion.

I have kept a sporting diary for years, usually a bare record of fish caught and birds shot, in some years an attempt to preserve for myself something of the individual flavour of my shooting and fishing days. Two years ago I decided that the time had come for another diary of the more ambitious sort. I decided too, perhaps in response to the despondency of my shooting and hunting friends, to use it as a means of exploring my beliefs as a sportsman, in the hope that I might see more clearly why fishing and shooting are so important to me and why I have always held them, properly pursued, to be blameless activities.

This diary was not written to convert others to my way of thinking; it was written rather for my own benefit, to elucidate to myself the nature of my thoughts about killing birds and fish for pleasure. If it should happen that it turns hunt saboteurs into aspiring masters of foxhounds or shoot captains, I shall be delighted. More likely is that it will help fellow fishers and shooters to unravel a few strands of their attachment to fieldsports and may stimulate some of them to develop arguments more convincing, and perhaps more succinct, than any advanced by me.

Most of this diary is not directly concerned with the morality of killing animals. It is about the countryside and, unavoidably, it is about me. I should have liked to keep me out of it as much as possible. But it has proved very difficult to keep me out of my own diary. I think that I am probably the worst thing about my diary, and my advice to anyone who buys this book and bothers to read this preface is that, in reading what follows it, he should try to forget all about me and to concentrate instead on the fields and the woods and the riverbanks where I spend so much of my time. For, if I have managed to convey some impression, however adumbrated, of the beauty of that part of England which it is my privilege to call home, then this diary has not been written in vain.

Laurence Catlow
Sedbergh, August 1996

In Memoriam

J.C.P.G.

THE DIARY

1 February

There were torrents of rain all morning. The fells are seamed with gushing lines of water. Rivers are brown and foaming and intemperate. There are pools in every hollow of the sodden fields. For me there was no shooting. I did not even bother to go out to Brough after morning school; and so it was a wretched end of the season and not at all as it should have been.

For the pheasant season should end with a few birds bustled out of gorse and bracken by Merlin the spaniel; it should end with a few flurries of excitement, with some sadness that it is all over again, with grateful memories of the sport that has filled the last months and with intimations of spring in the longer light, the feel of the air and in the singing of a few birds.

By the end of January, there come days that are not wholly of winter, days when the sun shines with something like a waking power and the wet earth seems to breathe out a yearning to be done with doing nothing, a yearning to be busy again and growing things. Then everywhere there is a sense of aspiration. Already there are snowdrops under the trees, and already this January I have heard dunnocks singing; already robins are piping and whistling all day long. Mistle thrushes are shouting and there is a restless edge to the cawing of rooks.

1

I did go out in the end, but not to Brough and without a gun. I took Merlin to the woods at the foot of Dentdale and ran him through the rhododendrons. He gets sharper to whistle every day. He is a fine dog with a foolish master and his virtues may yet triumph over all my incompetence.

The wind was very strong, tossing crows through the sky like black rags, and the screeching of gulls was blown on the air in piercing shreds of sound. There was a brief burst of stinging hail and an even briefer patch of blue sky. I almost regretted not going to Brough and fancied there was still time to leap into the Land Rover and thunder off there. But it was no more than a fancy; it was too late, and so I went back to Sedbergh and fed the dog and did some work.

It is an odd time to start a sporting diary, with shooting over, except for rabbits and crows, and with the first trout still almost two months away. It will help to pass the time and, while I wait for the first day of the fishing season, I shall plan my next season at Brough and think about blood sports. For it is strange, I suppose, that killing birds and fish amounts for me to an act of worship, that I thank God most sincerely for the blessings of life at the end of a day's fishing or shooting. It is certainly strange; it is also true, and I should like to understand more clearly why it is so. And, if I discover that this worship of mine is a perverted form of piety, then I suppose I shall have to give it up and write a diary about my life as a schoolmaster instead. God forbid!

2 February

It hurt to be trapped in a classroom this morning, and there were bitter thoughts about yesterday's weather and today's contrast. For today, with its bright sunshine and still air, would have been perfect for a last outing in search of a pheasant or two. The sky was blue today and everywhere there were vernal stirrings.

It was half way to spring today; it was more than half way and there seemed a message on the air: that winter was old and fading fast and doomed, and that the spring of the year was just round the corner. And yet it was not warm. There was a sharp edge to the sunshine, but somehow its light was not a winter light. Starlings were sitting in the bright branches, making chortling and gurgling and whistling noises. From every tree the chiming of tits rang confidently through the air and for the first time I heard a chaffinch rehearsing its spring song. I took Merlin for a gunless walk, trying in vain to find a rabbit for him to flush and trying to find words to define the quality of late winter sunshine. But appropriate words were as elusive as rabbits. February sunshine is different from bright days in December. It is just different.

3 February

There was no longing to be outside today. The wind was howling through the sky and tearing through the trees, snapping off great branches and tossing them on the air like strands of dried grass. Wet snow came slapping against the panes and every window in my classroom whistled and moaned. As I gazed through them disconsolately, sleet went sweeping over the fields in white and swirling sheets. It will be lying deep over the fells now and my pheasants at Brough will have a cold night of it. If their thoughts were turning to love, they will have turned back to food and shelter. My thoughts at the moment are centred upon whisky and a warm fire.

4 February

The sun is shining and old men have come out onto the streets to talk of their green days. On the hills the snow has almost gone. The top of Baugh Fell is just white, shining at the sky like a man's bald patch. The air is cool but lively and, as I walked Merlin before school this morning, a chaffinch began its song and then thought better of it. Then it began again and got the whole way through and managed the

3

complete performance a second time. Before long it will be so like spring that I shall start cursing mortality.

9 February

Winter is old and feeble and so am I. On Sunday I went to Durham to play fives, an obscure game of which I am inordinately fond and for which I never had much aptitude. It is not unlike squash, except that the ball is hard and you hit it with gloved hands, both of them. And since the ball is hard it sometimes hurts, and this recommends fives to public schoolmasters, who believe, of course, that pain is character-building. And, because it is a doubles as well as a singles game, there is just a whiff of teamwork about it; and we public schoolmasters dote on teamwork. Anyway, whatever moral virtues fives may promote, I love the game. I was never much good at it and I am getting worse fast.

I drove home on Sunday, with no trophies in the back of the Land Rover, but in the sure knowledge that I had caught a cold and with a brooding sense of decrepitude. Once I got home I was so stiff that sitting down and then standing up again were a creaking discomfort, and it hurts in the mind to acknowledge the signs of physical decay.

It is worse for the single and the childless for we have no companion in decline and there is no waxing flesh and bone close enough to us to compensate for the waning of our own bodies. It comes in fits and starts, this preoccupation with progressive enfeeblement. It was particularly strong yesterday, as I blew my nose until the skin was torn and raw, as my eyes streamed and turned red and looked like a drunkard's eyes, as my throat rasped and grated and complained. I looked at myself in the mirror and was disgusted by what I saw; and my teeth are dropping out and my eyebrows are like unclipped hedges and there is hair sprouting out of both ears. And the worst of it is that I am only 44. What on earth will it be like in another ten years?

Today was much better. I went out to Brough and took down hoppers and filled those I have left hanging to keep birds on my shoot. There were more pheasants to be seen than there have been for weeks past. I suppose it is three weeks with no shooting that has brought them back, which makes me think that next season I should perhaps harry them less frequently and see if I end up with more of them in the bag. But fifty birds for the season just past amounts to success; it is exactly 40 per cent of the 125 released and it was only the second season that I have shot the place. I am sure that I can improve on 40 per cent; and there are plans for strips of kale and for other things to sort out before long.

I love my shoot and loathe the thought of losing it. It looked very beautiful this afternoon, with its miniature stands of firs and larches and its steep banks of gorse. There were catkins shaking in the pale and windy sunshine. And Merlin flushed pheasants and came back to the whistle without chasing them and without asserting his independence in the deep and tangled temptations of the gorse. And it is very pleasant, after the end of a season's shooting, to watch without the onset of predatory urges, pheasants flying, to watch them with admiration and with hopes of eggs and chicks to come and with a whole half year ahead of you before they turn again into objects of desire.

I enjoyed this afternoon. The gentle exercise was good for my old muscles; the bracing air was good for my cold and I cannot have blown my nose more than twice. I came home quite at peace with a life already more than half-way towards the grave. Tomorrow I shall play fives. Now I shall mark some examination scripts. In an hour and a half I shall go to the pub and drink three pints of bitter beer.

10 February

The last lingering traces of my cold had fled by this morning. I was in tune with the chaste sunshine and the singing birds. Chaffinches are

5

proclaiming themselves everywhere now and song thrushes have begun to explore the possibilities of repetition. At midday there was a charm of greenfinches, trilling and whistling in the bushes beneath my classroom. I could hear then whenever I paused in my vain attempts to explain the difference between pronouns and adjectives.

I was in my ageing-pedagogue-despairing-over-the-incorrigible-ignorance-of-modern-youth mood. I am in it a lot and it should probably be complemented by a gown and perhaps even a mortar board. There was good reason for my mood today, for I was more than once assured that 'they' is an adjective; and it did no good to point out that we never say of someone that he is a generous and 'they' person. It hurt, when I asked a boy if 'his' was an adjective or a pronoun, to see the hunted look in his eyes and to know that, even if he came up with the right answer, it would be no more than a desperate guess. 'Why is it', I intoned dolefully, 'that boys can no longer recognise simple parts of speech?' 'And what on earth,' I muttered under my breath, 'does the modern English master impart to his charges?'

We classicists enjoy our pedantic indulgences, but there are times when teaching Latin seems an impossible aspiration. Those greenfinches were a very welcome diversion. It also amused me to watch a crow splashing droppings onto the headmaster's office.

Different robins sing differently. There are, of course, those broad similarities that make the song of every robin unmistakably robin-like. It seems a song so laden with the sadness of mortal life that you can scarcely believe that, to an audience of robins, it throbs with virile aggression and warns potential interlopers to fly elsewhere. It seems a song so sunk into introspection that its singer has lost all awareness of any presence in creation but that of his own melancholy thoughts.

I say so much as a general observation on the singing of robins. But individual robins interpret the inherited theme in their own way.

There was one this morning that sang, to put it pretentiously, like late Mozart, with a serenity of sadness; there was one just before lunch that sang a heavier song and sounded more like Brahms. There was another robin this afternoon, perched somewhere in the beeches around the fives courts, and this one seemed almost cheerful. But perhaps it was just me, flushed with health and victory, convinced that Winchester fives (the most obscure variant of this obscurest of games) is the best game in the world and that I, at the age of 44, am still one of its finest exponents. On Sunday, if all goes to plan, I shall lay a hedge.

12 February

Half term has come, with the pleasure of lying late in bed. It is a fine thing to be warm and supine and semi-conscious, harassed by no more gnawing thoughts than a vague awareness that tea will not make itself unless you first plug in the kettle. There comes a time, of course, when guilt sets in and continued sloth seems a waste of the day's opportunities. This usually happens to me at about half-past nine, although it did not get me from bed this morning until shortly after ten. It was because I had started thinking about my shoot at Brough and the prospect of buying it, and how High Park, for that is what it is called, would then be mine by right and not by favour, mine until I die.

I could fence off Blackberry Hill and dig a flight pond in the meadow, I could plant trees and strips of kale all over the place and spend long days there feeling proprietorial. I could even join the Country Landowners' Association and put a sticker proclaiming my new status on the back window of the Land Rover. The possibilities are endless. The fact is that Mr. G. seems keen to sell, that I am sick with longing to buy his land and that I have the money he wants for it. I suppose it is madness to buy 65 acres of rough grazing and woodland when I do not own a house. It is the madness of the wise and I am more than happy for the world to think me crazy.

For my own part, I think that the world, as represented by almost all politicians, animals' rights activists, the Children Act, most head-masters, modern popular music, the European Community, strident homosexuals, feminists screaming about their right to murder the unborn, town-dwellers ranting about no one's right to murder foxes, liberals simpering about everybody's right to do virtually anything (except, of course, to hunt foxes or to disapprove of sin) - I think that the world, as represented by such people and such convictions and such institutions, not to mention tabloid newspapers, pornographic magazines, the irresistible enfeeblement of our language, the anti-smoking lobby, the views of most men with beards, the almost universal contempt for self-restraint and chastity as ideals tantamount to a perversion, the absurd assumption that all values are relative, the pervading and pernicious sensuality that taints the air like a miasma and which makes men and women think cheaply of each other and of their own bodies; I think that all these abhorrences make the modern world a disgusting, demented and insufferably tedious place. Which is, in fact, another good reason for buying sixty-odd acres of land on the edge of the Pennines, for rearing and shooting pheasants there and for walking my boundaries thinking reactionary thoughts.

I enjoy intemperate rhetoric for its own sake and it is for others to judge how much of what I have just written is seriously intended. Most of it is. But do not think that I am a misanthropist. My best friends are all human beings and I agree with Doctor Johnson that a tavern stool is the very throne of human felicity. I crave company as a drunkard craves drink. I also love solitude, and I love it for hours on end, whether walking or fishing or just sitting in a chair; but I love it only when I know that the end of it will be a table with someone else there, or a bar with easy talk to season the tang of bitter beer. I find eating alone depressing beyond words and I like pubs only when I have someone to share them with. This is all because I like people; and it is because I like people, and think that each one of us is precious beyond measure, that I hate so much of what today's orthodoxy holds sacred.

8

I rather think that it is time I changed the subject.

I was very pleased with the dog Merlin this afternoon. We went to the woods together and he plunged into brambles and plunged out again whenever I called him; and, whenever I blew the stop note on the whistle, he froze like a statue, but like a statue with miraculously moving parts: one with a thrashing tail and a lolling tongue. And then he would gaze at me in silent longing to be busy and questing again.

There was a blue sky above the larches, a very pale blue sky, a sky more of winter than of spring, and there was no enlivening feel to the air. There were tits making noises in the tops of the trees, and the finches round the house spent the whole day talking to each other. But these were scarcely spring sounds. It is freezing fast now and they talk of snow for the next days. I shall be tempted to lie abed again tomorrow, for the hedge-laying has had to be postponed.

13 February

It was a quarter past ten when at last I forced myself from bed. Diaries of life in the country should, I suppose, be full of early risings and vigorous activity before breakfast. This one will be an exception, although I may manage a dawn or two when my pheasants arrive in August. But I had better confess that there will be no morning flights in these pages, no prose poems in praise of sunrise over the mudflats. And this will not be the result merely of indolence. It is also because morning flight is the wrong way round. I love waiting for duck in the evening, especially early in the season when soft air and the warm half-light turn lying by a pond into a form of self-indulgence. In later months it becomes a a test of endurance, but in September it is still a sport for easy livers.

The coming of darkness is very slow. It begins to gather in the angles of walls; sharp perceptions turn slowly into less distinct and dimmer forms. But this all happens so gradually that you wonder if it will ever be night, for the sky is still filled with what seems an invincible brightness. Crows flap raucously into the trees; owls begin to hoot; the barn across the pasture sinks into the thickening light and turns black. You realise that the processes of nature have not been arrested and that the night will come; it is time for the first rush of wings.

The whistling of mallards' wings is unmistakable, although straining and hopeful ears still try to persuade themselves that they can catch the sound of approaching duck in sighing rushes and whispering leaves and in the breathy noises that the wind makes in dry-stone walls. But the real sound is not like these, which are drifting, indeterminate and pulseless sounds, wandering aimlessly through the night and dying away imperceptibly. The true sound is a sound of muscle and sinew, regular, purposeful, and its strong rhythm charges the dark air with sudden excitement, until it turns into a brief vision of outstretched necks, of beating or cupped wings and of webbed feet thrusting forwards.

Two shots ring out and a shape plunges from the sky. Merlin leaps the wall and returns within seconds, carrying a drake. And then a brief waiting; and then the sound again and the loud shot and the swift retrieve. Soon it is over and I am walking back across the fields, enfolded by the comfortable intimacy of September darkness. For sport has ended with the ending of the day, with the lighting of lamps, and that is as it should be. It is wrong to start in darkness and to finish with the coming of light, to be spied out and exposed by the sun and then tramp back to the busy tedium of working life. It is far better to be enveloped by shadows, to sink into the darkness and to think, when it is all over, that it is time now for the quiet things of evening, for food and company and beer.

I am a flighter of evening duck, dreaming of the pleasures of autumn sport on a cold February afternoon. It is bitter cold now, with a sharp piercing wind buffeting the dry and tangled stems of the clematis outside the window. It is a lean and lifeless wind blowing from winter; it is not blowing with the vital cold of a spring wind. And the sky is leaden and makes everything beneath it look dull.

But it is part of the pleasure of February that it keeps you guessing, that one day stands on the threshold of spring, while the next takes you back to December. And so one day brings winter pleasures, the pleasure of defying the wind and finding beauty in withered and faded things, while the next is quickened by a restless impulse of eager life. I pity people who spend these weeks abroad in warm places; for how can you love the true spring of the year, when at last it comes, if you were not around to witness the harsh struggle that brought it to birth?

14 February

When men still believed in God there was no questioning the morality of fieldsports. For then we possessed souls, being creatures made in the image of our creator. Animals did not have souls and had been put into the world to serve the needs of man. They were trapped and netted for food. They were hunted for the glory of the chase and that was that. There were individuals, of course, who felt a special sense of kinship with animals; there was, for example, St. Francis of Assisi, but it is difficult to imagine St. Francis disrupting the local boar hunt or petitioning the pope in the hope that he would declare blood sports a mortal sin.

And the hunter was more secure in his sport in the age before Marks and Spencers; for today's urban meat-eater has lost contact with the origins of his dinner. He finds it very difficult to connect the stuff on his plate, which came out of a neat and bloodless packet, with the living creature it once was. And this makes it all the easier for him to rend flesh and enjoy its flavour (what there is of it), then to drain his

11

glass and wipe his lips and roundly condemn the barbarities of rural sportsmen.

I am not sure this gets me very far, but it is a start. Any defence of killing animals for human need or pleasure must rest on an assessment of the relative status of men and animals that sets humanity in a class quite apart from all other creatures, that insists, in fact, that the difference is absolute rather than relative. This is more difficult in an age that has little time for the soul and regards man as the result of purely material, evolutionary processes. There can be no doubt that the growing disapproval of hunting derives from the decay of Christianity; that Western men now think of themselves as mere animals and so feel closer to foxes and rabbits and pheasants and trout than they did when they believed that each one of us had been touched in his innermost being by the breath of God.

Few sportsmen realise that it is the decline of religion that now threatens their immemorial rights, and I shall not attempt to argue that shooters and hunters and fishers are a less godless crew than those who shout abuse at them. But almost all sportsmen are at least dimly aware that their opponents come mainly from large towns, and that they are men who have almost forgotten that they are carnivores. Some of them, in fact, are carnivores no longer, but that is a different matter and will need separate attention.

It so happens that I believe in God. I believe in the soul, and that animals do not have them. But, even without these convictions, I think that I should continue to shoot pheasants and kill trout without so much as a prick of conscience. And this is because, quite apart from my allegiance to the teachings of the Church of Rome, I do not believe that a pheasant, or a fox or a rabbit or a trout, possesses the self-awareness, the sharp sense of individuality, the moral possibilities, the emotional sensitivity, the ability to think, to choose, to grow in both its intellectual and spiritual faculty, the craving for love, the capacity to rejoice

12

and to grieve; I do not believe that an animal is born with or develops these qualities that make every human being a unique and precious creation.

I do not believe that a pheasant aspires or longs as we do. I do not believe that it can improve or brutalise itself as we can. I do not believe that, when a pheasant falls from the sky, or when a trout is pulled from a river and then knocked on the head, its death inflicts the agony of loss on the lives it leaves behind. I do not believe that, as killers of flesh and fowl, we make mothers despair, or ravage the bliss of lovers, or that we blight the contentment of whole families and communities.

Neither in its potential as an individual nor in the bond of affection that links it to others of its own kind is there anything in the life of a pheasant or a trout that makes the extinction of that life a significant loss. This is the conviction that lies behind my willingness to kill animals; and perhaps I can put it more succinctly by saying that animals live instinctively and unreflectively, untouched by that higher awareness that is both the blessing and the burden of man. Blot out a human life and you have reduced the possibilities of creation. Kill a creature that lives at the behest of thoughtless impulse and nothing that matters much has changed.

If I did not believe this to be true, then I should never again sit by a flight pond as the light fails, I should never again go fishing on a bright morning in May; and I should never again eat lamb or sausages or feel that it was right to swat a fly. And if the man at the meat counter of his local Marks and Spencers thinks that these thoughts of mine are depraved and wicked thoughts, then he must turn away from Chicken Kiev and buy himself a lettuce instead.

There is much rubbish talked on both sides of the debate about fieldsports. Supporters drone on irrelevantly about incidental benefits; opponents draw ridiculous distinctions, between eating meat through

13

necessity and killing animals for fun. 'All gibberish', say I. 'Forget about such trifles and consider the one issue upon which the whole argument hangs. Man's long history as a carnivore and his long-assumed right to hunt and to shoot and to fish both rest on the same belief regarding the status of animals in relation to himself: that animals are subordinate to his needs and that he is therefore entitled to kill them. If he is not entitled to kill them then he can most certainly no longer go out shooting pheasants. But I shall be surprised if it turns out that he can continue to eat the creatures that he can no longer kill (unless perhaps he waits for them to drop dead of old age). And if our traditional attitude to animals really is wrong, then this is likely to change more than our rural pastimes and our diet. What about the rats in our granaries and the mice in our kitchens? What about the bugs in our beds and the lice in our hair and what about the locust and the mosquito? It seems to me that they deserve as much mercy as the fox.

15 February

Once again my diary is a refuge from an unwelcoming world outside the front door, from a biting wind and a sullen sky and a countryside drained of all but dreary colours and silent except for the sound of creaking and complaining branches. The trees sound stiff in the joints, like worn-out old labourers, stiff and sore and aching in every arthritic bough. And the hedges are sighing in the wind, cold and weary of this return to winter. I have exercised Merlin and I am glad to be inside again, sitting in front of the word-processor and thinking about field sports.

I do not believe that the modern eater of meat is in a position to condemn us shooters and fishermen. It is true that, when we lived in caves and gnawed bones by the fire, we needed to kill in order to stay alive. But meat-eating is now an indulgence; we can keep hunger at bay without resort to lamb chops and rump steak. In exactly similar fashion, fieldsports derive from the same primitive necessity, and they

14

have been similarly transformed by human progress from the grim activities they once were, driven by the urgent compulsion of hunger, into pleasures that grace spare hours and feed our souls. Today's carnivorous opponent of blood sports can no longer draw a distinction between eating meat for need and killing pheasants for fun. For we can all ward off starvation with a rich variety of appetizing and nutritious fruits and vegetables. And so opponents of fieldsports, hunt saboteurs, suburban housewives, members of parliament with bizarre sexual appetites, must all express their horror of my sporting pleasures on bellies blamelessly full of lentils. Let flatulence be the proof of their consistency.

16 February

Last night I dreamt of a carnivore with a passion for red meat and for drawing distinctions. He kept me late in bed this morning, sipping tea and arguing with him. For my carnivorous drawer of distinctions, having abandoned his distinction between eating meat for need and killing animals for pleasure, continued to be a distinction-drawer by contrasting different sorts of pleasure, by commending the innocent pleasure of taste and then roundly condemning the depraved pleasure of bloodshed and slaughter.

I felt for a time that he had got a point. It is one thing to say, 'this lamb is quite delicious; every mouthful is sweet and succulent and its flavour is perfectly complemented by your Mouton-Rothschild '70. Yes, I should love another slice and thank you for refilling my glass.' It is quite another thing to say, 'I have just murdered my mother-in-law with the carving knife; the kitchen is awash with her blood and the sight of it sends me into a transport of the purest pleasure imaginable. Excuse me while I go and have another look.' There is a difference here between acknowledging a pleasant and harmless sensation and admitting to an diabolical delight in the spilling of blood and the spectacle of death.

It is quite clear that some pleasures are harmless, while others are disgusting and immoral. So far I went along with my flesh-eating distinction drawer and for a time I sipped tea with a thoughtful air. But before long I was saying to him that, although I accepted his distinction between innocent and guilty pleasures, I was not at all certain that he could regard his pleasure in roasted flesh as an innocent pleasure, if at the same time he was determined to classify my pleasure in shooting pheasants among the unspeakable and guilty ones.

'You seem to have forgotten,' I said to him, 'that your taste for meat cannot be satisfied without the killing of animals. If you tell me that I should not kill them, then I shall tell you that you should not eat them. For if an immoral act is necessary to provide an otherwise innocent pleasure, then the pleasure no less than the enabling act is corrupt and abominable. The pleasure of drinking first growth clarets is a blameless, refined and altogether civilised pleasure (to judge from my very limited experience), but, if it is a pleasure you can only satisfy by first robbing banks (which is the case with most of us), it has turned into a reprehensible and dangerous pleasure which you ought at once to renounce.

'And it will not do to get someone else to rob banks for you. That would be even worse, for not only would it be the behaviour of a coward, but it would also be asking others to do wrong on your behalf. And, excuse me for saying it, but it rather seems to me that you are in the same position as the wine-lover who robs banks by proxy. You will not kill the animals you eat. You expect someone else to do it for you. You have not the belly to provide your stomach with the meat it craves and, to make matters worse, you give yourself moral airs and graces and you look down your nose at men like me who are happy to take a gun and shoot their supper for themselves. Will you be offended if I suggest that you are, in fact, a hypocrite?'

'Not at all,' replied the sensitive carnivore. 'You do not understand the distinction I have just drawn. It is too fine for you. I do not object to killing. I object to killing for pleasure; I object to enjoying killing. Utilitarian slaughter, that of the abattoir, is another matter altogether and it sets meat on my plate untainted by human delight in the death of animals, which is why I refuse to eat pheasant and always have lamb with my claret.'

I think I filled my cup at this point, with tea rather than with wine, and mused for a few minutes.

'Your distinction is a fine one indeed,' I said at length. 'In the matter of distinctions you seem to believe that the finest are always the best. I think that I understand it and I am not certain that I go along with it. One difficulty is that it seems to exclude animals entirely from consideration of the morality of killing them; it makes the human feelings that accompany the killing of a sheep or a pheasant or a trout the one factor that determines its moral status as a blameless act or a heartless outrage.

'I had rather expected that you, as an opponent of fieldsports, would want to grant animals certain absolute rights. And yet I find that you are denying them any rights at all and approach the question of their proper treatment with no regard for the animals themselves. Rather, your gaze is fixed unswervingly on the heart and mind of man. This puzzles me, as too does your obsession with what I shall call the pleasure-factor.

'Your preoccupation with this pleasure-factor disturbs as well as puzzles me. For it seems to suggest that the emotions accompanying an act are more important ethical guides than the nature of the act itself. It seems to suggest that you can go ahead and poison your wife as long as the hand that sprinkles the arsenic into her morning tea pauses a while to wipe away a tear and then carries on sprinkling with infinite regret. I accept that whether a given act is right or wrong very often

17

depends on the circumstances that surround it. Famously, for example, there are many occasions when it is not a sin to tell a lie.

'But the deciding factor should surely be something other than the pain or pleasure the performer will derive from his act. Are not those affected by an act more important than the feelings of the man who carries it out? In the matter of killing animals, are the animals not more important than the emotions of the men who kill them? I think, on reflection, that your distinction is a dangerous and false one. It is your way of distancing yourself from the killing that puts meat on your table and it is sophistry. If you want to eat animal flesh, although you may not want to kill animals yourself, you most certainly want them killed. Anyway I do not have time for any more distinctions. My tea is finished and it is high time I left my bed and let the dog out.'

17 February

As I lay late in bed this morning, on this last day of half-term, I drew distinctions for myself and they ran along these lines.

Most fishers and shooters, including me, regard badger baiting and cock-fighting as cruel and abhorrent practices, rightly banned. And most opponents of fieldsports, I think, would acknowledge that there is something especially monstrous about torturing badgers that sets it apart from pheasant shooting and catching fish, and even hunting foxes, as an immeasurably more degrading and repulsive activity.

The distinction is obvious and uncontroversial, but I think it will be worth my while to examine the thoughts and attitudes that lie behind it. And the first point to be made is that cock-fighting and badger baiting and other outlawed and barbaric forms of sport with animals are all spectator blood sports, and they are sports that truly delight in blood and violence, in bared teeth and snarling jaws and torn limbs. They appeal, in short, to the worst impulses of our human nature and they satisfy these same impulses in a fashion that is peculiarly base

18

and craven; for they provide pleasure in bloodshed and violence and death without personal exposure to either danger or pain. Their sole purpose is to glut revolting appetites. They serve no need except this and they are abominable beyond words.

Blood and violence and cruelty lie at the heart of badger baiting. This is not the case with, say, pheasant shooting, which seeks the instant extinction of pheasants without the spectacle of bloodshed. And if we shoot a pheasant and fail to kill, then we take action to secure our prey as quickly as we can and to despatch it with all possible speed. Moreover, although shooting pheasants is not essential for human survival, it puts food on our plates and thus satisfies a basic and blameless need. Badger baiting ends up with a mangled corpse. The final result of a day's pheasant shooting, or a day's trout fishing, is roast pheasant or poached trout.

The pleasure of a day in the coverts or of a day by a chalkstream or by a tumbling northern river is not easy to define, but it does not partake of the savage delights of the bear pit; it derives from the touch of the wind on our cheeks, from the slow moving of the sun through the sky and the changing patterns of shadows beneath the moving sun. It derives from light in waving trees and running water, from a sense of Nature's teeming bounty and a conviction that it is right for man to take part in the harvest. Now there are those who question man's right to participate in this harvest when it involves the taking of animal lives. That is not my concern here, which has been rather to demonstrate to myself that my love of fishing and shooting has no kinship with the depraved pleasures of the badger baiter and his kind. I am satisfied that this has been done.

I am less certain that the fox-hunter will think my arguments useful. But he should take heart and point out that he gets on a horse and charges round the countryside and periodically breaks his own bones. At least he is no coward. And he is very rarely in at the death

19

and the death is normally very quick and the sight of blood means very little to him. He is a poet at heart, your fox hunter, delighting in the sight of twenty couple of hounds streaming through field and covert, transported by the strength and beauty of the mount beneath him, by pink coats and shining horses and wide winter skies. He should not claim, in my opinion, that fox-hunting is necessary to control foxes; he knows it is a lie and that lamp and rifle are ten times more efficient than a pack of hounds. He should argue that hunting transforms necessity, the acknowledged necessity to control foxes, into art; that it makes beauty out of the basic things of life and is a tribute to the aspiring spirit of man.

Not everyone will agree with him; but I think he has got a point and it is a point to which I shall doubtless return, though not until I have gone back to school and got on top of my work. But, before I return to Latin and Greek and leave my diary unvisited for a few days, here are some more thoughts on cruelty, which should, I think, be considered from two points of view: that of its victim and that of the man who imposes cruelty on the creatures around him. The badger baiter inflicts pointless suffering and violence on the badger. This is one aspect of his cruelty and it is disgusting. The second aspect of his monstrous conduct is what it does to him; it degrades and corrupts him. It makes him a worse man, a man more likely to beat his wife and batter his children and laugh in the face of human pain.

I do not believe that a pheasant shooter similarly brutalises himself. The pleasures of fishing and shooting are complex but they have no connection with delight in the contemplation of suffering. Nor do shooters seek to inflict pain (there is perhaps a problem with fishing here) but to bring swift extinction to a life that is individually almost meaningless and which exists on such a primitive level of self-aware-ness that it cannot suffer in any sense remotely analogous to human suffering. I acknowledge that these last observations are dangerous, in that they might be used to justify any treatment of animals. But

20

remember that we must always consider arguably cruel acts from two points of view and avoid conduct likely to deprave. And remember this too: that, although animals treat each other with pitiless indifference, we, in deference to our higher nature, should look upon them with more respect than they perhaps deserve as individuals. And so, although a wounded pheasant is incapable of mental suffering, we are dissatisfied with ourselves until our dogs have brought it to hand and it has been released from its discomfort. And what shooter, when he comes upon a rabbit disabled by the putrid blindness of myxomatosis, is not, out of pity, moved to knock it on the head? We shooters are ready to kill certain animals, because we believe they belong to a category of creation quite apart from ourselves. But anything that smacks of cruelty, of the deliberate imposition of pain or of pleasure in beholding it, is repellent to the true shooting man. And, although nature litters the world with the wounded and the dying, whenever we come upon her victims we are stirred by compassion to help them on their way.

A concluding thought or two about fear, for opponents of field-sports often accuse its practitioners of spreading panic through field and woodland. And so, if not guilty of deliberate cruelty, we might be said to cause it indirectly by the dread our dogs and our guns and our human presence inspires. I want to make two points here, apart from sounding a warning about attributing specifically human emotions to animals. The first is this: that fear, whatever we really mean when we talk of fear in animals, is omnipresent in nature. It is a constant condition of existence for most wild animals and the fear that the shooter arouses with his gun or the fisherman with his rod is just one of a thousand fears that beset the lives of pheasant and trout: fear of the fox, of the mink, of the falcon, of the otter, of the heron. This fear, which is an instinctive response to anything that might threaten danger, is a perpetual feature of the lives of animals. It is of the nature of the beast. It is there whether we are there or not.

Moreover it is not just sportsmen who provoke fear among our wildlife. When two of us go for a Sunday afternoon stroll, the blackbird in the bush flees our approach with startled notes of alarm, the rabbit in the meadow scuttles into his burrow, the trout feeding in the stream shoots off for his lair beneath the stones. If the shooting man is cruel for arousing fear, then I cannot see how Sunday afternoon strollers are less reprehensible. They should stay indoors and leave the animal world in fearful peace. They should sleep off their lunches in their easy chairs. And that is more than enough argumentation for one day. It is time for a whisky.

26 February

I have been a schoolmaster for more than a week and have thoroughly enjoyed it. Today I went out to Brough with Austin, to be initiated into the mysteries of laying a hedge. It was a soggy day, with the vapour from melting snow merging into the greyness of the sky, while from the sky itself there came rain and drizzle and the wet earth breathed out dankness.

I sat happily on the wet earth and listened, while Austin talked of liggers and stools and shooting tongues, and of the necessity, in deference to the habits of sap, to lay your hedge uphill. The hedge that starts at the weir-gate, running back along the rise above the meadow, is a long-untended hedge, full of gaps and sheep wire, but Austin proclaimed that, although it could not have been laid for at least twenty years, there was still a wealth of suitable wood just waiting for the shaping action of his bill-hook. It is a hedge of hawthorn and hazel, with some holly further up the slope. I watched, as Austin got to work, cutting out the old liggers and the dead wood, then slicing almost through living shoots and stems and branches, through gnarled and lichen-covered hawthorn, with its loose and crumbly bark, through smooth and silver-brown hazel, pushing down the laid wood and weaving it into a dense and thorny tapestry of stems that will deter even the most foolhardy sheep.

As the work progressed I could see cover being created before my eyes, and I began to dream of nesting pheasants in April and lurking pheasants in November. I went to inspect the hoppers and found that three of them were almost empty, even though I had filled them on Wednesday (during a couple of hours snatched from schoolmastering). It must have been the heavy snowfalls of Thursday and Friday that have convinced my pheasants that home is where the hopper is. Everywhere there were droppings, and pheasants' feet have trampled the ground beneath the hoppers into little quagmires. And there were footings running this way and that through all the ragged patches of snow.

Austin had nearly finished when I returned. I was relieved to find it so, for it had been impossible to ford the beck without letting some of it into my wellingtons at each crossing. It was icy water and five minutes of standing froze my feet. Austin staked the section he had finished and we looked at his handiwork while I admired it loudly. Then we squelched down the meadow and climbed into the Land Rover and drove back to Sedbergh. I am very eager now to start wielding a bill-hook myself. Austin tells me that I have about six weeks to do something useful with it, for by then the sap will be rising strongly and it will be too late to lay hedges.

28 February

It is a joy to me, this diary of mine. It is a privilege to write about the things you love, about gentle rain and damp earth and singing birds, about the soft coming of spring. And soon I shall be able to write about rivers, about the Wharfe and the Eden and the spotted trout that swim there. I have kept a sporting diary of sorts for many years, but it has been little more than a record of pheasants shot and trout killed, with occasional comments on wind and water and the obvious things that have made or marred my sport. There have been no entries for days when I did not go out with a rod or a gun; and so days like today have passed unmentioned; and, although today might have seemed to be entirely unremarkable, it has not in fact been so. It has been a day of drizzle and low cloud, but with a mild and quickening air. And I have felt for some reason that, whatever may happen tomorrow, winter is at last over. Frost and snow will from now on be features of the spring, of the inconstant northern spring that is soft as butter one day and as hard as a headmaster the next.

Today was an unexceptional day, except for some quality of the grey light and the moist air that expressed all the hope of the reviving year. And there was a chaffinch that sang with unusual virtuosity, trilling not only at the end of each burst of song but half way through it as well. This was a bird that realised that today was less ordinary than it seemed; and, if I were not keeping this diary, I should soon have forgotten both about the day and the bird that saw through its seeming drabness and recognised it as a day of celebration: a day that deserved its own song.

1 March

I was right when I said yesterday that winter was past. Last night, as I walked Merlin just after ten, the sky was full of the sound of birds, full of pipings and long, sad whistles floating on the air. And those cries were all the more haunting because the birds making them were high and invisible in the dark sky. They were curlews and golden plovers, flying back to their breeding grounds on the fells, and there was also the breathy squeaking of lapwings. They were all spring sounds and they were beautiful to hear.

Today it is March which, however raw and unfriendly it may prove, is unquestionably a month belonging to the spring of the year.

It is the month when my trout rods stir from their long winter sleep and emerge from their covers and cases one by one. I cannot believe that they are instruments of torture. I feel instinctively that fishing is somehow the purest of fieldsports. In fact I am convinced that fishers are better men than they would have been if they had never come to love fishing. And yet it seems to me to be more difficult to defend fishing from the charge of cruelty than is the case with shooting.

This is, of course, because playing a fish is undeniably a large part of the pleasure of angling and, even were this not so, it would still be a necessary preliminary to the catching and killing of trout or salmon. You cannot , if you angle for fish with rod and line, eliminate the fight that precedes the capture; and, just assuming that you could, how many fishermen would want to find that a mere wave of their rods had brought a hooked fish straight to net and that it was all over?

It is the tension of the fight, with a tight line and a bending rod, with a roused and angry fish running and leaping in his wild longing for freedom, shaking his head and lashing with his tail; it is your fragile contact with this struggling creature; it is the sensations he transmits to you through cane or carbon; it is the fierce desire to possess your prey and the fearful knowledge that your attachment to it is so precarious; it is all this that makes the fight so thrilling and that turns the moment of victory, when a fine fish surrenders at last and is drawn beaten over the net, into a moment of such marvellous and memorable fulfilment.

The glory of fishing is that success comes in stages. First there is the rise. You have fooled your trout; he thinks your fly is food and he wants to eat it. Next there is the strike; you have timed it perfectly and he is on. Then follows, if the fish is big, the great drama of the fight, which absorbs an angler so completely that, as long as it lasts, his happiness hangs upon the hold of his hook and the strength of his nylon. Losing a fish is a form of bereavement; it inspires disbelief and incomprehension; it takes time to come to terms with it. But what of success? What does catching a big trout or a huge salmon mean to a fisherman? It means more than those who know nothing of it could ever begin to guess and, in the case of an exceptional fish, it possesses more than a purely transient significance; it is a permanent joy and a lasting enrichment. And every fisher in the world knows that I am speaking the plain truth.

But the plain truth is also that the surpassing pleasure of catching a great fish lies in the the fact that it is the culmination of a long struggle. The killing, of course, is quick and painless; but the drama that precedes it is necessarily prolonged. And it is in the drama, and in the relief and satisfaction that follow, in the quiet contentment that steals over and stills more turbulent emotions, it is in this wonderful sequence of feelings, at once conflicting and complementary, that the angler finds his addiction and his delight. There are those who say that this is the delight of a torturer and, although I feel certain that they are wrong, it is clear that they deserve an answer. And I shall fish with less easy a conscience this season if I cannot say to myself that I have dealt with their objections to the sport I love best and shown them that they are wrong. I should like them to take up fishing themselves and so turn themselves into better people.

2 March

I went out to High Park this afternoon, filled the hoppers and spent an hour or so, not laying the hedge, but laying cover in the copse above the weir gate. It was a thought that came to me yesterday evening: that I could hone my mastery of the bill-hook by practising in places where it would not really matter if things went wrong. And so I spent an hour or so laying young shoots of hazel in the hope that they will thrive and sprout and thicken to provide cover for pheasants in summer and in September, persuading them that my land - with its hedges and hoppers, its dense stands of gorse, its thickets of hawthorn and bramble, its firs ideal for roosting, its beck with the purest of pure water for drinking, and with its new and welcoming luxuriance of undergrowth - is the very place where they want to settle down and remain warm and sheltered and well-fed for the winter. What will happen to my new cover, of course, is that it will never come to anything, for the sheep will munch each bud and leaf just as soon as it shows itself.

One of the arguments that fishermen are always producing in defence of their sport is that it is good for fish. And so it is; but this most certainly does not mean that fishermen are therefore right to go fishing; all it means is that they are willing to take pains and fight battles and spend both time and money in order to make sure that there are fish around for them to catch.

It would be good for the world if its human population were half its present size, but we should hesitate to commend the man who made such a reduction his purpose in life and set to work with gusto. We should all benefit, as long as we were not on his list: the whole planet would breathe more easily; everything on it would lead a less crowded and precarious existence. And the whole business would stink to high heaven. The fact that an immoral activity produces incidental benefits does nothing to change its nature; it is still immoral and still to be condemned.

Shooters do exactly what fishermen do. They point out that, if they did not like shooting pheasants, there would be many fewer, not more, pheasants to adorn the woodlands and stubble fields in autumn. They claim, and their claim is truthful, that grouse moors need grouse shooters if the heather is to thrive and delight the eye in August, if the merlin and the harrier are to make their homes there and rear their young. And who cares for the fate of the grey partridge except for those who enjoy killing them? And how much woodland would be lost to the plough, or would fall into barren neglect, if there were no longer shooters with an interest in its maintenance?

I could go on for pages and pages and it would all be an irrelevance. First demonstrate that it is proper to kill birds for pleasure. Only then proceed to the myriad blessings that flow from the sport, enriching the lives of both pheasants and men. I have so far produced some of the reasons why I feel killing animals for sport is a justifiable activity. I am sure there are more waiting to be discovered, and I have yet to show how fieldsports, far from being brutal and degrading, are expressions of reverence for the life of nature. I feel this very strongly. I shall perhaps come to understand this conviction more clearly in the course of the year's sport. But, although there is much to make clearer, I think that I am making progress.

Fishing, however, continues to puzzle me. I am worried by the thrill of the fight and the vital contribution it makes to the pleasure of angling. How can it be cruel, since we fishermen are so kind and gentle and bring peace home with us from a long day's sport? But how can it *not* be cruel to drive a hook into a trout's mouth and then to drag the poor creature this way and that until it is too tired to wave its tail and can struggle no longer?

3 March

We sportsmen too often refuse to acknowledge any difficulties with the ethics of our treatment of animals. We waffle on about the hunting instinct and about how we go hunting and shooting and fishing in response to the deepest urges of our nature. The problem with this approach is that theft, murder, rape and adultery, to mention four examples of questionable conduct, are all the result of urges every whit as deep. I regard urges with profound suspicion. Most of them need resisting. It is certainly no defence of fieldsports to claim that they are natural activities; it is natural to hate your enemies and yet there are some of us who persist in thinking that it is wrong.

It will not do, in defence of fishing, to say merely that it reunites modern man with his origins as man the hunter, that it is the expression of a human instinct and the satisfaction of an internal need. We have risen above our first beginnings. And flyfishing, at any rate, far from being a primitive business, is a highly sophisticated activity, about as close to the hunting practice of early man as is the music of Mozart to the rhythm of bongo drums. Nets and dynamite: these are the tools a reincarnate caveman would take with him on his fishing trips. He would most certainly refuse to waste his time with a Tup's Indispensable.

I do not feel, when I take one of my fly-rods from its case, that I am stripping away the centuries and stepping back towards the dawn of man. Nor do I want to feel this. But I am forced to acknowledge that, in hooking fish and fighting them until they are spent and helpless, I may seem to some to be displaying a callous disregard for suffering of the sort that men ought to have left behind them when they abandoned the caves that were their first homes.

5 March

Spring means much more to the middle-aged than to the young. You do not need spring when you are 21 and so absorbed in the vigorous currents of your own blood that the season of the year is an irrelevance and that death still seems meaningless. But, when you are 44, it is marvellous to take the dog out at midnight and to feel the breath of the wind, raw and vital, like a gift of new life. Perhaps it was the wine I had just drunk. Whatever it was, it felt like a renewal and I was grateful. And another pleasure of early spring is that it is warm enough to leave the window open when you go to bed, but still cold enough to feel that a hot water bottle is a necessity ra'her than an indulgence.

I sat up late last night, after my wine and my midnight walk with Merlin, reading Plunket Greene and enjoying the effortless good humour of his prose. He loved the trout he caught and killed. Had you suggested to him that he was heartless or cruel, I doubt he would have bothered with words. He would have leaned back in his chair and roared with laughter until the tears were dripping from his chin.

6 March

If someone forced a hook into a dog's mouth, a hook tied to a length of rope, and made a game out of hauling the dog around the garden, until the hook broke free or the dog dropped from exhaustion, I should think him a monster of depravity. But to do the same with a trout, in a river rather than a garden, seems to most of us unexceptionable conduct.

The fisher would argue that such treatment of a dog would be gratuitous, whereas he must first hook and play his trout if he wants to catch it and kill it and then eat it for his supper. He would point out too that he does not prolong the fight a moment longer than necessary, and, although admitting that he enjoyed taming the power of a big fish, he would vehemently deny that he drew any pleasure from the thought of inflicting pain, whereas the dog-owner addicted to exercising his pet with a hook and twenty yards of rope could scarcely deny that he took a cruel delight in the spectacle of suffering.

These would all be fair points, but the true explanation of our different attitudes to the dog-baiter and the fisherman lies in our very different attitudes to dogs and fish. We think that what is appropriate treatment of trout and salmon is most definitely unsuitable for dogs and cats, and for deer and hares and for rabbits as well. In the course of time we have constructed a sort of hierarchy of animals, with horses and dogs somewhere near the top and with fish and rats and bluebottles down among the lower orders. The presence of rats among the peasantry is interesting; it shows that our classification rests upon more complex, or perhaps more random considerations than the establishing of a divide between warm and cold-blooded animals, or between mammals and all other forms of animal life. Most of us, moreover, are better disposed towards trout than we are to rats. Fishermen regularly spare trout and return them lovingly to the water, whereas the rat inspires kind thoughts in few hearts. And there would be few tears shed, were it discovered one morning that there was not a rat left living in the whole wide world.

We have made friends and partners of the dog and the horse. We have entered into a contract with them and it is only fair that they should enjoy quasi-human status. They, together with cats and ferrets and pet rabbits, belong to a class apart: to that class of animals that have entered our lives and our homes and become a part of them. To hunt or kill such a creature would be to break the agreement we have reached with ourselves on our own and on their behalf. It would violate our sense of justice and would be intolerable.

The deer and the wild rabbit belong to a different category and I have no time to think about them today. In five minutes there is mass, and this afternoon there is a hedge at High Park waiting for the attentions of my bill-hook. Our attitude to animals is very puzzling. I begin to despair of ever sorting it out.

7 March

Today I seem to be seeing things clearly. Perhaps it was the hedging that did it; perhaps thought fermented inside me as I assaulted hazel and hawthorn, and then matured slowly with each further slash of the bill-hook, clearing to shining brightness as the lees settled to the bottom of my mind. The metaphor is a poor one, for my wild activity as a novice hedger could only have shaken thought into muddy confusion. Anyway, what seemed baffling yesterday now seems as plain as could be. We grant the higher animals privileged status partly for reasons of false sentiment, because the look in their eyes seems to express emotions like our own. And we think it wrong to torture them because it degrades the torturer and because the animals themselves can very obviously experience pain and communicate their experience of it.

With a trout this is not the case. It is difficult to look at a trout and to imagine that it is sad or happy or that it is enjoying the company of the other trout in its pool. A trout seems to live in a world completely remote from human feelings. A trout never gazes at us, as a deer or even a wounded duck can, with reproachful eyes. And so we are not worried by playing a trout, because it makes no sound and casts no glance that stirs our sympathy and makes us feel ashamed.

But we feel justified in imposing the fight upon a trout not merely because it is the trout's misfortune to have been born mute and unblessed with expressive eyes, but also because we believe that suffering has no meaning for it, that its brain and central nervous system are so primitive that a trout cannot feel pain. Traditionally we support this argument by claiming that the trout would not pull against the pressure of hook and line if it were painful so to do; it would run away from the agonising pressure of the angler's rod by running in the direction of a slack line.

I am not sure that this is true. I do not think a trout has the intelligence to realise that the hook is most uncomfortable when the nylon attached to it is tight. And I also think that, in animals, fear is a more potent force than pain. The hunted beast still runs from its pursuer, even though its lungs and its heart and its limbs are telling it every step that they can bear no more. Fear overrules pain. The urge to escape is stronger than the longing for rest and recuperation. I suppose there are occasions when this is also the case with man. And so it may be with a hooked trout; though the touch of the barb and the pull of the line are an agony almost beyond endurance, yet fear and the urge to be rid of the uncomprehended object in its mouth drive it towards its lair, drive

32

it on in the blind hope that safety and rest will be found there, and in noble disregard for the contrary restraints of exhaustion and pain.

I distrust the argument that the way a trout fights proves that it cannot feel pain. But everything I know about trout tells me that, although they undoubtedly feel the barb and run in the effort to be rid of it, they experience nothing that even approximates to human fear, human pain or human suffering. They respond to impulses not to emotions, and any attempt to interpret these impulses in terms of our own feelings, although we must necessarily resort to the language of human sensation to describe them, is quite simply false.

If I learned that I was wrong in this belief, I should put away my rods immediately. Yes, and I should do more than this; I should burn them and hang my head in deepest sorrow and shame. And it is time to extract some general conclusions from my ramblings of the last weeks. But I shall not begin today. It is too late now; it is time for the pub.

8 March

A sodden grey day, uninviting and uninvigorating in spite of the mild air, but it has been one of those days when I have enjoyed being a schoolmaster. I have enjoyed reading Juvenal with intelligent and appreciative sixth-formers. I have enjoyed my third form and they now (almost all of them) know the difference between pronouns and adjectives; and almost all of them are very pleasant boys. It is a privilege to be paid money for reading great literature and sharing your pleasure in it with others; it is a privilege to help boys to understand the rudiments of two wonderful languages and to be given a large amount of money for it every month. And I suppose I am paid for playing fives as well, however badly I do it. Do not believe me when I moan about my life as a schoolmaster. It is merely a passing mood.

I have prepared tomorrow's lessons: I have finished my marking. Now there is time for those general conclusions which I promised myself yesterday:

a) I do not think it is wrong to kill animals, because I do not believe that individual animal lives possess a value akin to a human life. I do not believe that there is, in the existence of an individual cock pheasant, anything that amounts to personality, or anything of the spiritual and moral awareness that makes each one of us both unique and uniquely precious. I elevate mankind so far above other sentient beings that I believe one of our kind to be worth more than, say, all the rabbits in creation.

I remember, when my aunt died in October last year, how after the funeral I fled from all the gloom of a grieving family and sat by my duck pond, waiting for evening flight. A few mallard came with the darkness and I shot a couple and missed as many. Merlin brought me the two I shot and I can recall thinking, as I took them from him and stroked their beautiful feathers smooth, that to imagine their extinction belonged to the same order of things as the death of my aunt would be an unforgivable nonsense. For death to matter, there must be loss, and I could not see how, either for those two duck or for the world they had left behind, there had been a loss of any importance. I know it sounds heartless, but how does killing a duck differ from turning off a machine?

b) I do not believe that meat-eaters are in a strong position to criticise those who kill for sport. Eating meat is an act of pleasure rather than of necessity and to eat meat is most certainly to sanction the killing of animals.

c) I disapprove of cruelty in sport. Cruelty lies in inflicting pain for pleasure, in which case it is called sadism, or in causing pain and not caring. Cruelty corrupts the man who inflicts it upon others. Shooters are not guilty of cruelty, because they aim to kill instantly and painlessly. When they fail to kill they take immediate action to find and despatch their wounded prey. The imposition of pain has no part in the pleasure of their sport, and it must be remembered that a pheasant lives on such a rudimentary level of awareness that it cannot experience anything analogous to what we mean by pain and suffering.

d) Fishing poses a more serious problem, in that playing hooked fish is a central and pleasurable element of the sport, which might thus be thought intrinsically cruel. But anglers are not driven by the desire to impose pain, but rather by the desire to catch fish. There is nothing in the fight of a trout that arouses or satisfies sadistic urges; there is no blood; there are no screams or snarls. The fight moreover is not deliberately extended to prolong the discomfort of the prey. And trout belong to so low an order of life that they exist in a world where the vocabulary of human feeling has no meaning.

I think this is a fair summary of the reasons why I am undisturbed by my activities as a shooter and a fisherman. Underlying them all is the conviction that man is absolutely different from all other animals, which I believe much more passionately than I believe in fieldsports. I fear that it is now an unfashionable view and is likely to be condemned as both callous and arrogant. When at last it has been universally abandoned, when everyone believes that all animals are equal and that man, for imperfectly understood reasons, is only slightly more equal than the rest, then we can look for the collapse of civilisation.

And I am not sure that this is too far distant. Already, here in England, we live in a society that seems in danger of setting more value on the life of a fox than it does on the life of a human foetus. It seems an ominous indication of the times in which we live that the sight of men and women on horseback, that the sound of a horn and the baying of a pack of hounds now excite stronger emotions than the thought of the unborn men and women that are every day denied their birthright. And you only have to question the morality of our present abortion laws and you are immediately dismissed as a ranting papist, whose disquiet does not deserve serious consideration.

If for no other reason, then I shall continue to support fox hunting for this one: that it is a means of insisting on the absolute difference between men and foxes. Tomorrow I shall ponder the rat, and I hope that he will help me to open my dialogue with the vegetarian. At the moment I am looking forward to tomorrow's lessons.

9 March

Comparing killing a duck to switching off a machine is unlikely to win much praise and it is open to the obvious objection that machines can be turned on again. And a living duck stirs us by the beauty of its flight and its feathers and with the rough music of its call. We associate mallard and teal with pleasant places and they mean more to us than machines. Nevertheless I feel that it is fair to compare what happens when a duck dies to what happens when a computer is unplugged: a set of programmed impulses is lost and that is all. The analogy is not exact but it is instructive: killing a duck is more like switching off a computer than killing a man.

And so to rats. I turn to them as my temporary allies, hoping to find help from them in a tight corner. For rats, in my opinion, with their dark underground ways, with their repulsive tails, their conspiratorial squeaks and their sinister associations with infection and plague, are instructive little creatures. They expose the extreme selectivity of our attachment to animals and of our tendency to project our own feelings onto brute creation.

And yet they are going about their business just as blamelessly as the fox or the badger. But whereas badgers fill most men with warm thoughts, and although many of us are loud in praise of the fox and scandalised by the disgraceful behaviour of men in pink coats, yet no one speaks out in defence of the rat, following its nose and its instincts in the same way as more fortunate creatures blessed with elegance or with playful ways.

Of course there are good reasons for hating rats and for killing them with pitiless efficiency. The man who argued that it was immoral to poison them would be regarded by most of us a dangerous lunatic. It is right, is it not, to kill animals for the common good of mankind? Rats, maggots, house flies and blue-bottles menace human health and are exterminated ruthlessly. Wasps threaten a trivial sting and we swat them without so much as a prick of guilt. Few defenders of animals' rights care to champion the cause of the rat or the maggot or, for that matter, of the earthworm, which spends its whole life working tirelessly for the benefit of gardeners.

I would never try to claim that the necessity to kill rats is a justification of fieldsports. I turn to the rat because our attitude to him interests me. For it is not merely because he spreads disease that we hate him; it is because he is furtive and ugly and squeaks in a repulsive way. Of course it is right to wage war on rats in defence of human health. But if it so happened that they were miracles of grace and beauty, and twice as dangerous as they are in their present hideousness, I do not doubt that there would be angry voices raised against the campaign to control them.

Are those who hate fox-hunters and love foxes inspired by an impartial admiration for the whole animal kingdom or by a sentimental affection for an elegant creature with gambolling cubs and a bushy tail? And is it fair that gardeners, digging their plots with the entirely frivolous purpose of growing perfumed roses or enormous marrows, should spear worms on the prongs of their forks and wage heartless warfare on greenflies and slugs? They do not need their flowers or their bloated vegetables. Perhaps it is permissible as long as they do not derive a secret delight from the fatal hiss of the spray or draw a cruel satisfaction from the artful laying of the poison?

Do wasps deserve to be declared enemies merely because they can inflict a passing discomfort? And what of the spider that is harried and hunted from the house in the erroneous conviction that cleanliness is somehow connected with godliness? Why is he less deserving of protection than the fox? Why should he not be left to spin his web - or is it her web? - in some secluded corner of the drawing room?

I could go on indefinitely and the point I want to make is this: that all animals are as God or evolution or the two in partnership have made them: they are all equally blameless because they have no control over their actions (which is another reason for comparing them to machines). And yet we are hopelessly inconsistent in the way we treat them. If animals such as badgers have rights, then why do worms have none? Is it only mammals that have rights? Then what about the rat? Does an animal forfeit all its rights as soon as they run contrary to the legitimate interests of man? Do only animals that melt our hearts have rights? Then on what grounds are unattractive animals denied them? Do animal-rights only apply to creatures that have reached a particular point in the evolutionary process? In which case my argument in defence of the pleasures of angling may be secure. Do pheasants have rights and trout none, or pheasants some and trout fewer? Or is the whole notion of animals' rights the misapplication of a specifically human concept to a sphere where it can have no coherence?

I cannot make sense of it. I wish that I could. I am as partial as the next man in my attitude to animals. To shoot a pheasant seems to me to be a blameless act, whereas to kill a robin would to my eyes be an outrage. Sentiment inevitably colours our thinking about the creatures that surround us, and there is nothing much wrong with this. But there is something wrong, something misleading, at work when we confuse sentiment with sense and make it a basis for moral judgments and for high-minded condemnation of the activities of our fellows. It is the rat that has led me to this conclusion and I thank him for it. He has not, as I thought he might (although I cannot remember why), helped me to persuade the vegetarian that his diet is a mistake.

10 March

One of the pleasures of keeping a diary is that it does not need to be coherent. And so here is a random thought. If it is wrong to hunt foxes because it subjects the fox to pursuit and to the fear which this is thought to inspire, then is it also wrong for a man to let his dog chase rabbits, sniffed out of hedgerows and rough cover in the course of an evening stroll? Presumably the rabbit is as capable of fear as the fox? And the rabbit - except when it decides to swallow its own children - is a harmless herbivore, whereas the fox spends its life tearing other creatures to pieces. Should not our walker call off his dog and so save the poor rabbit the suffering of pursuit? And suppose the same walker actually enjoys the sight of his dog legging it after the startled coney; is he any less culpable than a master of foxhounds? Certainly he is enjoying, if only as a spectator, the pleasures of the chase. But then most hunting men are no more than mounted spectators of the hunt. I suppose that, in the case of the man and his dog, the whole business is less premeditated, but I cannot see that this makes a world of difference. And, anyway, it may be a regular occurrence, something that happens most evenings, something anticipated with eager relish during weary hours in the office. It seems to me that dog walkers who disapprove of hunting need to examine their consciences.

I spent the afternoon hedging out at High Park, and cursing the brittle ways of hawthorn; but I was better at it than on Sunday and an efficient saw made things much easier. I can hardly wait to see what happens to my hedge when the sap rises and the leaf bursts and the year becomes a riot of thrusting growth. It will probably wither and die. But it was lovely this afternoon, with a curlew calling somewhere behind me, and with a red squirrel in the tall ash tree above the hedge. The wind was fresh and keen, a typical March wind, and the clouds were hurrying through the sky. From time to time sunshine came sweeping across the meadow and over the steep bank beyond the beck, so that faded grass and withered clumps of brambles shone briefly under its influence.

The landscapes of earliest spring are nothing if not tasteful. There are no vulgar colours and there is no ostentation. There are pale fields with the spare shapes of trees: delicate, drooping birches; tall and elegant beeches; there are knobbly ash trees and stiff, angular oaks, sticking out their branches, with hanging clumps of brown and withered leaves, like ragged scarecrows. The sun lights upon the subtle and shining browns and greens of hazel and sycamore trunks, on smooth and silver beech bark. The sky is a merging of soft greys and quiet blues. Nothing jars and the sheep merge into the drab pasture. It is a landscape of impeccable taste, but it is taste seasoned with vigour, with the raw vigour of the wind and the restless vigour of cawing rooks. It is, in fact, that rare combination: good taste with rising energy and a strong pulse.

13 March

High Park again, with a gale chasing sunshine and shadows across the sloping land. I could feel the warmth of the sun in the shelter of the Rise, but it was windy work up on the line of the hedge. I have been using my bill-hook more as a hewer of timber than a layer of hedges, cutting through rather than down the wood, wounding and splitting and leaving ugly scars that will not be quick to heal. It went better once I had realised this, and I have also realised that I cannot possibly lay the whole hedge this year. It will take two or even three years to complete, even if my enthusiasm for hedging puts down strong roots and does not wither in the bud.

As I wrestled with thorns and briars I thought of grey and red squirrels, and another aspect of our attitude to animals was revealed to me. I am still thinking and it may be a day or two before I have anything more to say; for the season of report-writing is here and it takes longer to write these documents than those who are not school-masters might be inclined to think.

14 March

Another blessing of keeping a diary is that it offers escape. It invites you to postpone unpleasant duties in the name of art. For we think of our diaries as literature. We think that, in our own way, we are as interesting as Pepys or Boswell; and, yes, we do write them with an eye to posterity. At least I do. I hope some professor unearths my diary when I am dead and proclaims me a genius. And so writing it seems more important than writing reports, which are not generally composed with thoughts of future publication and are unlikely ever to be revered as treasures of the nation's literary heritage.

And then there is the daily involvement with words, the daily effort to express thoughts and feelings in language that communicates their force. I like words, and it is a delight to abandon the sloppy imprecision of speech and to try to use them properly. And if my diary were to be given to the world in the next year or so, I could retire and live off the proceeds and devote myself to laying hedges and shooting pheasants and catching fish. And you can dream dreams in a diary, which is yet another good reason for keeping one.

16 March

On the Eden the season for trouting has begun, with hail and snow and a wild wind. Today brought dense sheets of cloud, with a gale howling beneath them and with driving sheets of snow. One moment there was a lowering, eschatological gloom, with the wind roaring through it like a preacher denouncing sin from a Scottish pulpit. A moment later great holes had been torn in the clouds and the sun was streaming down with a glory that seemed expressive of redemption. It has been a marvellous day, with changes of light and mood every five minutes. It has been a set for *Macbeth*, darkly ominous and rumbling with the sounds of doom; then it has changed its mind and started rehearsals for *A Midsummer Night's Dream*; but soon realised that it is months ahead of schedule and has summoned back the clouds and the darkness.

Today has been March to perfection, for March, like me, is an old conservative by conviction. It belongs to the spring, it is part of the spring, it is charged with the vitality that is the essence of spring. But it prefers to forget all this; it prefers to pretend that nothing has changed since January died, as though winter were fixed and immutable and here for ever. It tries to remain loyal to the past and so it surrenders only unwillingly to the forces of its own nature. For, try though it may, it cannot control itself and suddenly starts smiling when it was meaning to frown; then it flushes with sudden warmth when it was wanting to remain cold; it breaks into song when it was shaping up to growl, and it is swept by bouts of sudden joy when it was settling down to feel depressed. I love March, especially when it is as confused as it has been today. But, unless it starts imitating May, I shall be happy to postpone my first fishing trip until the end of term.

Red squirrels and grey squirrels are not as fascinating as rats but they are interesting nonetheless. It was the sight of that red squirrel a few days ago that set me thinking. And the truth is that, with regard to animals, we are xenophobes. Grey squirrels are nasty foreigners with unpleasant habits and bad manners. Red Squirrels are British and thoroughly commendable. The coypu, an illegal immigrant from America, has been trapped to extinction as an intolerable alien. The mink touches a sympathetic chord in few hearts. But show these same hearts, cold to the attractions of the mink and the coypu, a pair of otters on a film and they will melt immediately.

There is doubtless some sense in all this chauvinism. There is a proper desire to protect vulnerable species and to preserve threatened habitats. But it is mainly a matter of sentiment. And sentiment, as I have already pointed out, is a misleading guide for those in search of the truth. I wonder if some further conclusions are beginning to brew within me, conclusions that will take into account hunters and fishermen, rats and rabbits, vivisectionists and vegetarians. Perhaps I should try some tomorrow. My reports are all finished.

17 March

Since men emerged as feeling and reflective beings we have inter-
preted nature in the image of our own minds. We have put spirits in
trees, in rock and water, in earth and sky. We have filled creation with
life born within us. We have fancied life and intelligence to reside
where they are absent. It has been an expression of wonder and reverence. It has been the yearning to feel at one with the world around us.
It has been natural at all times.

We no longer people nature with nymphs and satyrs. What we do
now is to put out thoughts and feelings into the brains of animals, so
that we think of the hunted fox as a hunted man and of the hooked trout
as a suffering human, of the lamb in springtime as an innocent victim
doomed to undeserved extinction. And when we persecute animals,
such as the rat and the grey squirrel, we do so more happily because
we charge these creatures with our own failings and persuade ourselves
that they are wicked. We do this although we really know that the rat,
the fox, the rabbit and the squirrel are all equally beyond moral blame
or commendation because all of them can live in one way only: in blind
obedience to their inherited natures.

When we regard animals as roughly equivalent to men then we
draw wrong conclusions about the way they live. We value them for
what they are not, blinding ourselves to their true worth in the
economy of nature. We see a cock pheasant strutting in the arrogance
of his breeding plumage and fancy that he is pleased with himself. He
is no such thing.

When I see a cock pheasant I think that he is beautiful and that I
should like to shoot him. It seems a pity to me that such delicious meat
should be wasted on the undiscriminating belly of the fox. It cannot be
an accident that dead flesh feeds still-living organisms. It cannot have
been intended, by the shaping forces of nature, that we should refuse
the food she so considerately provides for us. It would be a waste, a

43

nonsense; it would be a denial of nature, which has so designed things that, in death, the rabbit and the pheasant provide nourishment for the living. It is part of the great cycle of life and I can see no reason why we should cut ourselves off from it.

To hunt and to shoot a pheasant, admiring its shining beauty in the air and its speed on the wing, and then to turn it into food, eating it with red wine and reverence, is the expression of a very proper regard for its value in creation. This is, I think, why I regard shooting and fishing as acts of praise, whereas to grant a pheasant rights akin to our own rights, to think of its life as in any way comparable to the life of even the most degraded human creature, and finally to condemn the eating of its flesh as a barbarism, is to transform the pheasant - and the rabbit and the trout - into something that it is not. It is a denial of the nature of things and it is wrong.

22 March

Blackbirds are singing in the evening now and I listened to one with delight as I marked a set of exercises. It made a competing thrush sound dull and unmusical, for it was such a warm sound and there was such joy welling from every note. It means nothing of beauty to other blackbirds. It needs a man to interpret the song of the blackbird in terms of emotion and aspiration and affirmation. There is no doubt that these qualities are there, but blackbirds are unaware of them; they are unaware of the meaning of their own song.

A world without blackbirds would be a sadder place; a world without men would be very much worse. For then the seasons would come and go with no one but God to reflect on the changing glories of creation, and no one but God would appreciate the beauty of the blackbird's song. I rather think, by the way, that birdsong is a proof of the existence of God, for, by transcending its purpose and turning into art, it suggests the activity of a shaping and creative mind. I am more inclined to attribute the song of the blackbird, and our capacity to be moved by it, to the activity of God than to the action of the unaesthetic forces of evolution.

The end of term is only a day away. I enjoy each term, most of it, and I hate the ending of each one of them. The boys are bad-tempered. So am I and most of my friends. It is only the prospect of what lies beyond these last days of term that makes them tolerable. And, to make matters worse, they are accompanied by functions that demand attendance when what you are really wanting is a taste of the hermit's life. I do not disapprove of end-of-term functions. I recognise their importance. But they are not the best medicine for weary schoolmasters.

Slipping out of a concert this evening, for a breath of fresh air and a few lungfuls of tobacco, I sniffed the smell of manure blowing off the nearby fields; it came to me like a blessing from a world where there are no end-of-term functions. It reminded me that in two days I shall be fishing, and it made me very happy to be working in a school where the air is sometimes laden with the evocative fragrance of well-rotted ordure.

24 March

It should be my first day's fishing at Kilnsey on the Wharfe, but it is too wet and windy. I shall leave the river unvisited today and drive over this evening for the keeper's supper. Twenty years ago nothing would have kept me from the Wharfe on the opening day. Now I am more selective in my choice of fishing days, especially early in the season when the trout are unlikely to stir for more than an hour or so. Flyfishing for trout is the most refined of fieldsports and I enjoy it most in quiet weather. There is satisfaction to be drawn, it is true, from casting your fly with something like accuracy into the teeth of a downstream gale, but it is a grim sort of satisfaction and the wind blows away most of the delicacy that is the essence of the dry fly and of the upstream wet.

Trouting in early spring can be very tedious: hours on end without sight of a fly or a fish, so that casting becomes an empty ritual performed without pleasure or purpose and with all hope of a rise long dead. Any weather, with the exception of teeming rainfall, is good weather for shooting. You can shoot with pleasure in anything but a cloudburst. And there is something appropriate about fishing a noble salmon river in a roaring gale: fishing a great surge of water with heavy tackle designed to cope with the large effects of nature. But trouting with the fly calls for warm air and a soft breeze. The forecast for tomorrow is more promising.

Instead of fishing today, I took Merlin for a walk, glorying in the prospect of four weeks without entering a classroom. Bluebells are sprouting in the woods, bluebells and dog's mercury. The colour of the new growth is startlingly green. The earth is sodden with weeks of soaking rain. The air is soft and the very touch of the sun seems to stir a fresh current of life. Merlin flushed a rabbit from a patch of brambles. He stopped to whistle and, as I patted him and praised him, I thought that perhaps I should have gone fishing after all.

26 March

Last night we had our keeper's supper, with guinness and good cheer and not even the ghost of a hangover this morning; which was just as well, for to have greeted today with jaded and complaining senses would have been an impiety. To have stood in today's sunshine regretting last night's intemperance would have been unpardonable, and it would have bred within me an even deeper self-loathing than excess usually inspires.

It was half past eleven before I made the first cast of a new season. It would have been earlier, but I had filled the Land Rover with diesel and then driven off without the fuel cap. Luckily, the day was so beautiful that I chugged back to Threshfield to reclaim it with scarcely a curse or an angry thought. Half past eleven was quite early enough.

There was no fly all day and I never saw a fish move. I spent my time wandering along the banks, listening to the insane laughter of a woodpecker in the woods on Knipe Edge, flushing mallard and goosanders from the water, watching dippers skimming up and down the river and squeaking at me as they sped past. The water was full and clear, foaming and sparkling down the long runs and the splashing falls upstream from Black Keld, catching the sunlight and throwing it back into the bright air. The river shone ahead of me, blue and white and silver, smooth and broken and rippled and singing on its way. I relearned the various flicks and jerks that pass for my roll cast. I covered spots which have brought big fish in seasons past. I blessed the gentle breath of the breeze and revelled in the temperate glories of spring sunshine. I spent much time looking at the sycamores and ashes that line the river below Kettlewell, at the flaking bark of the sycamores, green or grey with lichen, and at the furrowed trunks of mature ash trees.

The shape of sycamores varies greatly. Typically, I suppose, the branches form a broad dome above the trunk, forming a general impression of sturdy grace. They are comely rather than elegant trees. But there are some that aspire heavenwards with long, slender trunks and with an outgrowing of branches and subsidiary stems that does not interrupt the rising line of the whole tree. There are two such on the beat where I was fishing today. They are right on the water's edge and there are great trout down among their roots. But, in spite of these fine specimens, sycamores are not my favourite trees.

The elm is best of all, especially when hung with blossom in late May, and the more so since you must now look at every flowering elm in the sad certainty that it is doomed to die before its time. And the low canopy and the concave lines of a typical English elm make it very beautiful. Second comes the beech, with the silver shining of its bark, with the slender intricacy of its shoots and buds, and with the marvellous translucence of the young leaf. Birches are fine trees, with that startling winter contrast between the white bark and the purple branches. A large birch is very fine, for it combines the impressiveness of size with all the refinement of smaller specimens. But they are never big enough to be truly noble and they do not soar with the easy elegance of the beech. But look at the birch and the beech and at their intricate tracery of tapering shoots; then look at the stubby fingers which a sycamore points at the sky, and you will acknowledge that the sycamore is no aristocrat among trees.

I have forgotten the oak, but northern oaks are too often stunted. Young oak leaves, gleaming brown with the spring sun shining through the distinctive shape that can be confused with no other leaf, make all oaks precious. And pheasants love acorns, which make oaks dear to the keeper unless they are just over his boundary. Ash trees are in all respects undistinguished, with knobbly branches and buds like clotted scars, with no grace of form and with unmemorable leaves. Only the hedger likes the ash. The branches of chestnuts droop like sagging breasts. Willows are untidy trees, but they flush shining brown in spring and, on windy days in summer, the silver undersides of their leaves make the season seem almost young again, whereas in March pussy willows insist that is spring when cold winds are trying to tell you that it is not. Alders are sturdy but graceless; the pale orange profusion of their catkins in spring is the best thing about them. Blossoming cherries are miracles of beauty. Rowans are lovely and lonely trees. Summer foliage is dispiriting in its heaviness. Blankets of conifers are an abomination. A small planting of firs or pines or larches is a different matter. And trees in autumn are unquestionably a separate subject.

I am off to London tomorrow. I shall be there for close on a week, watching boys play fives and meeting old friends and seeing what beauties the spring of the year can bring to the streets of North Harrow.

2 April

I enjoyed my four days spent at the back of the fives courts in St. Paul's. I was delighted by the achievements of my players and proud of Jamie, my captain, who is now the national schools' singles champion. But there is something almost pitiable in the way we coaches identify with our players. It is a form of vicarious fulfilment. It is a way of reliving in others the days of our youth or of attaining a level of success of which we ourselves were never capable. And, at the end of it all, instead of the happy exhaustion produced by vigorous exercise, there is the weariness of long standing and prolonged tension. There may be a hint of envy too and, in my case, there is certainly a feeling of regret: that I only discovered the delights of competitive games when I became a schoolmaster, that I spent my own schooldays despising the sweaty antics of games-players and posing as an intellectual, which meant skulking by the river Hodder and thinking pretentious thoughts and smoking Woodbines.

Anyway that is fives over for another season (except for the Scottish doubles in May) and I shall not see London again for another twelve months. The best things about London are the beer, which is very good indeed, and the plane trees, which are very beautiful, especially the bark. But I shall be happy to wait a year for both of them.

This morning I drove to Gisburn to collect Merlin from kennels. On the way back I realised that I have been unfair to ash trees, for some tall specimens certainly achieve elegance. It is an elegance that should be appreciated from a distance, for the features that go to make it are not lovely in themselves. But I have been unfair to the ash. A tall and well-proportioned one is a fine tree. I have also been unfair to the northern oak. I saw some today that were unquestionably noble trees, with each large horizontal bough turning upwards and swelling out, in its own shoots and branches, to form a dome, so that the canopy seemed a succession of small cupolas. Beech trees stroke the sky with countless slender shoots; sycamores clutch at it. The branches of chestnut trees turn away from the light and then have second thoughts.

There is no fishing weather in prospect. There has been sleet and hail today, and snow is lying on the high fells. Blackbirds have stopped singing in the evening and the hawthorns are only just beginning to turn green. Sloe blossom is still shut tight within the bud, while the wind is sharp and they talk of heavy rain for tomorrow.

3 April

Easter Sunday. A sullen sky and a raw wind, with no birds singing to greet the day of redemption. I went to mass in an ugly little church, where a shabby band of worshippers - I was as shabby as the rest of them - keened resurrection hymns with a complete disregard for melody and with utter contempt for the wheezings and moanings of a revolting electric organ. Half the congregation probably had hangovers; perhaps some of them were fornicators; doubtless others hated their wives or husbands or had just defrauded the Inland Revenue.

It was mass as it ought to be. The tokens of sin were stamped on every face. There was no mood of rejoicing. There was no beauty in any outward feature of the ritual. But the church was full to overflowing, full of men and women drawn there in the knowledge of their unworthiness, in their need of pardon and in their common belief that there, amid surroundings of surpassing dreariness, they would encounter God as truly as the disciples stumbled upon his risen presence on the first Easter of all.

Mass is much better when it is devoid of aesthetic appeal. When there is a fine choir singing Palestrina I listen to the music. But when a tone-deaf congregation is coughing and screeching its way through tuneless hymns, and when there is no incense to carry my prayers to heaven, then I shut my eyes and close my ears and think about the real presence.

I should have liked to go fishing today. It is good to celebrate the resurrection with a fishing rod in your hand. But the wind is howling outside my window and the first raindrops are slapping against the panes. And so I shall think about blood sports for a while and then take Merlin out. This afternoon I shall talk to my diary about my dog.

Western man feels guilty about the way he has treated many of the human societies with which he has come into contact. Red Indians and Eskimos - I think you are meant to call them something else now - are obvious examples. We also feel guilty about the way we have plundered and polluted the natural world; and it is fashionable to believe - it may also be true to believe - that Eskimos and Red Indians display a very proper respect and reverence for nature, and that we have much to learn from them.

Now the Indian's admiration for the buffalo was inspired by its strength and its speed, by the fact that it is edible and because its hide can be used for many purposes. He admired it and he killed it. If you had suggested to him that he should limit his diet to fruits and berries, leaving buffaloes to roam in peace, he would have thought that you were mad. He would also have thought that you were a dangerous heretic, because he knew that for men to hunt and eat the buffalo was part of the divine scheme of things.

He held the buffalo sacred and believed that it was its power to nourish himself and his fellow Indians that made it a holy creature. He saw no inconsistency between his high regard for the buffalo and his fondness for killing it. He hunted it with joy, he killed it with a reverent thankfulness, he ate it with holy relish. He was, in his relations with the buffalo, rather like me and the pheasant. And he shared, with me and with most sportsmen of today, an eager desire that the creatures he hunted should flourish and multiply. He killed the individual and prayed that the race would continue to prosper and fill the plains.

I have to admit that I am relieved not to find myself a Red Indian of old. All that chanting and dancing would have been very tedious; I should have had to creep off at every opportunity to smoke solitary pipes of peace. I am also very happy to admit that the analogy between the hunting Indian and the shooter of pheasants is inexact. My point, if I can remember it, is this: that the Indian loved his buffalo both dead and alive; he loved its magnificence as a living creature, he loved to match his skill against its living power and he loved to feast upon the sustaining flesh that it yielded him in death. For all these reasons, he wanted a world full of buffaloes, just as I, who enjoy the beauty, the challenge and the taste of a high pheasant, delight in well stocked coverts.

And it seems to me that the Indian and I, hunting with admiration and eating with thankfulness, both show a very proper regard for the true value of the creatures we hunt and kill and eat. What I want to know is this. Why does your bearded liberal in Hampstead or Hammersmith think that the Indian, in his involvement with the buffalo, got it right, whereas I have got it so hopelessly and harmfully wrong in my dealings with pheasants and trout? Why does he stroke his beard reflectively and think that the world would be a better place if Columbus had never climbed into a boat and discovered America, and if, unbeknown to us Westerners, vast herds of buffalo still thundered over the plains with the Apaches in hot pursuit, whereas, at the very mention of hunting for the pot here in England, he starts pulling out whole tufts of beard and starts bellowing about his hatred of blood sports as an affront to the values of a civilised society?

He is a strange creature, your bearded liberal from Hampstead or Islington. His very beard is a statement, an expression of yearning for a time when men lived less artificial lives in closer communion with seed and beast. When he meets such men in books or on television - if he has one - he is lost in wonder and admiration. But any approximation to such men and their ways in his own country is quite intolerable to him and calls for instant legislation. It is quite likely that he is also opposed to organised games on the grounds that they are inegalitarian and foster sinister competitive urges. I wonder if he is happy for his Red Indians to play lacrosse? And I have spent so much time with buffaloes and Indians that I have no time left for my dog.

4 April

I enjoyed my diary yesterday and was perhaps swept beyond the bounds of common sense by delight in the absurd. Of course I was not trying to suggest that I am generally similar to Red Indians as they were before the coming of the cavalry, except, that is, in one respect: that I admire the creatures I kill, that I regard the sweet flesh of the pheasant as part of nature's bounty - there to be harvested and enjoyed - and that, although I am happy to kill individual pheasants and mallard and grouse, I want a world full of them, and not merely because I like to shoot them.

It strikes me as odd that many of my friends, whether or not they wear beards and live in Hammersmith or Islington, are inclined to approve of the old Indians' involvement with nature, arguing that it puts our habits of exploitation to shame, whereas they are disposed to look down their noses at my similar, though necessarily less intimate and more artificial, attachment to fields, woods, rivers and the creatures that live there. I think that my unsentimental admiration for the pheasant and the trout is correctly founded and recognises their true place in the economy of nature. I see an attitude similar to my own in the way true hunting peoples look upon their prey. Since their treatment of nature is widely recognised as wise and reverential, I look for a similar approval of my own conduct. And that will do, at least for the time being.

Hail is the weather's special offer for today. There is pale sunshine with a sharp wind blowing through it, a wind that every hour or so brings in a cover of cloud with a brief battery of hail. It is violent while it lasts, but soon the sunshine hurries back and the greenfinches start talking again. Rivers are brimful and gurgling. You cannot walk five paces off the road without an ooze or a squelch. It is the wettest spring I have ever known and I should love it were it not that I want to be fishing. I should love the vigour of the wind and the swift onmarch of dark clouds, the clatter of the hail and the probing brightness of the sun. I should delight in the rushing energy of streams and the yielding wetness of the earth. But I want to be fishing and I am fretting like a child. It is too wet, too cold and too windy for fishing, and so I shall have to be content with training the dog.

I have owned Merlin for just over two years and he is just over three and a half years old. He is a big springer, bigger than many labradors. He is liver and white and altogether very handsome. His breeding is impeccable, with field trial champions scattered all over his pedigree. He is a neurotic dog, frightened of children and strangers. He is inexhaustible in the field and will face any sort of cover. Gorse seems to be his favourite; he drives right through it with a manic relish while more sensible dogs are still sniffing around the edges and deciding that they would prefer not to bother. When I got him he was undoubtedly well trained. His faults are now as follows:

His mouth is less soft than it should be. He does not break bones or crush rib-cages, but occasionally he chews flesh. Most birds are undamaged and brought quickly to hand and, the more difficult the retrieve, the less likely he is to damage a pheasant or duck. I can live with his mouth, although it causes moments of embarrassment. He has never delivered a bird that was ruined for the pot, for, when he does chew one, it seems always to be on its back.

He has developed into a pegger of birds, by which we mean a dog that picks up unshot game before it flushes and then carries it back proudly to his master. I fear this talent will develop with age, although, in Merlin's defence, it is mainly in thick gorse when he pounces on the birds, where they are very slow to get on the wing. I have worked him in the beating line at my syndicate shoot in Wigglesworth and he has never touched an unwounded pheasant. But, last Boxing Day at High Park, when I shot with Austin and the bag was seven pheasants, three of them were Merlin's sole responsibility. I would hear a sudden commotion in the gorse, mingled sounds of flapping and snorting, and I would think to myself: 'Blast him; he's got another.' And when Merlin pegs a bird, he is not always eager to deliver it, and his mouth is at its roughest when he decides to help himself.

But his worst fault is one he shares with many springers, for he is, bless his heart, an unpredictable beast. He will flush four rabbits and gaze at me proudly, with a look almost of reproach for my ever doubting his steadiness. And then the fifth will prove too much for him and he is off in frantic pursuit, deaf to my whistle, deaf to my anguished roars, returning only when temptation has gone to ground, slinking back with a doleful and apologetic air and seeming to be promising me that this is the last time and that he will never do it again. And I can never be sure when he will decide that he prefers chasing game to flushing it. He will work for half an hour, or for a whole day, with exemplary obedience. And then suddenly, when I try to stop him as he is hunting out a hedge and pulling too far ahead, he insists that he is a free spirit and does exactly what he wants. It rarely lasts more than a minute, but it turns me purple with rage and it means I cannot work him on rough shoots other than my own, because hosts are rarely amused when a guest's dog flushes a dozen birds just out of range of the guns.

One more fault and then I can begin to sing his praises, for he is a dog with many virtues. But he does, curse him for a wilful and refractory spaniel, run in to the fall of killed or wounded game. Thank God he does not run in to shot and, to be fair to him, he will sit at a peg all through a drive and wait more or less patiently for it to end. But, if he is hunting cover and flushes a bird and if I shoot it, he rarely waits to be told before setting off to collect it. And you cannot punish a spaniel for coming back to you with a pheasant in its mouth, especially one that looks so inordinately pleased with himself.

He has a variable mouth. He pegs birds. Sometimes he chases rabbits. There are occasions when, even without the temptation of fleeing game, he treats my whistle with contempt. When out with his master rough shooting he retrieves at his own pleasure rather than at mine. There are times when I almost hate him. But then I think of his boundless enthusiasm and his readiness to plunge into the thickest and sharpest cover. I think of him in the gorse at High Park, where the only clue to his whereabouts is the sound of urgent motion in a jungle of gorse scratching and tearing growth. I see his bleeding tongue and his bloodied nose at the end of a particularly rough excursion. I think of the headlong speed at which he works and of the tireless energy with which he tracks a pricked bird and almost always finds it. I think of the day at Wigglesworth when five pheasants were down, way back behind the guns in an untended and impenetrable spruce plantation, and how Merlin had gathered them all before the other dogs had managed to find a single one. Yes! There are times when I feel proud of him, as well as other times when he fills me with anger and shame.

And he is a very gentle dog and there are many faults of which he is free. He never whines at a peg. He never runs off with a retrieve. He never refuses to enter cover and he never bears a grudge. There are days when he works impeccably and, on such days, I forgive him unconditionally for those days when he has not been perfect. I think that, at the moment, he is getting better rather than worse and I look upon him as a friend. Given my stated opinions of animals, I suppose it is inconsistent of me to think of a dog as a comrade. I do not care a fig. He is my partner in sport, my companion on summer walks or on winter evenings by the fire; and I know that, when at last he dies, I shall bid farewell to him with tears.

5 April

Merlin's faults stem, I think, not from his intrinsic nature or from defective early training; nor really from me. They are faults bred by circumstance, in particular the fact that, before he came to me, he had been used to pick up on a large shoot where there were bags of four and five hundred birds. And so, passing into my ownership, he found little days, with bags of half a dozen pheasants, frustrating and unsatisfying. Moreover he had never been shot over. He had worked occasionally in the beating line, but he had spent most of his shooting days sitting way behind the guns and waiting to start retrieving when the shooting stopped. He was not accustomed to a master with a shotgun, or to the wild excitement of flushing a bird and seeing it crumple and fall a second later.

Of course it is my fault! Of course I should have realised that he was still an inexperienced dog and needed time to come to terms with different conditions of work. And perhaps his first trainer gave him too much retrieving too soon, so that, once he started collecting birds, he expected it to be a pleasure that went on and on, and then found it difficult to understand, when out with me, that there was only one pheasant to collect, that it was time to forget about gathering and to start hunting again. He found all this difficult to absorb. He became excitable and impulsive and prone to forget himself. And I failed to realise that he was a dog confused by the unfamiliar demands that were being placed upon him. I was wrong to absolve myself of blame at the beginning of this entry and I am now reaping the harvest of my own foolishness.

It may just be possible to eradicate some of Merlin's worst failings. I should like to stop him running in. I should like to feel more confident that he will stop when I blow the stop whistle and then come back to me when I call him in. I work him every day and try to insist that he obeys me. It is only rarely that he does not. The last half-dozen rabbits have proved resistible temptations and today, although he met no game, he needed no correction of any sort. I shall devise stratagems to tempt and to teach him. I shall refuse to despair when he refuses to learn. I shall report on his progress. It is, of course, too late to turn him into a model gundog, but too many shooters are far too complacent about the failings of their dogs. I shall not go into next season without having made the effort to improve mine.

6 April

My diary today is a fairy story with a happy ending. It goes like this.

More than twenty years ago, when I was a student, I used to spend my long summer holidays fishing the Wenning. I caught a few trout and countless hordes of parr and thoroughly enjoyed myself, for the very top of the river, and the two becks that came together to form it, were wild and lovely waters, flowing through a wide landscape of rushy pastures and green meadows and white limestone, with the bold and distinctive lines of Ingleborough rising in the near distance.

The years passed and I fished the little Wenning less and less, for by now I had fallen in love with the Wharfe. Then men with diggers came to the river I had almost abandoned and thought they would improve it. They thought what a good idea it would be to gouge out the gravelly runs between the small pools, to chop down any trees and bushes that might get in their way, to heap up the banks way above the normal height of the water, so that the Wenning would turn into a well-behaved little river, accepting its confinement and flowing on its way in an obedient and orderly and thoroughly obliging fashion, having renounced its former habit of occasionally spilling out into the surrounding fields.

By their own standards they did an excellent job, but when I paid a rare visit to the Wenning and saw what they had done, I was heart-broken. I gazed in disbelief at the scarred banks, at the stumps of trees and at the channel of water that had once been a river. I realised how much the Wenning had meant to me and knew at once that I could never fish there again. And so I said a solemn farewell to the nursery of my fishing life and left it, as I thought, for ever.

That was fifteen years ago. It is a sad story best told in a few words. I thought it was the end of the story. But at the keeper's supper in Kilnsey the other week, I met my friend Derek Law, who used to fish the Wenning in the old days and deserted it as I did. He told me that he had bought a ticket again last season, that the river was begin-ning to recover and that his wife Anne had caught a fine seatrout from it in the back-end. Before I went to London I put fifteen pounds in an envelope and sent it to the estate office. My permit was waiting for me when I returned north, and today, for the first time in fifteen years, I went fishing on the Wenning.

There was sadness waiting for me there, for it can never be the same again. There are pools and runs that have gone for ever and there are neatly profiled banks that belong to a dyke, not to a trout stream. But Derek is right; the Wenning has proved more resilient than I had thought possible, and up above the top corner, where the river turns by a copse of sycamores and oaks and alders, it seems almost unchanged, and the Clapham and Austwick becks are both as wild and lovely as they were in the days of my young manhood. And the spring olives hatched in dark droves between noon and three. And the trout rose to greet them and I took five weighing four pounds four ounces and I missed several at the strike and put some down and returned half a dozen.

My first trout was the smallest, a mere half-pounder that I would certainly have spared if I had known what was coming. But I remembered the Wenning as a river of small trout and I thought that this one and another of the same size would make both my day and my breakfast. The next two trout were both a couple of ounces over the pound and they both fought deep and hard before they yielded and were drawn over the net. A fish of fourteen ounces came from the bottom of Austwick beck and by now I was a very happy fisherman.

The wind was gusting upstream and blowing pale sunshine over the fields and over the bright stream. The water was full and clear and singing and shone back at the sun. There were redshank piping querulously on the breezy air. Curlews were greeting the spring with sorrow-laden calls. There were pheasants shouting in the woods and strutting along the margins of cover. Mallard lifted and quacked off the pools. A sand martin flew rasping above me. A pair of teal whistled through the sky. A single partridge burst from a rushy hollow and sped away on noisy wings. It was cool and windy. There was snow on the steep flanks of Ingleborough. But it was spring and the olives were hatching and everywhere there was life and movement; and I had come where I had not been for fifteen years and found it better than I had dared hope.

I forgot about fishing and roamed up Clapham beck, sitting and smoking for a while. Then I searched out places from the past before I turned round and wandered downstream. I killed another fish, one of twelve ounces, and then ambled back to the Land Rover and to my sandwiches. On the way home I shouted aloud in thanksgiving to the good God and to the kind friend who had between them given the Wenning back to me. And almost the best of it is that now I can begin to reclaim my memories of those long university summers more than twenty years ago.

Until now I have avoided them, because they brought too much sadness. But, as I fish the Wenning this summer, they will come back to me without bitterness. I shall welcome them as I sit by the river and smoke. And the seatrout will come with the summer floods and, who knows, I may even catch a salmon from the junction pool.

That is the end, or the beginning, of my fairy story about the Wenning. I finish this entry on a practical note, advising fishers never to forget the dry fly in spring, and I say this in spite of my general preference for wet flies. Of the five fish I killed today, three of them came to a floater: Kite's Imperial was the downfall of three of them; another seized a Waterhen Bloa and another an Orange Partridge. I started with wet flies, fishing them upstream as almost always. I caught the first two fish I covered, but more fish refused my flies, and when the hatch thickened and the trout began to feed with enthusiasm, I rose no more fish until I realised that they were eating duns and tied on a dry fly. It was what they wanted and it stayed on my cast for the rest of the day.

It is hardly an over-simplification to say that, at this time of year, the only fly that matters is the large dark olive. The Eden breeds a few true march browns and I remember an afternoon on the Wharfe when the trout rose with gusto at some small black fly, with a red spot on it, that I have never seen before or since. Further south the hawthorn fly comes early, but here it is a creature of the May. I have seen iron blues on the Eden in April, never on the Wharfe. Their season coincides with the may-blossom; they are creatures of Mary's month but sadly they are much less common than they used to be.

In early April it will almost certainly be large dark olives (I like to call them spring olives) or nothing, which makes choosing your artificial a simple task. But do not assume that, because it is early in the season and the trout are hungry, they will swallow whatever you throw at them. I have known days on the Wharfe when they scorned a Waterhen and wanted only the Orange Partridge. I have known days on the Eden when nothing but a Snipe and Yellow would convince them. I have known more days, on both rivers, when they disdained sunk patterns and had eyes only for the dry fly. Perhaps the duns sit longer

61

on the surface when the day is cold, and are thus easier victims than the nymph. Whatever it is, when the trout are on spring olive duns, it is unlikely that you will need any artificial other than a Kite's Imperial on a size fourteen hook.

7 April

I was to have gone hedging today, but rain and wind have put paid to that. Instead I am still thinking about yesterday. I never caught such a bag of trout from the Wenning in the old days. A single fish of a pound was the triumph of the season for me. I suppose I was an incompetent fisherman, charging up and down the river, full of youthful eagerness and short of skill. I cannot believe that the Wenning has actually improved in the intervening years, although it may be that a reduced run of seatrout has helped the brown trout to thrive. Those vast shoals of parr must have consumed a huge amount of food.

The trout I killed yesterday were very beautiful, with red spots and shining flanks and broad tails. They looked lovely, lying together in the grass, and I kept taking them out of my bag and setting them beside each other and gazing at them all over again. I did not feel guilty. I did not feel cruel, or like a murderer, and I do not set this down to blunted or depraved sensibilities. I caught them and killed them. I blessed the God that has given us pure water and the trout that swim there. I ate two of them for breakfast. Their flesh was pink and delectable. The other three I shall cook tomorrow and eat them with friends. We shall eat them reverently, with *premier cru* Chablis in our glasses. We shall drink to my surpassing skill as an angler, and I shall think that in catching five trout, in killing them and cooking them and sharing them with others, I have brought pleasure to myself and to my fellows, and that, in a world full of wickedness I have managed for once to avoid it and done good rather than evil. *Deo gratias.*

10 April

I am a weak and sinful man. The trout were delicious, as was the Chablis that accompanied them. The pheasant had been casseroled in port wine and I thought it went very well with *Chateau Hortevie '85.* Cotherstone cheese, from near Barnard Castle, is one of the finest of English cheeses. I like to drink it with a glass or two of Olga Raffault's incomparable Chinon. The coffee was dark and strong, just as coffee should be. But then a convivial evening turned into a booze-up. I went to bed cursing myself as a hopeless drunkard and woke up feeling guilty and with a dry mouth and a headache.

I hate hangovers. I hate the way they take all the pleasure out of being alive. They nag at you all day long, reminding you that excess is avoidable, that sin is corruption. There is no answer to anything they tell you. They are right, and anyway you feel too weary to argue with them. The sore head, the rough throat, the tired and aching limbs: these are all very unpleasant. But worst of all is the unceasing moral rebuke that a hangover brings with it. It is the reason why I do my best to avoid them. Hating yourself is a foretaste of hell.

Intemperance, in the form of a bottle of Glenmorangie, ruined what would have been a delightful evening, and poisoned the remembered pleasures of food and wine. As a penance I went hedging, in cold and windy sunshine that turned, at about four o'clock, into heavy snow. It was a cathartic sort of day. In the biting air I hacked through old wood and laid new wood until my wrists would have no more. Thorns pierced my gloves and tore at my face. Briars lurked and pricked. The saw stuck fast in thick branches when it was almost through. My bill-hook grew blunter and blunter and the hedge I was trying to shape was generally uncooperative. When the snow came I gave up. I filled the three hoppers that are still hanging. I smoked and shivered and listened to pheasants shouting all around me. Then I drove home and sat in a chair and felt like a worm.

Today clouds are floating serenely through a blue sky and there is kind sunshine. Yesterday's snow is shining on the high fells but the air down in the valley is soft. The breeze is whispering of forgiveness and I feel well again.

Merlin has developed a new aberration. At the beginning of his daily exercise he ignores the recall whistle completely and goes questing on his own. I rant and rave and in a minute or two he returns, looking guilty and ashamed. I shout at him again and pull his ears and then he behaves himself. I do not understand dogs. Tomorrow will be a fishing day, on the Wenning or the Eden. If I catch any trout, I shall see to it that the eating of them does not degenerate into a carouse.

11 April

A fishless day on the Wenning. There was some fly, but never more than a trickle and I never saw a fish rise and never moved one. But it was pleasant in the sun and the birds were busy along the banks and in the surrounding fields. I wandered along Fen beck, slow and deep and just the place for a big fish on a summer evening. I dreamed of days in May, and of later days when the seatrout will have come. I am very happy to have returned to the Wenning. I shall spend much of the summer repossessing it, and I shall explore the becks much more thoroughly than I ever did twenty years ago.

The Wenning, I feel it already, is going to be my chief delight this season. The Wharfe and the Eden will be neglected, and I shall probably catch fewer trout as a result, for the Wharfe and the Eden are undoubtedly finer trout streams. But falling back in love with a river is an intoxicating experience. It is like discovering a long-lost treasure. It is like coming home from years of weary exile. There is all the thrill of first finding and there is all the warm contentment of finding again. It is the connection with the past that makes the whole affair so special, but not in a sentimental or self-indulgent way. I do not walk the banks, thinking about the young man who walked there two decades ago. I do not yearn for summers gone or for departed youth or for any nonsense of that sort. But the past is very much a part of the present; it is there with a gentle and unspecific potency and it makes me feel very glad to be back.

I have been unfair to ash trees and I shall sing my palinode now, before the leaf bursts and blurs the distinctive lines of trees unhung with foliage. I saw at least half a dozen ash trees today which were very beautiful, lifting their branches with an airy sweep and curve that was all their own. The sycamore is a tidy sort of tree, with its neat and regular dome. It looks very pretty when it stands, with several others of its kind, on a rise of ground against the horizon. But the ash scorns such easy symmetry and achieves a more careless grace; and there is an expression of yearning in the way it raises itself to the sky. There is no interruption of movement, for the branches do not break the uprising of the trunk; they transmit and channel it into fresh and flowing lines. I was wrong about the ash. But it must be a solitary ash, standing tall in the corner of a field. Such a tree makes the sycamore seem earth-bound, and the horse chestnut, by way of further comparison, strains after elegance and still looks stout.

12 April

Another day with, as Skues used to put it, a toom creel. To judge from his books such days possessed the charm of the unusual for him. I confess that I could do with less of them. My creel today came home toom from the Eden and Scandal beck, one of its tributary streams. The beck is new water for me, for the club has just taken it. And very inviting it is, with long glides over gravel, short runs over the living rock, little pools on corners and between boulders and under hanging willows.

I spent most of my time wandering along the banks and wondering how it will fish when at last the trout acknowledge that the season has started and that it is time again for them to be caught. Away from the wind it was warm in the sun, and there were huge white clouds floating through the sky. There was a good hatch of olives and it was disappointing to see no response from the fish, but I am sure there are big trout waiting to be caught here. It is a beck made for fish and for fishermen.

13 April

My conscience drove me to High Park, armed with a bill-hook rather than with a fishing rod. And now I have done all the hedging I am going to do this year - I make it sound as though I have been at it for years - and I have done a rotten job of it. When I compare my work with Austin's, I feel ashamed and wonder why I bothered. But the truth is that I have enjoyed it, that I have improved as I have gone along and that most of my work will live and put forth shoots. An expert would quite properly laugh to scorn my efforts at hedge-laying, although Austin will laugh only in his heart and will doubtless tell me that I have done well. Your tactless expert can laugh as long and as loudly as he likes. I have enjoyed it and I shall be better at it next year. And next year it may be my hedge, and then I shall be able to hack away to my heart's content. The point of it all is to hold birds. I shall have to wait till November to see if it has fulfilled its purpose. If it seems that it has and especially if by then the hedge is mine, I shall set to work again with frantic enthusiasm.

Today was almost the best sort of spring day, with sunshine and a lively wind and a few sailing clouds, spreading the sense of peace that white clouds, moving unhurriedly through the blue sky, bring to the land and to the people beneath them. There was some power in the sun, but it was a power tempered by the touch of a breeze. It was a bracing day, a vigorous day full of the noise of birds. Cock pheasants were

66

strutting and calling hoarsely. Chaffinches were singing across the beck. I heard my first willow warbler, sounding sad to be back in England. There was a blackbird singing sweetly from the hedge and a song-thrush repeating itself in an ash tree across the meadow.

I went to fill the hopper in the Douglas firs and, looking up into the branches, I saw an extravagant tail and a red squirrel staring down at me with curiosity. It is time to stop feeding my pheasants now, but there are still two binfuls of grain. I shall indulge my birds this spring. I shall pamper them through the first weeks of nesting time in the hope that they will lay lots of fertile eggs. And it is not only pheasants that will benefit from my generosity. So too will the crows, curse them. They will eat my grain and then show their gratitude by helping themselves to my pheasants' eggs. But finches frequent my hoppers as well as crows and pheasants, finches, tits and red squirrels. And so, given half a chance, do the sheep. But they are not here yet. It will be August before I need bother about sheep and, in August, they will be the least of my worries. The farmer next door tells me that he has seen a fox. I wish I could see him too and find out where he lives. If only I could, he would not be alive much longer.

As I drove home late this afternoon, the trees seemed further on than when I passed them in the morning. Near Grange, hawthorns are almost in full leaf. Willows can wait no longer and are turning greener by the hour. Horse chestnuts are spreading wide their sticky buds and the sycamores are greeting the beginning of warm days. Nothing is as beautiful as spring, and nothing has the same power to make middle-aged men seem young again.

17 April

It is an evening of complete serenity: windless, cloudless, with chattering greenfinches and singing blackbirds outside the window. It is the sort of evening when sin and sorrow seem to have no place in the world, an evening for calm reflection and quiet happiness. The light is pale and pure, the air is just touched with cold but not unkind. The trees are still. The leaves too are resting and waiting to unfold more tomorrow. The sloe-blossom has opened, startlingly white and soft and rounded against its setting of dark and prickly shoots. Celandines have closed up for the night. There is a blue shimmer of water across the bay with the blue shapes of hills beyond. It is very beautiful and it defies description. I list details, mere accidents. The essence of it all eludes me.

On Thursday and Friday I was fishing in Wharfedale. A cruel north wind blew through both days. Olives were lonely creatures and there were few rising fish. Even mittened fingers ached with the cold. I saw two trout move and I caught them both. The fly that deceived them was a Waterhen, seized with an eagerness that made setting the hook an easy business. The strange thing is that I rarely felt bored. I fished for hours with no real hope of a trout, but I enjoyed it never-theless.

Two or three years ago I feared that I was growing tired of fishing. Thank God the fear has passed. I know already that this summer I shall want to do nothing but fish. I shall resent teaching in May when the iron blues are hatching on the Wharfe and the Eden. I shall sit in my study on evenings in June, reading Ovid resentfully and marking heaps of exercise books in a mood of rising anger. I shall rush to the water whenever possible and, almost certainly, I shall fish badly, because I shall be nervous and impatient and too eager for the first trout.

I shall frighten fish before I cast to them. I shall bungle the strike or play heavy fish too hard. I shall lose my temper and end up throwing stones in the water and I shall curse myself for being the worst fish-erman in the world. But there will come an evening when things go well, when the trout rise to my flies and splash loudly in the failing light as they struggle against the pressure of the rod, struggling in vain until they surrender and are drawn over the net. There will come such an evening, and with it will come peace, sliding down the silver water, rising white with the first curls of mist from the pools, hanging and gleaming and tangible on the still air. There will come such an evening and, when it comes, I shall thank God for many things; but above all I shall thank him for making me a fisherman.

Thoughts of term are beginning to loom. Tomorrow the Wenning. On Tuesday the Eden. Wednesday will be for one or the other of them. And then on Thursday I turn back into a schoolmaster.

18 April

The morning was cloudy and the wind had swung westerly. The air was softer. It was a gentle sort of spring day, a day for slow growth, for slow and steady unfolding rather than for an impatient pushing out of the earth or for an impetuous thrusting from the bud. I started fishing at eleven o'clock.

There was no fly until after one, but there was plenty to divert me. There were snipe drumming above the rough pastures, a sound that is rarely heard these days, but in old fishing books there are always snipe drumming their way through spring days by the river. It is an odd sound, rather like an aerial bleating, rather more like fast and rhythmical blowing into a milk-bottle. It is too breathy a sound to be adequately represented by its conventional name. It goes well with the wheezing call and airy wing beats of tumbling lapwings. There were lapwings falling about the sky today and scarcely a minute passed without the mournful call of the curlew.

I am sure that the curlew is a guilt-laden bird. Its song throbs with sorrow, a mournful confession of some primal sin that can never be expiated, a plangent lament that has rung down the centuries in warning and repentance. It is one of the saddest and most beautiful sounds in nature and, in spring, curlews float through the sky like lost souls.

Waiting for the rise - if there was to be one - and walking slowly upstream, I amused myself by listening to birds and fitting their songs to a human type. The curlew, of course, is a despairing sinner, whereas the wren is untroubled by guilt. Its song is one of affirmation, with no burden of suffering or sorrow. It is a beautiful song, but it is perhaps a shade too assertive, and it rings out with just a hint of arrogance. The wren has no time for doubt or for doubters. I think he may be a born-again christian, inclined to intone 'hallelujah' at inappropriate moments and to say 'amen' in a loud voice. But his moral regeneration, praise the Lord, has not blinded his love of beauty. He is a born-again christian who will have nothing to do with guitars.

The willow warbler - I heard several today - is a poet: a poet that sees all the beauty of the spring and knows that it will pass: a poet of the shadows and of melancholy thoughts, an introspective poet that avoids company and perfects his sad art in lonely contemplation. The chaffinch, by contrast, is a completely different sort. He is an uncom-plicated soul, happy to enjoy the pleasures of the present day without thought of tomorrow. He sits in the sun and enjoys company and his chief failing is that he is incurably cheerful. He is very tiresome when you are feeling jaded or depressed.

Round every corner there was a pair of redshank, rising on pointed wings and piping plaintively. I did not get very far with the redshank, although I decided that he was definitely restless and probably neurotic. I was still analysing him when I noticed that olives were beginning to hatch and, from then on, teal were just teal - there was a pair again at the bottom of Austwick Beck - and sand martins were plain and simple sand martins. I was glad to see my first swallow and my first sandpiper, but I paused no more than a second to welcome them back. I was stalking along the riverbank, watching the olives floating down the water and fluttering onto the air, willing a trout to rise and willing others to follow his example.

But the response to a fairly thick hatch of fly was disappointing. I heard a fish rise in a fast run. Then I saw him and saw too that he was feeding confidently, that he was swallowing a fly two or three times a minute. But then I did a foolish thing, for I was above him and I fished my flies down to him. I knew that it was wrong, even as I lengthened line to cover him. He rose, of course, and I felt him briefly and he was gone. I am incompetent with downstream flies. Even the experts miss a good number of rises, but I miss almost all of them. I do not enjoy fishing wet flies downstream. My motive for employing the method today was pure indolence. I could not be bothered to get out of the water and get beneath my fish. And, because of my indolence, I bungled what seemed as though it was going to be the day's one chance of a fish.

I paced upstream and, although the olives were hatching strongly, I did not see another rise. I came to the meeting of the waters, decided to explore Austwick Beck and there, round the first corner, was what I had been longing for: three or four trout eating olives as they floated down a gentle glide. I made myself put on a dry fly, an Imperial. It was a struggle, but I could see that the trout were on the dun. It is an absurd confession, but I have to admit that the hands that tied on the new fly were trembling with excitement. I have caught thousands of trout. What do a few more or a few less matter? When they matter no longer, I shall no longer be a fisherman.

Here at last was what I wanted in the form of rising trout. But I also wanted to catch some of them. I had been waiting all day and now was my chance and my hands were trembling with the happy prospect of success and with the dark fear of failure. Sin was a dim memory. Mortality was an irrelevance. Trout were all that mattered.

Once or twice the Imperial floated over the nearest of the feeding fish and was ignored. I tried again. A neb broke the surface and he was on. He fought like a trout twice his size. He dashed up the pool and then down and round the corner. I was forced to follow him and was very eager not to lose him. I had seen his turning flank and knew that, even though no monster, he was a good fish. He was a very strong trout and it must have been two minutes before he splashed to the surface and acknowledged defeat. He weighed one pound four ounces and he made the day. He had put down all the fish above him, for I had not dared to pull him away from them. I caught a second trout, again on the Imperial, from the very bottom of the beck. Then the hatch petered out and it was all over.

I wandered downstream, happy with the Wenning and with the two trout in my bag. The sun came out and a pair of roe deer splashed across the shallows below me and bounded off. Mallard sprang from the margins of the stream. Pheasants shouted in the woods. There was the dark silhouette of a blackbird, singing its heart out from the top of a hawthorn. I felt like singing myself and drank a cup of tea instead. Now I am looking forward to trout for breakfast.

20 April

The day before the beginning of term and a visit to the Wenning. It was meant to be the Eden but the pull of the rediscovered Wenning proved too strong. It was probably my last fishing trip for at least a fortnight, for I shall be burdened by a sense of duty and I shall not get my rods out until I know that my classes, especially my examination classes, are in proper order. I may steal an hour or two somewhere on the Eden, although I am not very fond of fishing for just an hour or two (except on summer evenings), but I shall not set off at twelve with no intention of returning before seven or eight o'clock. And, to be honest, it is not just conscience that will restrain me; as much as this, it is the knowledge that I cannot confidently expect to find rising fish until May is a week or two old. It is very frustrating to rush from work and find the river lifeless. It can happen, of course, at any time of the year, but it is much less likely once the trout have properly rediscovered the pleasures of surface feeding.

And this is something that has yet to happen. There was a big hatch this afternoon, between one and three o'clock, and I did not see a fish rise. At the bottom of Austwick beck the olives were jostling each other down the current and I could scarcely believe that no trout wanted to eat them. I waited for twenty minutes and then went searching for hungry fish on the river, returning half an hour later to find the fly as thick as ever. I shouted at the sleeping trout and ordered them to wake up and start feeding. I pointed out how temptingly the surface of the beck was littered with a profusion of juicy olives, but they would not listen and they would not rise. If I had not seen trout feeding there a couple of days ago, I should have refused to believe that there was a single fish within a mile of the place. I gave up in disgust and stumped off to the Land Rover.

I have fished eight days these holidays and I have killed nine fish. There have been better starts to the trout season and there have been starts much worse. The best thing about this season's early days, apart from my delight in returning to the Wenning, has been my hunger to go fishing. It is a fever with me again, as it was ten and twenty years ago, as it has not been for some years past. I have never lost my pleasure in fishing, but this April it has turned back into a passion. I do not know the reason, but I am very happy to acknowledge the fact that I am once more a man obsessed. Praise be to God.

24 April

The beginning of term has kept me from my diary for a few days. But I am in good humour. What a pleasure my five upper sixth formers are!

Reading Ovid with them is a pure delight. Meanwhile showers and warm winds have brought leaves to the trees and flowers to the earth beneath them. Sycamores and chestnuts are virtually in full leaf; to have written slightingly of them in earlier entries seems ungenerous when I gaze at them in their present loveliness. All the hedges are green now. The larches are turning. Anemones shine white in the woods and the fields are spread with a blue haze of speedwell. Daisies and dandelions have decided that their season has come; and very soon I shall have to admit to myself that it is too warm to go to bed with a hot water bottle. The very thought encourages me to pray for frost.

I went shooting clays this afternoon, with Austin and three boys. I managed to hit more than I missed and it was pleasant in the sun. Writing this has reminded me that my guns are still to clean, and so I had better finish this entry and attend to them before I go to the pub. I have my mind's eye set on Wednesday for an afternoon's fishing, and sometime this week I must go out to High Park.

25 April

I went along the river Rawthey late this afternoon with Merlin. There were swallows in plenty and, after the morning's rain, the air was shining with the marvellous purity that turns ordinary landscapes into visions of paradise, especially once the light begins to slant towards evening. The landscape around Brigflatts is no ordinary landscape, with the gleaming and sparkling of the river and the green spreading of the fields around it, with the swooping of swallows and with the rounded rising of the Howgills in the background. In this afternoon's transfiguring light, and with young foliage on many of the trees, it was more beautiful than I have ever seen it.

Oaks, beeches, ashes and elms have yet to open a leaf. The buds of alders are still not ready to burst. The full glory of spring is some time away. But this is the best time of all, for now the pulse of the season is at its most compelling; there remains something of the spareness of a winter landscape, but softened by the first flush of growth and transformed by the awakening touch of spring sunshine.

Even Merlin seemed moved by the beauties around him. He sat to the stop whistle and came to my call with prompt obedience. It was as though he did not want to spoil things, as though he sensed that discord would be out of place on such an afternoon. The truth of it is, of course, that there was no game to excite him, for there are no rabbits around Sedbergh now. They all died of myxomatosis last autumn and it was most inconsiderate of them. For rabbits are what I want, countless hordes of them, so that Merlin will be tempted and will fall, will be corrected and will then fall again; so that he will learn at last that chasing rabbits is a bad idea and renounce it for the rest of his life. I wonder how he will behave at High Park tomorrow, where there are a few rabbits, although not enough. Perhaps the breakthrough is near.

3 May

The true splendours of the spring have come to Sedbergh, and I have been too preoccupied to celebrate them in my diary or to revel in them along the banks of the Wenning or the Eden. Primroses are in bloom. The grass is suddenly thick and long and very green. The air smells of mown churchyards and cricket fields and, all day long, blackbirds are singing. Yesterday evening I saw a single swift and the sky will soon be full of their screaming.

A week has turned the season from promise to profusion. There have been moist days of sagging cloud and warm air. There have been bright days of breezy sunshine and floating clouds and, every day, I have yearned to go fishing and acknowledged grimly that there were more pressing calls on my time. But tomorrow it should be possible to get away for a few hours, as long as I do not spend all evening talking to myself in this diary.

I should have gone fishing this weekend past, but I had committed myself to going to Edinburgh for the last fives of this season. I played badly and enjoyed myself and, in Musselburgh, the sun was shining and the cherry trees were thick with blossom, welcoming the first days of Mary's month with lavish tribute and celebration.

My mind at the moment is full of High Park. Very soon I shall know whether I am going to buy 62 acres of rough grazing and tangled woodland, with a winding beck and a small meadow at the heart of it all. I am sick with longing for it. I want to cherish the sloping fields, to plant the climbing banks, to sit smoking by the weir-gate, while my pheasants shout at each other and think that it is all mine. I never believed that I was much bothered by the urge to possess things, except for books and guns and fishing rods and bottles of wine. I was wrong and, if it all comes to nothing, I shall be heart-broken.

I cannot bear to go to High Park again until I have learned whether or not I am to become its owner. I can scarcely bear to write about it. But I think about it all the time. I go to sleep counting up my assets and wondering how much I can raise my offer, if one of the neighbouring farmers decides to bid against me. Perhaps tomorrow I shall hear something and, if it is what I want to hear, I shall forget about fishing and laugh uproariously if the dog runs riot, and I shall most certainly drink a bottle of champagne.

4 May

To the Eden and Scandal Beck this afternoon, with wind and brief showers and a moving cover of grey clouds. There was no hatch (perhaps it happened before I got there), but chattering crowds of swallows were flying low over the water and I thought at first that the olives must be coming off the beck in profusion. I was mistaken, and I wonder what it was that brought the swallows dipping and swooping over the stream. Was it an act of joyful repossession by birds lately returned to last summer's haunts? Certainly it seemed like some sort of celebration, but I suppose it was nothing of the sort. I suppose it was merely hopeful investigation provoked by hunger.

There was precious little to satisfy a swallow's hunger. I saw perhaps a dozen olives and no sign of a moving trout. And the wind, which had been strong to begin with, soon turned into a howling gale. I fished a little in fits and starts, but there was no pleasure in it. I spent more time pacing the banks, thinking about money and the price of land.

As I paced and thought, I stumbled upon two mallard's nests, disturbing the sitting ducks in the course of my brooding progress. I admired the pale lining of down and the pale olive of the eggs. In one clutch there were seven of them, in the other there were nine. But both nests are in exposed places and I shall be surprised if they escape the attentions of sharp-eyed crows or questing weasels or hungry stoats. I expect, should I fish the same water next week, that I shall find them both plundered. Ground-nesting birds must be particularly short of brains.

It is still early in the trout season and, without hatching flies, you cannot hope to see rising fish. It is when the black gnats and the reed smuts come, when the riverside trees buzz and hum with myriads of flying things, that you find occasional fish feeding at any time of the day. But it would have been comforting to see a rise or two today.

Scandal Beck is new water for me and I do not know what to expect. But the stretch of the Eden upstream from the inflow of the beck to Eastfield bridge has been one of my favourite haunts for more than ten years. I have caught fine trout there and made some fine bags. But last year, whenever I came to the Eastfield stretch, I found few signs of fish and I caught next to nothing. And, when I met local fishermen, they muttered darkly about the wretched state of things and the disappearance of the trout. They have been doing just that for more than ten years, but last season I began to believe them and in the end I almost abandoned the Eden, spending all my fishing days on the Wharfe.

This season it will be different. I shall fish often and hard at Eastfield and, by the end of September, I shall know the truth of it: whether I was just unlucky last year, coming to the Eden on the wrong days, or whether the locals are right in saying that the river is sick, and that the great trout that used to live off the richness of pure water have themselves sickened or died or abandoned their old home.

5 May

I had not planned to fish today, but a morning of heavy drizzle put paid to any thought of cricket and so, counting the loss of cricketers my gain, I drove off to the Eden in a quietly festive mood. It was gone two when I left. It was three o' clock before I made my first cast. It was too late to be starting but it was far better than not fishing at all.

The conditions were superficially similar to those of yesterday, but the feel of the afternoon was completely different. There was wind and drizzle and the sky was grey. Trees only a few fields away were dim and misty shapes. But the air was soft and there was more light beneath the clouds. And very soon the wind sank to a gentle breeze, a warm breeze full of the sound of swallows. And, though the water was grey, it was gleaming as it murmured on its way through the lush pastures, with sloe-blossom still painting the hedges and with early parsley whitening along the lanes.

Once again I went up the beck and, almost immediately, I realised that there was some fly coming down the water, not in any quantity, but in a steady trickle that gave hope of a rise or two. They were olives mostly, but mixed in with the spring olives were brook duns and a few iron blues. I had barely started fishing when I found a feeding trout. And I hooked him and lost him and then hooked another and caught it and killed it, all in less than five minutes. It was then, of course, that the hatch petered out. I wandered off upstream and found no more rising fish. Yesterday's duck was sitting - the other is on the edge of the river and I went nowhere near her - and so I made a detour to avoid disturbance. I met a fisher coming down the beck, who confirmed what I already suspected: that the main hatch had happened before my arrival and that the trout had now gone off the feed. He had caught three, he told me, and missed others and kept one. And he pulled from his bag a great yellow trout that must have weighed two pounds and made me sick with envy. I did not show him mine, which was merely a plump three-quarter pounder, an entirely run-of-the-mill trout better left in the obscurity of my inside pocket.

And that was more or less it. I fished another pool or two and dreamed of summer evenings on Scandal Beck. I walked back downstream, glancing at the swallows and the sand martins and the noisy oyster catchers. I released Merlin from the confinement of the Land Rover and let him bound along the lane and sniff his way along the hedge-bottoms for twenty minutes. Then I met the river-watcher on the wooden bridge over the Eden.

We come across each other once or twice a season and always we talk together for a few minutes: about the state of the river (he seemed fairly hopeful today), about the problems of releasing pheasant poults and the many pleasures of fieldsports. It is clear that he loves his job. He cherishes his river. He wants to see the Eden bursting with trout. He wants the banks fenced and planted. He wants the water pure and teeming with shrimps and nymphs. He wants the Eden to deserve its name and he told me today that otters have returned to its upper reaches.

Yesterday I forgot to mention that I met an old mole-catcher just as I started fishing and that he told me the same news, assuring me that he had seen the otters himself. I made startled noises and inwardly disbelieved him, saying to myself that what he had thought to be an otter had surely been a mink. He looked to me like a short-sighted old mole-catcher. But perhaps he was right after all. I hope so and I enjoyed this afternoon. It will be a week before I can go fishing again.

8 May

This afternoon I shot at clay pigeons and missed nearly all of them. The sun was shining and I did not give a fig. If it had been November and they had been pheasants rather than little black discs, I should have cared passionately and gone home in a dark mood. Shooting clays is a game. It is rather like playing darts and it does not seem to matter very much. It can be useful practice. It can be a pleasant way of spending an afternoon. But it fails to stir me and, if I had not promised to take a boy or two shooting with me, I should certainly have gone fishing instead. I sense that tomorrow will bring a half-holiday and that I shall spend it on Scandal Beck and catch a bagful. And if it also brings the news that I am to become the owner of 62 acres of land near Brough Sowerby, then undoubtedly I shall be the happiest man in the world.

9 May

There was a half-holiday today and I did go fishing. But I did not catch a bagful and I did not enter into the spirit of things. I could not surrender to the delusion that is the essence of fishing: the absurd conviction that what matters most in life is catching fish. It was an afternoon full of incidental pleasures, bright with sunshine and shining water. The wind was light and warm. Casting a fly was a delight. The young leaf waved over the water, yellow and green or gleaming brown. The slow movement of clouds brought subtle changes of light. The river and the beck were sliding and singing miracles of purity and brightness. There was some fly on the water and I caught two trout and kept one of them, a most beautiful fish just under the pound with the reddest fins I have ever seen.

But, although the afternoon was the perfection of spring in that best phase of the season before growth runs riot and engulfs beauties of form, I stood outside it all and saw how lovely it was and longed to be a landowner.

At five o'clock I was sitting by the river some way downstream from Eastfield bridge, listening to a linnet singing somewhere nearby and wondering what I shall do if I lose my little rough shoot. I have not lost it yet. I may well still buy it. But today I learned that one of the surrounding farmers may be interested. And today, as I sat by the river in the sunshine, I felt certain that he was a millionaire and would pay whatever it might cost to get his hands on even more acres than he already hoards; I only want 62 and then I shall be happy for the rest of my life; what could he want with a few rough fields and a tumbledown wood? I felt certain that he just wanted to spite me.

They were foolish and unreasonable thoughts, but they swallowed up the pleasure of the linnet's song and of the dipper that came darting and chattering downstream. And knowing that I shall now have to wait at least another week before my future at High Park becomes clear only made matters worse. It made me grind my teeth with bitterness. If I lose the land and the shooting I shall have very little to tell my diary this winter.

And what will Merlin do if he can no longer flush pheasants from banks of gorse and search them out along the hedges and in the rushes and brambles of High Park? He will have half a dozen driven days at Wigglesworth. He will go flighting duck with me on perhaps a dozen evenings. He will walk the estuary from time to time and the odd snipe may come his way and even the odd grouse this August. But it is High Park he loves and it is High Park I love and with each passing day I want it more. It is a new feeling, this passionate urge to possess, and I am not sure that it is altogether commendable.

12 May

Yesterday afternoon I went back to Scandal Beck. There was a strong east wind blowing under a blue-grey sky. The high Pennines above Appleby were massive shapes against the horizon, huge and indistinct forms in a haze of milky light. They seemed to belong to a world of distant and unattainable stillness somewhere beyond the reach of the wind. Down by the beck the willows were bending and moaning and the water was ruffled. Sudden squalls chased themselves along the flats. Thank God they were chasing themselves upstream, or I should have turned round without bothering to fish and driven straight home.

In only two days the beck had fallen back very noticeably. Another week without rain and we shall have low water and arduous sport. Once again it seemed, as I wandered upstream, that I had come fishing too late in the day. There were some medium olives, and some olive uprights, riding the choppy water or flying helplessly on the wind, but I felt certain that they were stragglers and that the main hatch was over. I searched hard for rising fish, but I had come almost to the old railway bridge before I found one, and he melted away before I could cast to him, behaving like a fish that had eaten enough already and was now thinking of taking a rest.

Above the bridge I found another trout, rising against a willow in a little run down the far bank. He ignored my Imperial and rose again, and I realised that he was feeding under the surface. For once I did not fish on in hopeful indolence, but stopped casting long enough to change flies, tying on a Snipe and Yellow and spitting on it to help it sink. You need about two minutes for all this. Too often it is time I refuse to spare. Although I know that my fly is wrong, I cannot persuade myself to make the minimal effort of trying a different pattern. It must cost me scores of trout.

Yesterday I made the effort and the Snipe and Yellow was seized second cast. It was not a big fish but it was plump and twelve inches long and it went in the bag. Another trout showed a few yards upstream, but it was a difficult throw under hanging branches; I cast clumsily and this one went down. I thought that would be the end of it, for by now fly was very sparse. I walked up to the top of our water and was not surprised to see no sign of a feeding fish.

It was time to turn round now and walk back through the wind, time to check from a distance if my duck was still sitting - she was - and to glance casually at likely pools and runs in the half-hope of finding a trout that felt hungry enough to help itself to a rare olive. There was no longer even a trickle of fly, but if I stopped and watched the water for a few minutes, then this was usually long enough to spot a lonely silhouette bobbing down the current or struggling into flight.

I was watching just such an olive huddling against a rock on the edge of the beck when, an inch or two away from it, the water shaped itself into the unmistakable signs of a trout rising in a sliding run; there was a dimple at the centre of a small humped circle, a dimple that vanished before it had time to spread; it was not the lazy and perfect circle formed by a trout rising in a still pool: rather it was a brief and irregular impression, etched on the surface of the grey water, which melted away just as soon as it had been seen. But it was there again a few seconds later and in no time at all it was there again.

'Line drag,' I said to myself and sat down to think, for I wanted a brace badly and it seemed just the place for a heavy trout: a narrow run against the bank, with a richness of food passing through it that would in other places be spread over the whole width of the stream, with twisted roots and, by the standards of the beck, deep water for shelter.

But, although this narrow run was undoubtedly an attractive spot for a trout in search of an ideal home, it was also a difficult spot for a fisherman. For, only a yard or two beneath the run, a ridge of gravel slanted across the beck and the way the water slid towards it unequivocally signalled drag. And I should not be able to keep my line off the slide and slip of the gravel, because in doing so I should undoubtedly show myself to my fish.

But if I got downstream and fished from the far side, then the set of the current gave hope that my fly might swim on its way like a real fly for just long enough to tempt a feeding trout; though, whatever I did, the wind would probably slap my line on the water with the force of a whiplash and ruin things at the first cast. And should I change my fly or stay faithful to the Snipe and Yellow that had already given me a trout? I felt an untypical urge to get out my fly-box and replace the fly on the end of my cast with some other pattern, but then the trout rose again and I felt certain that it was eating something just below the surface of the stream.

The Snipe and Yellow stayed on. I crept downstream and crossed over and then edged my way up the bank. My first cast was short. My second was caught by the wind and fell heavily. But at once the occupant of the run rose obligingly, not to swallow my fly but to assure me that he was not frightened and to point out to me exactly where he was feeding. The third cast had him. There was a nudge on the line and suddenly it was tight, and throbbing with the glorious sensation of a heavy fish. I should like to say that he fought furiously, that he dashed from pool to pool and shook his head and leapt and lashed with his tail and stripped my reel down to the backing.

But it would be untrue. He fought doggedly and he was slow to tire. Once or twice he flopped half out of the water and confirmed that he was big. But he never tried to leave the little pool where he had been hooked. He hung in the current, rushing a yard or two upstream and then falling back almost within reach of the net. But, if I offered it to him, he soon showed me that he was not spent. He was a strong fish, but there was little dash to him and less enterprise. I knew that I should catch him, if only the hook was firmly set and if only I did nothing rash. He burrowed down into the water and I turned him with side strain. I might have been worried by a stake and a trail of wire right at the top of the pool, but he never tried more than half-heartedly to reach them. He hung in the water and pushed through it and came down-stream again. And at last he was beaten and turned on his side and was drawn over the net.

His size surprised me. I had been thinking of a pound and three quarters but, lying in the net, he looked well over two pounds. The spring balance told me that he was nearer three. He weighed two pounds ten ounces and he was the biggest brown trout I have ever caught. He had dark spots and his belly was yellow and his tail was very broad. His eyes stared at me with no message of resentment or pain. I did not feel that, in hooking and fighting him, I had been guilty of torture; I did not think that, in taking him from the water, I was spreading sorrow through the little pools of Scandal Beck. I did not believe that, in knocking him on the head, I was snuffing out a precious and unique awareness.

I observed that he was fat and felt sure that his flesh was pink and would taste delicious. I praised God for giving sinful men great trout to catch and eat. I killed the trout in my net and then strolled down the beck, filled with a quiet happiness and a deep contentment that stayed with me till sleep. It is not every day that you catch the biggest trout of your life. If I did not think it a waste, I might even get him stuffed.

14 May

It is summer now, with swifts screaming round the house in the evening, with boys screaming in the house yard after evening prayers, with all the trees, except for oaks and ashes, smothered in leaf. And there is that tension in the air, which begins to gather in classrooms and libraries as important examinations draw near, as nervous sixth-formers recognise that their prospects of wealth and power and greatness now hang in the balance. We have finished our Ovid. Thucydides is almost done and the Athenians will soon have been left in the stone quarries of Syracuse. Meanwhile the east wind is still blowing and it is warm and dry and dusty.

This afternoon I drove up Howgill lane. The roadside banks are full of bluebells and dandelions and the delicate white of stitchwort. Dogwood is swelling with blossom and the sloe-blossom will soon have faded. Ferns are pushing folded shoots out of the earth and the lambs in the fields are as big as cocker spaniels.

I left the Land Rover at Fairmile and headed up Fell Head, with Merlin gambolling in the beck, sniffing through dead bracken, thrusting his head down rabbit holes and generally behaving like a well-behaved gun dog. It was hot down by the beck and out of the wind; it was sweaty work climbing up through the bent and the bilberries, pausing to look at the pink bells of their flowers and to whistle in the dog and to gather breath for the next stage of the ascent. The long ridge to the summit was fresh and breezy, with singing larks and parachuting meadow pipits; for an unfit man of 44 it was also very steep and much longer than he remembered. He stopped a lot; he wheezed and panted and was very glad when at last he reached the top and lay sprawling in the sunshine, smoking his pipe.

Some summers I walk up hills more often than I go fishing. This summer will not be such a one, unless it decides never to rain. But it is a fine thing to climb up towards the sky and to look down on the world for a time. And today the Shap fells and the lake-district peaks were sleeping in a blue haze, while windy cloud-patterns swept across the broad brown slopes of the Howgills. It was fine and fresh in the wind. I walked on to Breaks Head and scrambled down the steep slope to the beginnings of Long Rigg beck. Then it was on down the narrow valley, with Merlin questing on either side in tall and woody heather that has not sheltered a grouse for at least twenty years.

The valley of Long Rigg Beck is one of the finest in the Howgills, with the bold flanks of Fell Head on one side and the smooth slopes of White Fell and Bram Rigg on the other. It is deep and sheltered and half way down there is a stone sheepfold, where you can lean your back against a wall and smoke with your face in the sun, listening to the sound of the beck and to the endless bleating of the sheep.

Then you continue on your way and turn into a much smaller side-valley that winds up to the scarred ramparts of Fell Head. This seems a secret valley and the climb out of it is steep, taking you over Whins End, where you find a wide sky and a broad view again. You have emerged from loneliness and, though you meet no one, you are once again ready for the world and prepared for human contact. A grassy path leads along gentle slopes to the western ridge of Fell Head and it is back the way you came down Fairmile beck. I met not a soul today in the course of my walk, which is how I like it; not because I hate my fellows; rather because it is good, after spending four or five hours by yourself, to be glad to meet some of them again. I love solitary walking. A solitary life would drive me mad within a week.

18 May

It is a matter of regret to me that I do not have time to give to my diary at the moment. I do not have time to sit back and think, to probe into the experience of each day and to prise out its special qualities and its enduring value. All I can do is record a few of the things that happened, embellishing incidents with a few of the thoughts that accompanied them and with some subsequent and shallow reflections. It is a poor thing at the moment, this diary of mine.

But, although a source of general dissatisfaction, lack of time is a blessing in thinking of today. All I can bear to do is to sketch the grim outline of it, and then to forget. It was a day by a river when I might have done great things. All I ended up doing was catching a single trout and feeling that I was a star-crossed bungler who would have been happier if he had never held a fishing rod in his uncooperative and clumsy hands.

I went to the Wenning and found it lower than I had expected, low and clear and difficult, with an irksome north-easterly breeze blowing downstream, with a sullen light from grey clouds unsoftened by steely glints of sunshine. It was cold too and I wore a heavy jacket and did not feel that it was May.

But there was fly on the water and there were rising trout from two o'clock, when I started, until 5.30 when I had to leave. There were medium olives and olive uprights in a steady trickle, but at the start it was black gnats the trout wanted, for black gnats were floating down the thin currents in some profusion, both singly and, more enticingly, in coupling pairs. Trout eating black gnats are either easy or difficult. Today they were difficult and I tried them with several small black things before one took hold, a beautiful yellow trout that weighed twelve ounces and went in the bag.

Then the iron blues came, the first big hatch of them that I have seen for ten years, and the fish started eating them immediately. In no time at all, on a broad slow bend of the river, there were half a dozen and more trout rising greedily within a few yards of me; and it was clear that they were good trout, not two-pounders perhaps but trout that would bend a rod and strain a fisher's nerves before they were drawn over the net. On went an iron blue dun which was despatched over them and completely ignored. They were nymphing, of course. I watched for a few moments and not a neb broke the surface. There were humps and swirls and there were sightings of tail-tips, but there was never a snout and there was no sign of disappearing duns. It was time for the Snipe and Purple. Five minutes later I tied my hopes to a Dark Watchet and, very soon afterwards, with the trout still rising and still ignoring the floating duns, I decided that I was beaten and began to fish badly, trying patterns that I knew would fail and moving from trout to trout with a frantic haste that would have disgraced a raw novice.

I did pull myself together. I acknowledged that I was not going to catch trout with a wet fly and went back to the dun, hoping that, as the hatch slackened, the fish would become less particular in their taste and start picking off flies from the surface of the water.

I was right. The stream of iron blues became steadily less abundant and the trout began eating the dun as well as the hatching nymph. And I began rising them, good solid rises that should have produced firmly hooked fish. There were four or five such and every one I bungled, striking too soon or too hard or, in one case, not at all. I broke off the barb in the jaws of a trout that felt really heavy. Two or three times I felt the jarring pull of a big fish and then nothing but the dark conviction of my own ineptitude. I was relieved when it was time to finish and drive home. Now I am desperate to go fishing again. I said that I longed to forget today's disaster. That would be foolish. I must draw conclusions, but I shall wait until I can draw them more calmly. Incompetence is best recollected in tranquillity.

20 May

I spent the afternoon in the Howgills, with Merlin and a wild wind. It was grey and desolate and invigorating. I was in the wildest and loneliest area of the Howgills around Uldale Head and Black Force. It was just what I wanted after a thoroughly enjoyable evening on which wine and whisky were drunk in temperate excess: an evening that left behind no taste of sin but which sent me late to bed (without a hot water bottle) and which, at noon the next day, called forth in me a sudden longing for lonely hills and for tonic lungfuls of bracing air.

From Carling Gill Bridge I headed up Weasel Gill, while Merlin raced from side to side and leapt over the beck and rushed back impatiently as though in pitying disbelief that it could be taking me so long. Moorland gills are fine places, so hidden and secret are they. The hills themselves are lonely, but they are wide and open. The rocky waterways that tumble down their sides have carved for themselves a deeper and more withdrawn solitude.

They are also full of surprises. Panting up my gill this afternoon I found yellow clumps of primroses at a thousand feet and more, hiding away from the world and shining against the darkness of the layered rock. There are rowans there too and hawthorns; there are miniature waterfalls and little pools and, above all, there is a feeling of complete separation from the wider landscape, as though no external influence has penetrated this winding cleft since the hills were uplifted and the rocks were folded and lined.

Weasel Gill splits or, rather, it is formed by the junction of two smaller gills. I turned up the one that comes in from the right, grows ever shallower and eventually loses itself in the featureless expanse of moorland that is Uldale Head. The surrounding hills were grey and indistinct forms. The wind was very strong, and it held me as I came down to the Blakethwaite Stone, which stands at the top of Uldale, a narrow valley with curving and regular sides, unadorned, grimly beautiful in the bare simplicity of its contours, brown and grey this afternoon and unwelcoming. I did not even stop by the stone for a drink from my flask, but pressed on to the northern slopes of Fell Head and to Black Force, where the peregrine cut though the air with sharp wings as she shrieked her displeasure at my intrusion into her fastness.

Black Force is, I suppose, the Howgill's most impressive feature: a beck tumbling and cascading down a dark and almost sheer ravine, spilling over narrow ledges, foaming over great boulders and past great buttresses of rock, rushing past rowans that are wet with spray and cling precariously to the shattered hillside, until finally it splashes down to the valley floor and joins its waters to Carling Gill.

I sat at the bottom of it today, with the steep slopes and sprawling screes around me, with the cramped water of the gill at my feet, with the wind roaring down the deep and narrow valley that keeps the hills apart. I did not pause long, as I sometimes do on sunny days. I pressed on and in half an hour was back where I had started, glad to have been in the hills but happy too to have left them. Bright days are fine for loneliness. The air and the light are cheerful then and the solitude is uplifting. But, on grey days and wild days, the sombre mood sinks into you and saps your pleasure. On such days two or three hours is enough.

26 May

Yesterday it was back to the Wenning on an afternoon that was almost warm. Oaks are still young in the leaf, yellow and brown and very delicate. Beneath the trees in woods and copses there is still a haze of blue, and gorse is bright yellow now. All day long young jackdaws screech from the church tower; and from holes in walls and trees broods of starlings, summoning their harassed parents, send out muffled rasps and squeaks. Meadows are beginning to wave in the wind; buttercups are beginning to paint them yellow. Farmers are beginning to cut silage and to turn hen pheasants into tattered shreds of bone and feather. Boys have realised how imminent are their days of reckoning and some are close to panic at the prospect of their exams. Hiding away in the shelter of the leaf, shy apple blossom is blushing pink.

Rivers are running very low. I hear reports of downpours further south. But here never a drop falls and the land is very dry. The Wenning yesterday was creeping on its way. I crossed it through an inch or two of water where, in April, I had thought twice before wading out into the vigour of the current. I did not expect much sport, but the sun was warm and the breeze was light and there was still that feeling of return and rediscovery that made just being there a delight. There was also a garden warbler singing in a steep thicket across the shrunken streams of the river, singing in sweet and subdued celebration of the blessings of the summer, while, from every bush and tree, the sad song of the willow warbler drifted on the air.

I found nothing but parr rising until I had walked up to the stepping stones, which now break the current where once a rotten bridge spanned the river on rickety stakes. Above the stones there is deep water and, in this long slow pool, trout were rising to eat the black gnats that were floating on the surface. Appropriate artificials, both floating and sunk, were all refused, but the trout - there were three or four of them and they were clearly good fish - went on rising, picking flies from the sunlight or swirling at them beneath the surface.

There were some olives coming down and a few were being eaten. I decided to try a bushy olive, heavily dressed on a size fourteen hook, for there are times when smutting and gnatting trout will swallow such an artificial with gusto. It does not happen often. But when it does, sport can be exceptional, and it can go on for hours on end. I call yesterday's fly the Yellow Thing; it is a Rough Olive variant, with a thick body of yellow wool and two hackles, one ginger, one honey dun or grizzle cock.

There have been days when it has caught me trout after trout. Always it surprises me when trout busy eating tiny black things snatch greedily at something that is neither small nor black. But there are times when they do and I have known times when scarcely a fish refused it and when nine out of ten of them were firmly hooked. There are times when the Yellow Thing is an irresistible fly.

Yesterday it rose and hooked the first trout over which it floated, a plump fish of twelve ounces that was soon in the bag. Then I put a fish down with a heavy cast and missed a half-hearted rise. And then a brood of ducklings erupted with their mother from beneath the trailing branches of a willow, and I watched in helpless frustration as she sought to lead me from her young, now flapping feebly upstream, now beating the water with a trailing wing and frightening the trout that I had seen feeding in the next pool. It was no use explaining to her that I was no danger to her ducklings, that it would be September before my attitude towards them changed. There is nothing you can do when a mother duck leads you on, except to sit down and smoke or to follow her upstream and hope that she will decide she has taken you far enough before she has flapped and splashed her way through the best pool on the river.

The best pool on my stretch of the Wenning, to judge from recent experience, was just round the corner to which my mother duck was heading. I was relieved to see her turn and fly wide of me, on low and furtive wings, brushing the swaying stalks in the meadow as she sneaked back to her brood. I wondered whether the nests I had found on the Eden and Scandal Beck had produced ducklings, or whether they had fattened crows and foxes. Then I crept along the steep bank, through lush grass and red valerian and white parsley. I caught and returned a small trout and missed a better fish. Then I came to the long lazy pool where I met iron blues and rising trout last Wednesday.

They were rising again, and not with the hasty, splashing rises of inconsiderable fish. There were sucking noises and arrogant swirls; there were circles broadening across the pool from the point where a neb had pushed through the surface of the water to seize a drifting fly. There were big trout feeding and I had no need of the nymphs I had tied in readiness for a second meeting with iron blues. For there were black gnats everywhere; it was black gnats the trout were eating and I fished for these gnatting trout with a yellow artificial ten times as big as any black gnat that ever lived and flew and fell onto the sliding currents of a northern trout stream. It worked.

I missed a rise or two from trout that took the fly after it had passed the point where I had expected it to be taken. Then I covered a third fish and immediately he seized the Yellow Thing and weighed one pound four ounces. He was short and fat, very yellow in the belly, and I felt sure that I should enjoy eating him. The next cast brought me a pounder and now there were three trout in my bag. I rose and missed the next trout and, though he went on feeding and though I tried him with flies like the ones he was eating, he would not come again and at last he went down.

I wandered up to the head of the river, in warm sunshine and with flowers waving all along the banks. A few mayflies, the true mayflies that set the hearts of chalkstream fishermen beating with well-bred excitement, came fluttering down the breeze and floating down the river. They seemed exotic creatures in the shadow of Ingleborough and the trout ignored them. The bottom of Austwick beck showed no sign of a feeding fish, and so I roamed down again and found the river suddenly quiet.

Now I sat on the bank, listening to the swallows, smoking my pipe and feeling absurdly happy. Last week I sat there morosely, resenting the beauties around me and wishing that I had not bothered to come, all because I had failed to catch trout in a big hatch of iron blues. Now I was sitting in the same spot with three trout in my bag and I was happy beyond the compass of words, deeply and quietly happy and thankfully aware of the blue sky and the flowing water and the song of birds. It is ridiculous, the happiness that three trout can bring to a man doomed to die. But it is real and it is important. It is one of the best blessings that God has given us in a world full of sorrow.

2 June

I want it. I shall have it. It will be mine. I sat there this afternoon, in yellow sunshine and warm air, with birds singing around me. I looked up the little valley and saw the waving grass in the meadow and the tall firs standing by the beck, with the yellow-leaved oaks facing them on the Rise. I saw the graceful sweep and curve of the fields, their lines softened by the season's growth. I saw slopes to be planted in years to come and hedges to be laid, places for pheasants to strut and skulk.

I heard a shouting cock and felt conscience-stricken because I have done nothing this spring to protect the sitting hens from the plundering beaks of magpies and crows. There is little I can do, because I cannot be at High Park every day to check traps, but I could at least have made a gesture with my gun. It would have been better than nothing, but I could not bear to be there as long as I was uncertain whether I was ever to own it. And now I cannot bring myself to believe that I ever shall. I love it so much.

Tomorrow I must call on my solicitor and my bank manager. I shall be short of money before long, but there will still be a bottle of champagne for the day of completion (Bollinger, *Grande Annee '85*). But perhaps this entry is a premature celebration. There may be hidden snags and secret pitfalls. Please God may it not be so and forgive me, dear Lord, that on this day of Corpus Christi I went to mass and thought of fields and woods and meadows rather than of the real presence. I shall make amends to your mother; for, in the little plantation of larches by the meadow gate, I shall set up her statue. I shall hang it with garlands of flowers every May, and I shall kneel and pray there whenever I visit my land. And perhaps her presence will keep away crows and ward off foxes? And perhaps she will see to it that all who come there think only pure and peaceful thoughts and that they take away a joy and a blessing in their hearts?

Meanwhile I am hopelessly behind with this diary. There are three days fishing to be recorded, three difficult and instructive days. And I had hoped to write of flies and fly-tying. When I have called on the bank manager and the solicitor tomorrow, and when I have taught my lessons and marked a set of Latin proses and a set of Greek unseens, and when I have thought about Saturday morning's classes, then I shall give my mind to three days on the Wharfe, with swarms of black fly and shrunken pools and wary trout. But, as I cast my mind back over my half-term fishing, I shall be wondering whether to plant oaks or beeches on the Rise above the meadow, and where the best spot might be to dig a flight pond. And, within a year, I shall probably be out of work and bankrupt.

3 June

Black and bloated clouds have been sailing through the sky all day and, when the mood has taken them, they have sent down drenching bursts of rain to refresh the parched earth. I was caught in one as I went from solicitor to bank manager, and in another after I had decided to call on my accountant as well. There should be fine fishing in a day or two. I shall give my next free afternoon to Scandal Beck and the Eden beneath Eastfield bridge.

Trying to recall days by a river at the distance of almost a week is unsatisfactory. I can supply the statistics of my recent holiday on the Wharfe. I can tell you that in three days I killed five trout: two on the first day, both with the Yellow Thing, three on the second, both to a dry black gnat, and absolutely nothing on the third. I can tell you that the fish fed all day long and were so obsessed with the endless stream of black flies floating over their heads that, in spite of the shrunken streams and the diminished pools, they were not difficult to approach. But they were very difficult to deceive. I tried everything that seemed even remotely appropriate and, for most of the time, everything was a dismal failure. Even the stock-fish knew what they wanted and knew that it was not the fly on the end of my line.

I can tell you too that the summer half-term break is one of the best fishing trips of the year, that reaching the *Falcon* at eight o'clock on Saturday evening, after hiding from parents all day and then dozing through an hour of speeches and prizes, is a deep delight; that waking up on Sunday morning and realising that I have nothing to do for three days but to go fishing, is a moment of unalloyed happiness. And there is the first evening fishing of the year to look forward to, with all the serenity that still evenings bring to the quiet places where my rivers flow. Then there is the smell of honey that drifts from flowering sycamores at the end of May, and the sharper fragrance that comes from white chervil along the banks. Swifts scream through the sky all day long. Young duck dabble along the margins of the stream, and the trees are still different shades of green, while the hawthorn is in two minds whether to unfold at last into a soft and scented splendour of white. It is the last of the spring before the roses and the elder blossom and the waning of birdsong.

But these are general impressions of May, whereas I want the particularities of three May days and already they have gone, because I was too lazy to record them at the time. I remember cold cloud on the first morning, and how, in the afternoon, it softened to hazy sunshine and something like warmth. I remember a bright and vigorous air on Monday and a tearing gale blowing downriver on Tuesday. And through it all black gnats fell on the water and the trout rose to feed on them. At intervals flushes of duns, medium olives and olive uprights and brook duns and the first of the pale wateries, joined them on the water, and often the air was full of the yellow wings of fluttering stone-flies; and every gust of wind brought a shower of sycamore blossom onto the river.

The August Black was no use, which makes sense, since the trout were feeding on black gnats rather than on smuts or midges and since the black gnat is a land-bred fly that finds its way onto the water by accident and, for every black gnat a trout sees underwater it must see twenty or thirty sitting temptingly on the surface. The August Black (hook size: 18. body: crow or magpie herl over purple silk and ribbed with the silk. hackle: shiny feather from a starling's neck) is the greatest of summer wet flies, but this half-term was not the time for it. It will have to wait.

When the trout became briefly weary of black gnats and spent a few minutes eating duns, then the Yellow Thing was worth an airing. Mostly it was ignored, along with Imperials and Rough Olives and Pheasant Tails and any other fly that floats. Dry imitations of the black gnat were generally treated with contempt, whether tied with a white or a black hackle and however small the hook, although there was a period of perhaps twenty minutes on Tuesday afternoon when a very simple pattern, nothing but black silk and a tiny black hackle wound round an eighteen hook, brought me three trout in quick succession.

And on the evening of the same day two large fish on the Skirfare rose confidently to this same pattern. I missed the first and hooked the second firmly. He made two long and savage runs and then hung below me in the stream, shaking his head and looking huge and still untamed. But I thought that he would be mine and I could scarcely believe it when, very gently, the hook parted company with his jaws and he swam off slowly upstream. I am certain that he was well over two pounds; but, for once, I did not feel that sense of almost stunned bereavement that so often follows the departure of a big fish.

Perhaps it was the virtue of the evening that kept me calm, for the wind had died and the limestone walls were shining pink in the last of the sun, and the water ahead of me was smooth and white and the trees were standing in a holy stillness. It was not an evening for turbulent emotions. Moreover I was for once conscious of no folly or clumsiness on my part. It is the way of small hooks to detach themselves from the mouths of trout. If you make them your allies you must put up with their idiosyncrasies and accept their fondness for coming unstuck.

I was disappointed, but I did not turn crimson with rage or throw stones into the water. I moved on quietly, thinking how thrilled I should have been if I had just slid a trout of almost three pounds into my bag, and I found more fish feeding. They would not look at my Black Gnat or at the other flies I showed them, and on the edge of darkness I reeled in and drove off to the pub. I should have liked that trout; he would have made the whole day memorable. And I can never console myself for the loss of a big fish by reflecting, as I am meant to, that he has gained more by his escape than I should have won by his capture.

It is dishonest to set out to kill fish and then to pretend that you are almost pleased when they get away. And any fisherman, if he cares to be frank with himself, must acknowledge that he goes fishing because he sets little store by the feelings of trout compared with the pleasure he reaps from catching them. I love catching trout and I am often very upset when a big one throws the hook. Sometimes it spoils a whole day. But this time I managed to bear my loss with quiet resignation. It did not ruin the taste of Guinness and I did not wake up the next morning still brooding on disaster. But the wind spoiled the next morning, and the afternoon as well. By three o'clock I had had enough of it and was ready to go home.

They were a difficult three days and the trout, apart from the five that died, had the better of it. I did not make a mess of things. I did not bungle repeatedly, although there were some lost opportunities. On Sunday there were two or three fish that I should have caught; one broke me and I missed two or three at the strike. There were missed fish on Monday too and there were times when I persisted with patterns that were clearly of no present service.

But rain-fed rivers, when they drop low and clear beneath the summer sun, are very difficult rivers to fish. And, in such conditions, trout feeding on little black things are, in my opinion, the most difficult trout of all to bring to net. I have left one of my pipes in a hole in the wall above Spout Dub. I have rung Colin, our keeper, and promised him lavish rewards if he can recover it for me. I shall ring him again tomorrow to find out if he has managed to find the right hole.

9 June

I do not think I have ever driven to a river before and then driven away without bothering to fish. But the Wenning looked so small and tired this afternoon. There was a wild wind blowing up the river. There was useless drizzle flying on the air and the sky was grey. And I felt as weary as the river looked and, seeing the dark and windswept remains of its pools, and with no sign of a rising fish, I decided that I should be better in my study tying flies than stamping up and down a riverbank and cursing the wind and catching nothing.

Since half-term the weather has been cold and damp and dispiriting. Rivers are croaking out a desperate prayer for rain, but heaven answers their appeal mockingly, with moist air and spots of drizzle on the wind. I deplore hot weather, but I would rather endure a burning sun than these grey and sullen days. At noon I hate a cloudless midsummer sky and the fierce brightness that comes from it; but such days redeem themselves when they turn into still summer evenings full of summer smells and the shining patterns of spinners' wings.

I do not regret coming home without putting up my rod. I have spent the afternoon working, and then, while tying flies, I have dreamt of fishing. There is a sort of therapy in winding silk, fur and feathers round a hook. I could never spend a whole day at it. But for an hour or two, or even for half of one, it is very pleasant. And a well-made fly is a minor work of art. Sometimes I look at an Orange Partridge or a Waterhen Bloa, at a Brown Owl or an August Black, and, realising that for once I have got it all just right, I acknowledge to myself that I have made something beautiful and regret that some day it will be mangled by the unaesthetic jaws of a hungry trout.

And the old wet flies of the north are far more beautiful than any floating fly. It is a spare beauty of line and form not unlike the beauty of early spring, whereas dry flies are overdressed creatures of fussy and false charm. They are like trees when the leaf has smothered their grace of form. So at least are my dry flies.

All summer the vice is ready at my table. I put it away when friends come for supper, but it goes back where it belongs before I go to bed. And in idle moments, or when I know that another exercise book will be the end of my sanity, or when it is still ten minutes too early to go to the pub, I resort to my vice and fashion a fly or two. The time has come now for a couple of Orange Partridges. And, just as soon as they are finished, it will be time for three pints of bitter beer.

10 June

Summer trees are at their loveliest in the late evening, when the deepening light takes away the vulgar profusion of their leafage and they stand still against the sky, like upraised, imposing and graceful shadows, like substantial ghosts. Under the summer sun, or beneath grey summer skies, they seem overburdened with leaves, drooping and despondent. But, as the night closes in, this heaviness falls away and they raise up their massive outlines to the last light. They become embodiments of spontaneous shadow and they exude a solemn peace. So at least it seemed to me last night, when I had tied my two Orange Partridges and was taking Merlin for a brief walk before I went to the pub.

The bursar died at half-term and, this afternoon, I went to his memorial service in the school chapel. You can approach death more closely when you are not yourself too painfully touched by the effects it spreads among the living. You can admire the grieving dignity of families. You can reflect that you too will end up in a coffin before long. You can wonder what other people are thinking and whether they can brush aside the grim fact of mortality more easily than you. And, after the service, you can come out into the sunlight and discover a sad and precious value in the smallest pleasures and the most trivial duties that belong to being alive.

11 June

Once again I went to the Wenning and came home without wetting a line. This time it was not the weather; it was me. The weather was soft and warm and still: the sort of cloudy day that spreads a white light over the earth and seems all the while on the point of turning into sunshine. It was a quiet and welcoming afternoon, a good one, apart from the shrivelled state of the river, to be out with a fishing rod. But I am smitten with a cold and, this afternoon, I could not walk ten yards without sneezing and pulling out a handkerchief.

And I did not realise how tired I felt until I reached the Wenning and was standing on the bridge, gazing at the thin trickle of liquid that was creeping down the bed of the river, creeping over the clotted gravel and fringed with slime. I acknowledged that I was not up to it, for fishing a low river in the daytime is very demanding. It calls for bending and crawling and for quick and controlled reactions. It calls for delicacy and concentration and for the top of your form. I was not up to anything but blowing my nose and feeling miserable, and I knew that, if I did fish, I should make an utter hash of it and feel even more wretched and depressed.

And so I left my waders in the Land Rover and put on a pair of wellingtons and wandered off upstream for half an hour. And, in spite of my cold, it was pleasant and I was glad that I had decided on a little exercise and that I had left all predatory thoughts behind me.

There was nothing feeding but parr, splashing and dimpling in the thin runs and the shrunken pools. I saw no sign of a decent trout, although there were mayflies hatching and sometimes as many as three or four of them on the water together. But they seemed out of place, or at least out of time. I thought that they ought to have known better than to cast off their nymphal shucks on so still an afternoon when nothing else was active but tiny things, nothing but aimless smut and frivolous parr and neurotic shoals of fry.

It was an afternoon of high summer, the cloudy rather than the sunny sort, with trees heavy green and motionless, with long and leaning grasses all along the banks. It was an afternoon that had gone to sleep and would not wake again until the light began to darken. I was relieved I had no rod with me. It was much better sitting by the water, coughing and sneezing and smoking defiantly, and wondering whether the time was coming for the northern angler's answer to the challenge of low water and shy trout, wondering whether the time was approaching for the upstream worm.

It is only on the Wharfe that I fish the worm, and rarely before July. The traditional month of its best service is, of course, June. But June is a wonderful month for fishing flies. If I were staying at Kilnsey now, I should certainly get out my worm rod. As it is, it will probably be at least a month before it goes to the river with me. And if the weather breaks and the rains come it will have to wait even longer. I enjoy a few worming excursions in the course of a season. But some seasons pass without one and in others I have dug no worms before September. Last year I caught one trout on the upstream worm, and it was the last fish of the season. But perhaps, this coming week, I shall get out a fork and go to the compost heap and see what I can find.

14 June

I had planned to go fishing this evening, but two of my sixth-form Latinists were uncertain about their Ovid, and tomorrow is Ovid's special day in the form of the A-level Latin literature paper. We went through some passages that were puzzling them and I tried to explain the grammatical complexities. And then there was the dog to feed and exercise and I felt that fishing would be too much of a rush. And anyway the water is so low. I left my rods alone and went out with Merlin and it was very beautiful, with a clear sky and a shimmering blue light over the fells.

Purple cranesbill and red campions and yellow poppies are waving now along the margins of every road, bringing a summer glow to the hedge-sides. The wild roses have yet to open, for the season is backward, and I am still waiting for midsummer evenings full of the smell of elder-blossom. Very soon it will come and, if rain comes as well, I shall sniff the heady sweetness of summer blossom on the banks of the Eden or the Wenning and catch a bagful of trout as the blue winged olives flutter through the failing light.

I fear that I am about to buy another dog. It is senseless, for I have no need of two dogs and I certainly lack the skill to work two of them together. Merlin is quite enough for me, and I should do better trying to improve our partnership. But I have heard of a redundant keeper with a ten-month springer for sale, and my informant speaks well of the dog's breeding and behaviour. I have arranged to meet the dog on Thursday and already I know that, by Thursday evening, I shall be the owner of two spaniels. The result will be more expense at a time when my thoughts should be turning towards parsimony and, come October, I shall have two wild gun dogs for my shooting friends to deride and revile.

Suddenly I feel almost guilty about not going fishing, for spending time with Ovid and two diligent boys instead. The breeze has dropped and the air is warm. It is an evening that calls for anglers along the banks of trout streams. And no other sport summons its devotees, not merely to pleasure, but to the performance of a sacred duty. How can it be wrong to go fishing when this evening I feel that it is close to a sin to have stayed at home? I feel that God in his goodness made me a fisherman and that, at this moment, I am treating his blessings with contempt and proving untrue to the high and holy vocation he has laid upon me. And what I have just written is not entirely frivolous. Fishers have always thought of their sport as being in some mysterious way morally beneficial. Others now think of it as a barbarism. We fishers know that we are right.

15 June

I am looking, as I write, at a plan of High Park Farm, and I am feeling propectively and proudly possessive. I did not know that the wood where my pheasant pen stands is dignified with a name. It is called Brogden's Plantation, although I find it difficult to believe that the tangle of hazel and birch and alder, which makes up nine-tenths of Brogden's Plantation, owes its origins to the activity of a man called Brogden or grows there through the agency of any shaping intelligence other than God's. But I shall enjoy talking of Brogden's in future pheasant seasons.

I went out to High Park this afternoon, to discuss some problems of access with Mr. G. We went trespassing together, and he took me to a narrow field where an old track runs to within fifteen yards of what will soon be my boundary. It was this track that interested us, because, if extended, and with the provision of a gate in the hedge, it would allow convenient access to my land. It was this track that brought us to the narrow field. What caught my attention here was not the track, but a pond in the field's far corner, a pond with water in it, even in midsummer after weeks without rain, a pond with reeds growing out of its middle, a pond of inviting seclusion and of no great depth. It was, in short, a pond that announced itself to a flighter of duck as a pond where duck ought to be flighted.

I went off to see the owner of the pond and was fortunate to find him herding cattle into his lane. He belongs to the affable class of farmers, the other class tending to be downright rude. He did not send me packing with a curse or shake his stick at me and tell me to be gone. He smiled as he listened to my exposition of my interest in his field and the track running through it. He said he did not like to be awkward, but that he would like to think about things and talk them over with his law man. He mentioned the hay in my meadow as something he would like to have in his barn; and then he bade me a courteous farewell and went off to milk his cows.

I had been listening while he talked and nodding my head sagely, but, all the time, I had been thinking of his pond and laying plans. The hay in my meadow was the chief part of them, but for the time being I shall keep them to myself. Tomorrow I shall behave like an idiot and buy another dog.

16 June

He is not as big as Merlin, though he is a hefty spaniel. He is called Digby, which is not the name I should have chosen for him, but in time I shall come to think that it suits him admirably. He has the wide head and the broad nose that I like to see in his breed. Too many spaniels are snouty creatures with pointed faces. He is black and white, well marked and well feathered, the head itself all black. Undoubtedly he is a handsome dog. He is full of energy and I cannot believe he will be daunted by the jungle of gorse at High Park, although I shall be surprised, and perhaps a little sad, if he develops Merlin's manic drive. I do not want to acknowledge Merlin's hunting equal in a second dog. I want to point to Merlin's imperfections and to say that Digby does not share them, that he never runs in or pegs game or ignores my commands. Then I want to point out that, in spite of all this, Merlin still stands alone as a dog for rough places, for gorse that scratches and for rending brambles and for hedges full of thorns.

I resisted the temptation to bring Digby home with me and ruin him at once. The next two weeks are busy and distracting ones. I left him with Brian in Grindleton. Brian trains dogs and knows all about them. Merlin came from Brian and, as you know, he was an exemplary spaniel when first he became mine. I shall see Digby again in a fortnight, and then regularly in the course of the summer holidays. I shall be guided by Brian. I shall not take him shooting before he is ready for it and he will mature into a model sporting dog. But, however good he becomes, he will travel in the back of the Land Rover, while Merlin keeps his privilege of lying in the front.

My attitude to dogs is ridiculous. I do not believe that they are capable of true affection. I feel deeply sorry for those people who are either so unfortunate or so inept in their dealings with men and women that they seek from dogs what they cannot find among their own kind. It is a nonsense to believe, as some do, that dogs are the moral superiors of men. Certainly they are capable of less evil. They are, in fact, incapable of any evil at all, just as they possess no faculty for good. We should remember, we dog lovers, that our dogs bound through their lives with no powers of moral discrimination, with no burden of choice. They live in unquestioning obedience to their own natures, and there cannot be virtue without freedom.

But our dogs communicate a powerful illusion of friendship, and I am very happy to surrender to it, as long as I remember from time to time that an illusion is what it is. As I write this I am stroking Merlin's ears and feeling sorry for him because a rival is so soon to enter his life. If he died tomorrow, I should mourn the passing of a close friend and, though he lives without knowledge of good and evil, I shall continue to think of him, by turns, as the worst of sinners and as an embodiment of all the virtues. Digby, I feel certain, will prove a saint.

18 June

I have yet to fish this month, the best of all fishing months, and it is already more than half over. If I had been on holiday I should have gone out in defiance of wind and water and I should have managed to catch a trout or two. But in demanding conditions, I want a whole day for the river, not just a few hours: a whole day or a long, calm evening. I ought to have gone fishing on Tuesday evening. I wasted one of the very few serene evenings that the season has yet brought, for now we are back to wind and gloomy skies and taunting drizzle.

I console myself by reading about fishing each night before sleep. It has been Skues most of this week. Some time ago I published three articles on my favourite fishing books, which were, and I think still are, Lord Grey's *Fly Fishing*, Plunket Greene's *Where The Bright Waters Meet*, and Farson's *Going Fishing*. But, if these are my favourite fishing books, Skues is most certainly my favourite fishing author, and there is so much of him to read. It is the wit of his writing that I find so enjoyable. One sentence is full of ironic solemnity, another flows with an easy elegance, a third is perfectly balanced, the next is mockingly poetical. And there is that judicious blending of the intricate and the straightforward, the formal and the colloquial, that brings constant variety of tone and is the mark of a truly imaginative user of words. Here he is at his best:

In early June the valley of the Erlaubnitz is a dream of heat. On either side of its fringing water meadows there stand, either upon the level or stretching up the lower slopes of the hills, larch poles in serried rows, evidence of the heroic German endeavour to accomplish the impossible - to assuage the unassuageable Wurstphalian thirst - while higher up the slopes and clustering round the picturesque oolitic limestone crags, no less serried pines - planted by the same foreseeing and provident German mind - make provision to cope with the almost equally unassuageable national demand for toothpicks.

It is splendid stuff and there is plenty more like it. Skues' anecdotal writing is a continual delight. The style is self-conscious, but somehow the mood is relaxed and the flavour of a day is imparted without tedious recourse to the waving flowers and the singing birds and the sparkling streams that make up the stock-in-trade of hacks like me.

The only problem with Skues is that he caught so many trout. He does occasionally miss a fish, and now and then one or two of them drop from the hook. There are even times when he fails to bring them up to his fly. But, on most pages, the barb is pulled home, the little nine-footer bends like a hoop and, after a vigorous struggle, a lusty two pounder is drawn over the net. And if, once in a while, the trout have the better of it in the morning, they are invariably worsted in the afternoon and subjected to utter humiliation the same evening. Sometimes it makes me feel jealous. Sometimes I put down Skues in depressed admiration and go to bed with a complex, all too conscious that my favourite fishing author consistently wrote better sentences than I do and that his wizardry with a rod makes me no more than a pygmy of the fishing race. And what did he do with all the trout he caught? I hope he distributed those he could not eat himself among the deserving poor.

20 June

Yesterday evening it was the Eden. I had not realised that Saturday's rain had lifted the streams. But, while we were shooting clays yesterday afternoon along the banks of the Rawthey, one of the boys, who is himself a fisher, pointed out to me that the river was up a few inches. He was quite right. It was not in flood, but it was shot with colour and flowing with more noise and vigour than for many weeks past. There must have been more rain in the hills, or some heavy bursts during the night, for the drizzle that moistened Sedbergh on Saturday could have kept falling for weeks on end without refreshing a beck.

I set off for the Eden at six o'clock and found that it too had been touched. Scandal beck was as low as when last I was there, but the river was dark and peaty and full of promise. There was a brood of well-grown ducklings along the edge of the river. I hoped that they were from one of the nests that I found in the spring. I wondered whether they would survive into September and flight into my nearby pond while I was sitting against the wall with Merlin at my side. I climbed up the bank and found the remains of the old nest. I could not tell whether it had been plundered or whether the eggs had hatched and were now dabbling beside one another in the water.

The river was up and flowing. All that was needed was a hatch of fly or a fall of spinners. I was hoping for the season's first encounter with blue winged olives, and I was bitterly disappointed; for I saw not a single dun and, although a few troupes of yellow uprights tried to dance, the wind made a nonsense of their efforts and they soon thought better of it.

It was a disappointing evening. No fish larger than a six-incher showed itself, except for a trout of eight inches which I caught from the bottom of Scandal beck and returned. The evening could not decide whether it wanted to be dark and lowering and windy, or the sort of evening that settles into a damp grey stillness under a thick cover of cloud. Mostly it was windy, but there were periods of calm, when the heavy mood began to gather beneath the hanging leaves.

I was uncertain whether I wanted to be there by the Eden or some-where else, for it was dispiriting fishing through pools and runs and thinking of the great trout I had caught there in seasons past. I began to think that a pub would be a more comforting place than a river haunted by memories. I began to think again of two lean summers on the Eden at Eastfield and I began to feel that I was fishing a river that had entered upon its twilight as a trout stream. A great sadness came over me and I drove back to Sedbergh in search of the consolations of company and beer.

Skues would not have abandoned the Eden last night. He would have fished on into the last light and he would certainly not have been distracted by thoughts of pubs. But when I am fishing the evening rise, pubs are often a problem for me. Ten o'clock comes and I start thinking of beer. If I have caught a brace I do not think about it for long. For a brace of evening trout is all I want and I surrender to my thirst with an easy mind. But there are evenings that find me still fish-less at ten, and they are sometimes calm and sunny evenings when the blue wings are beginning to hatch or when the spinners are threatening to fall. On such evenings it costs me a struggle either to stay or go. It is not just alcohol I crave. Even if I fish until midnight there will be whisky waiting for me at home. It is the delight of sitting in a pub, swallowing mouthfuls of beer and talking about nothing in particular: that is what I want at half past ten of a summer evening.

It is a shameful admission for a trout fisherman, but it is true. And so midsummer evenings by a river often end with a brief period of frantic incompetence, with me dashing from pool to pool and fright-ening any trout that are at last settling down to feed, until at the end of half an hour I can persuade myself that the rise is over and that there is just time to get back to Sedbergh before the pub shuts. By the middle of July, thank God, there is no longer a difficulty.

22 June

There is a particular feature about bright and windy days in high summer that commends them to me: it is the movement of clouds. For, while trees stream in the wind and uncut meadows ripple and wave, while loose leaves and petals and stalks fly on each wild gust, with everywhere a bending of wood and grass and the sound of rushing air, yet up there in the sky the great white clouds float on in solemn and unhurried silence: untroubled, aloof and calm.

It was so today on the Eden. The wind was very strong, so strong that Scandal beck was out of the question. But, in spite of the wind, I was glad to be fishing and glad that the misery of schoolboys, in the form of examinations, had brought me the freedom of an afternoon with no lessons. For the air was bright and the clouds were moving with stately purpose. It was too wild for delicate fishing, but midsummer day had brought heavy rain at last and the Eden was up and singing. And the world seemed washed clean and seemed younger than it had been before the rain came.

I started just below Eastfield bridge, with wet flies on my cast: Brown Owl and Eric's Beetle. I had been tempted to leave the Eden and go off to Yockenthwaite at the top of the Wharfe. But, when there is only the afternoon for fishing, it is better to save ten miles at either end of your journey. And there was the thought too that I might find fish rising at Eastfield and come home comforted and hopeful for the future.

There were duck everywhere. I have never seen so many large broods of well-grown mallard. The early flighting should be very good. Bands of goosanders are less welcome and they croak malevolently before performing their party trick by charging off with flailing wings and putting the trout down in the best pool of the whole river. There was such a band today. They muttered and grunted and I expected the worst and was relieved when they careered away downstream.

It was not long before I caught a trout, from the run below the bridge. He took the beetle but was only nine inches and went back. Pale wateries were hatching in a trickle, genuine pale wateries as the yellow eyes of the males proclaimed, but I could not see them being taken, so I fished on with wet flies. Nothing stirred in the narrow, willow-fringed run above the bridge. Under the trees in the long pool beyond I put a fish down, suspecting that he was big. It was the wind really, blowing with such wild bad temper, and I was not too hard on myself. There were no fish rising in the broken water beneath the falls. I passed on to Quiet Corner and prayed that there I should see the rings of rising trout. I was not disappointed.

There was a time, not many years ago, when I was obsessed with Quiet Corner. It is a lovely spot, a long glide over shelves of red and yellow rock, arched over by tall trees. On hot summer days, it is a place of buzzing and droning shadows; and, in the old days, the droning and the buzzing were punctuated by sipping and smacking sounds, as huge trout moved in the slow current and helped themselves to another smut or another spinner or another dun.

It was a place where I used to spend hours on end, for, by the time I had worked my way to the top of the corner, the fish at its bottom end had recovered their composure and were busy feeding again. I would fish for them again with a different fly and, even when the water was very low, even in mid-afternoon on a blazing and windless day in July, there was hope of a trout at Quiet Corner. I have failed with countless fish there. They have looked at my Red Spinners and my Black Gnats and my Yellow Things, at my August Blacks and my Treacle Parkins and my Imperials, and they have despised them all. But I have killed big fish at Quiet Corner, almost to two pounds, and I have lost at least one trout that I know was a monster.

In recent years I have spent less time at Quiet Corner. I have spent less time on the Eden. I was very pleased yesterday to see three or four trout feeding quietly under the trees at the bottom of the pool. I tried them with the Brown Owl and the beetle and they would have none of them. They were smutting fish, but I feared that handling a tiny August Black in a raging gale would prove beyond me. I would try it. But first

I would try something else.

At least one of the trout was sucking in pale wateries between mouthfuls of smut. Trout taking an occasional dun to add variety to their diet are not always selective fish. I tied on a Yellow Thing, cast it over the lowest of the feeding fish and he promptly swallowed it. He was a fat eleven-incher and he went in the bag. A second trout came a few casts later, but he was smaller and went back. Then the Yellow Thing disappeared again and this time a big fish was bending my rod like a hoop, running hard and leaping and falling back with a splash. He did not fight long but he fought hard. He weighed one pound ten ounces and he made both the brace and contentment.

I passed on, back into the sunlight, and followed the river round the next bend and through a wool-strewn pasture where a pair of curlews rose complaining and floated on the wind. I found another trout feeding under the bank and he came to the Yellow Thing and was all of twelve inches. Two smaller trout I returned and then I stopped fishing and sat down and smoked; and, while the wind blustered through the branches above me, shaking the red keys of the sycamores, I gazed beyond them at the clouds as they marched slowly through the sky. There were still fish rising but I did not harry them. Three was enough for the afternoon. They had not told me that all was as it should be at Eastfield, that everything was as it had once been. But they had assured me that things were not as bad as I had feared, that it would be worth coming back.

Today there is no wind. The elders are turning white. The first wild roses are out along the hedges. The air is beginning to carry the heavy smells of midsummer and I hope to be on the Eden before eight o'clock.

23 June

It is strange that, in a season of general failure, a season of low water and few fish, I should have fallen so helplessly back in love with fishing. I cannot have killed more than 25 trout so far this year. Blank days have been commonplace. I have fished into the teeth of fierce and snarling winds. I have struggled by the sides of shrunken and shrivelled rivers. And all that I have wanted to do is to go back to them and to start fishing again.

But I could not go fishing yesterday evening, as I had hoped, and my next fishing trip is more than a week away, somewhere beyond the end of term. For a week or so rivers will flow without my presence on their banks. The wild roses will bloom and the elder flowers will scent the evening air without the honour of commemoration in my diary. I shall do justice to them both, and to whatever else takes my fancy, just as soon as July comes along and makes me free until September.

30 June

The term is in its death agonies and, with each passing minute, I am feeling more cheerful. It is a languorous evening, with cloud and a heavy stillness. I should like to go fishing, but some boys are coming round to say farewell and to drink wine. I shall enjoy their company this evening and miss them next year when they have gone. It would be wrong to go fishing and my conscience is more influential with me because, come tomorrow, I can more or less abandon it for the next nine weeks.

I went out to High Park this afternoon with my solicitor and roamed the fields with him. It was very beautiful, for the cloud did not come until six. The meadow was full of pink and purple orchids and bright with the yellows and reds of flowers that I cannot name. The high banks above the meadow and the sike are still ungrazed and the breeze moves over them with a rippling sheen. The water in the sike is thin and clear and there were clouds of spinners dancing over it.

115

They were ecdyonurids of one sort or another. There was a pair of curlews floating and moaning over the Hag. My solicitor talked of fences and water rights and I listened to one word in ten and made nothing of it all.

I do not care a fig about fences and water rights. I long to possess something that I love, and I shall not be truly happy until the formalities are complete and I know that I have it. Doubtless this lust to possess is a sin. In mitigation of my error I could urge that I yearn to have only so that I can cherish. I do not want to plunder, but to preserve and improve. I shall have to go out to High Park again sometime in the next ten days, before I head north. The pen needs checking, for my birds arrive almost as soon as I return from Scotland. It will have to be done, but I shall not enjoy it. Today I looked at wild roses, twining through the hawthorns on the high bank above the sike and glowing red. The thought that they were blooming on land that might still never belong to me made me shiver with dread. I do not want to be there until I know that the dream has turned into reality, until I can sit by the running water and sprawl in the long grass and listen to my pheasants shouting to each other across my land.

1 July

It is the evening of the best day of the year. It is the evening when to be a schoolmaster is the best blessing in the world. I drove out of Sedbergh at four o'clock in the afternoon, singing away to the chugging accompaniment of the Land Rover and wondering where to fish tomorrow. It shall be the Wenning, although I fear that I shall find her very low. But, however low I find the water, and however windy I find the day, I shall fish hard and long. On Sunday I go to see Digby. On Monday I go to the Wharfe and I stay in Wharfedale until Thursday evening. Then, whether or not contracts have been exchanged, I must spend a day at High Park around my pheasant pen, before ten days on

Speyside precedes a week on Tiree.

When I get back from Scotland it will be time to collect my birds. August will be filled with their care, full of fox-fear and fox-hatred, with a dash to Loch Lomondside for a day at the grouse on the thirteenth. In August I plan to fish most evenings. By the beginning of September my poults will all be headless corpses and the Brough foxes will have grown fat, or most of them will be roosting high in the trees; they will have turned into creatures almost capable of looking after themselves and I shall be sleeping more easily in my bed. I have been invited to Hartside for a driven day on the first Saturday of the month. The following Monday will find me back at work and depressed, and with less than a month to catch a few last trout.

I enjoy being a schoolmaster, and not merely because of summer holidays that seem, at their beginning, to stretch almost into infinity. I enjoy Latin and Greek and attempting to teach them. Boys are often very annoying. Often too they are charming and cooperative. Almost always, and even when they are at their most trying, they are amusing beyond words. I have no time for schoolmasters who do nothing but moan about the unbearable tensions of their vocation. It is a vocation full of fascination and laughter.

But I am very happy to bid farewell to it for nine and a half weeks. At some stage of them I must read some classical texts and make ready for next term. But at the moment it is this diary that matters most to me. I want to keep it this summer with care and love. There is my diary and there are, of course, 62 acres of land at Brough Sowerby. The best day of the holidays, better even than this first day of all, will be the day when I sign a contract and know that the land is mine. It looks as though it may happen before I set off for Scotland. It looks as though a week on Monday may be the day of days.

2 July

What is summer fishing by a little river in the north? It is briars by the edge of the water, shining with white and pink blossom and with bees buzzing among them. It is scented elderflowers the colour of clotted cream and banks painted with swaying dog daisies. It is hanging grass and leaning spikes of sorrel, and yellow monkey flowers where the marigolds bloomed in spring. It is the breathy rush of swifts' wings and the rasping chatter of sand martins. It is the gaunt shapes of the sheep after the shearing and it is fat lambs feeding in the pastures. It is the cropped yellow of meadows that have been mown for silage or for early hay. It is the sad falling away of the willow warbler's summer notes, or a blackbird that remembers spring in a few muted seconds of song. It is heavy air and a near haze and cows splashing down to drink. It is a listless angler, sitting and smoking for twenty minutes at a time, then fishing his unhurried way up another run and resting again at the top of it. It is trout sipping flies lazily and slow circles spreading over the pools.

I was tired today and the heavy midsummer mood was just right for me; so too was the Wenning, with its quiet pools and mossy runs and its welcoming loneliness. The water was not as low as I had feared. Certainly it was low, but it was flowing rather than creeping on its way and it was clear and free of slime. Ingleborough must have caught some of the soaking drizzle that fell in Sedbergh all Sunday and that Monday and at last brought the Lune up in heavy spate. I expected little sport today. In spite of yesterday's commitment to arduous activity, I was prepared for a lazy day ending with little to show for it. But, in defiance of what I had anticipated, I was given an absorbing and fruitful fishing day, and I moved through it with delight and with slow gratitude.

All day there were duns trickling down the stream. I spent as much time picking them off the surface and trying to identify them as I spent fishing. There were true pale wateries, but not many of them. There were purple duns in some quantity. They are like largish iron blues, but they have three tails and they hatch in high summer and seldom in more than ones and twos. They are an entomological rarity and I have never seen as many as I saw today. Trout are said to ignore them and I cannot be certain that, even today, when they came in moderate profusion, any were taken.

The flies the trout wanted were not purple duns, nor pale wateries, nor the few small dark olives that decided to hatch. For the dun most often on the water, in a steady trickle from one o'clock until four, was the large spurwing: *centroptilum pennulatum* to the entomologist, a puzzle to Skues many years ago, a delight to me today, and easily recognisable by its blue wings, its pale, almost translucent body and its relatively large size. It is a fly built roughly on the scale of the olive upright, much bigger than a blue wing. Just to be sure that you are looking at a large spurwing, get out your magnifying glass and gaze through it at one of the wings. Do not bother with the hind wings, even though the shape of them is diagnostic and has given the fly its vernacular name. Ignore the hind wings. They are too small for riverside inspection. Look at the edge of one of the forewings. Look for a single intercalary vein. Say *centroptilum pennulatum* to yourself and feel rather knowledgeable.

Flies are one of the great pleasures of flyfishing. They are a pleasure too often ignored. Knowing what the fish are taking sometimes makes the difference between a full and an empty bag. Often it does not matter a fig. I do not think it mattered much today, but it was a delight to come across an uncommon fly and to establish beyond doubt that it was just what I thought it was. I have seen large spurwings before, on the Wharfe and the Eden, but they have seemed lonely creatures, lacking the company of their own kind, and I have never seen one eaten by a trout. Today the trout wanted them. They were taking both the hatching nymph and the floating dun, and they seemed to think that the Yellow Thing was a passable imitation of the large spurwing dun.

I fished slowly and rested often. There were times when an airless

119

calm fell over the river. I missed a big trout from a little run at the bottom of Austwick beck. I put back a few parr and a few midgets and I killed four. All of them took the Yellow Thing. They were between ten and twelve inches long, plump and yellow, with red spots and amber fins and full tails. At the end of it all I felt quite pleased with myself.

There is a fashion for big trout nowadays. Many fishers look with scorn upon any fish under a pound. They are wrong to do so, and it is the stocking of rivers with large fish that has produced the false belief that size is all that matters. I would rather catch a half pound trout from the top of the Wenning, telling myself that, ever since it began life as an egg, it has known no other home but the Wenning; telling myself that, as alevin and fry and as a proud young trout, it has swum in no water other than the water that flows down from the deep limestone springs of Ingleborough. I would rather catch such a trout, and a brace or a leash to go beside him in my bag, than a dozen deformed monsters that gobbled pellets and grew pot-bellied until they were judged fat and misshapen enough to be tipped into a river and caught by fishermen. And trout of between half and three quarters of a pound are exactly the right size for a plate.

3 July

This morning I put Merlin in kennels and watched Digby gambolling around for twenty minutes. He is coming along well. Then I drove over the fells to the Wenning and spent the afternoon fishing. It was a warm and humid afternoon, the sort of summer afternoon when the hills are dim and uncertain shapes, when smooth water stares back at the sky with a milky gleam. There was never a breath of wind and I fished with my lightest rod, seven feet four inches of thin cane, a rod that coaxes line and cast and fly through the air and lays it gently on the water. It was made for a friend who died four years ago. It was made by Norman Goodwin in Skipton and it is quite unlike any modern rod of carbon fibre. It is not a particularly practical rod; its action is so slow and so gentle that using it seems like fishing in slow motion. It cannot put a fly into the wind.

But it is very beautiful, with yellow-brown cane and green whip-pings and with the subdued lustre of the varnish, and its character is perfectly suited to windless afternoons when the hills are sleeping in haze and a midsummer stillness has settled over all things.

I killed two trout, both on the Yellow Thing, fish of eleven and twelve inches. I put back some smaller trout and a few parr. A pair of goosanders came circling and croaking over me, and they flew back for a third and a fourth inspection as though they were affronted by my presence on their banks and wanted to make their disapproval plain. I fished up to the top corner of the Wenning and the long flat where the best of the trout lie. The little rod whispered as it worked for me and it caught me my two trout from the little pools on the way. At the top of the long, shadowed flat where the big trout live, there is a spot where a fish has been feeding almost whenever I have been there. It is a spot close to the bank, between two flat stones; it is a smooth glide of water beneath a leaning ash. He was feeding today, dimpling at things too small to see. I rose him and pricked him on that dark afternoon when the iron blues were hatching. He felt big. Today I changed my fly. I put on an August Black and was ready to cast over him when a thirsty cow splashed into the river and sent him shooting down the pool.

Half an hour later he was back feeding and I was back below him. The little rod whispered and the fly fell and the trout rose. Again I pricked him, feeling the pull of a heavy trout and the sudden collapse of tension as the hook came free. He will be there another day and I shall have him before the end of September. By modern standards I do not suppose he is very big. If he weighs more than a pound and a half I shall be surprised. But he will be worth more to me, when he lies beaten in the net, than trout of twice his size from other rivers. Not that

I have ever caught a trout of three pounds.

I wandered off downstream in search of my flask of tea. I sat on the bank and drank from it and realised that trout were moving in the still pool above the stepping stones, feeding on or near the surface with those violent and swirling rises that speak unambiguously of blue winged olives. And there, on the flat grey surface of the pool, blue wings were sitting with their dark wings raised in silhouette. It was past six o' clock and it was time for me to go. There was not even half an hour for the challenge of trout eating BWOs on an evening of low water. I did knot on a Poult Bloa and it rose the first trout to which it was cast. There was no time for more, and so I left the Wenning and the trout and the blue winged olives, telling them that I should be back in August with whole evenings to devote to them. Tomorrow it is the Wharfe.

4 July

Compared to the Wharfe the Wenning is no more than a ditch with water running through it. So at least it seemed to me when I reached the Wharfe at half past eleven this morning and began to fish. And this comparison puzzled me, because I drew it without for a moment resigning my regained affection for the Wenning and the trout that swim there. But the Wharfe looked so beautiful, with its deep pools, its bubbling runs and mossy glides, with its bars of shining white gravel, with its little waterfalls and its channels through ridged and fluted and yellowed rock - the Wharfe looked so beautiful this morning that I could not help thinking of the Wenning and how it fell short of such loveliness.

The day was hot and still and damp and hazy, with brief showers that promised to turn into downpours and then dried up before they had properly started. But they filled the silage makers with determined purpose and all day the clatter of their machines rumbled through the heavy stillness. I did not fish with yesterday's rod. It finds big fish too much of a burden and the Wharfe is now a river of big fish. Twenty years ago, when I first came to its banks, a trout of a pound set the whole dale talking. Now such fish scarcely merit a mention. Trout are only big if they are nearer two pounds than one and every season at Kilnsey brings some of the members fish in excess of three pounds.

It is the club's policy that has brought this change, for we now pour big fish into the Wharfe at Kilnsey, whereas twenty years ago our beats were stocked with trout of around eight inches, so that they were not worth catching until they had been in the river for a season or more. I am not altogether happy with the introduction of large trout into rivers, especially rivers like the Wharfe that already support a thriving population of wild fish.

But, if it has to happen, and there are reasons why it must, then the way we do it at Kilnsey is the best way: with one annual stocking, one only done in April and thereby giving the immigrant trout time to learn the rudiments of wisdom by the time summer comes along. And the river is so full of wild trout, and of trout from the stockings of earlier seasons, that each April's interlopers find nowhere to go but the big dubs, where they gather in huge colonies and can be harried by those who care for such sport. Moreover the high beats of the river are left unstocked. The big trout that swim there may well have begun their lives in a stew pond, but by the time I catch them at Yockenthwaite they are, except in size, indistinguishable from the smaller fish that have always been there.

I like trout with yellow flanks and dark backs, with amber fins and broad tails. I do not like the malformed fins, the torn and broken tails, the pallid grey gleam of trout from a stock pond, and it is rare for me to catch such a trout at Kilnsey. I should be happier with no stocking or with fewer introduced trout. But I am not discontented with things as they are, and there is no denying that Kilnsey trout are often very difficult, or that the real hope of a monster and the frequent contact with trout that know how to bend a rod both lend excitement to fishing there.

One of the reasons that Kilnsey trout provide such demanding sport is that they spend most of each summer obsessed with smut. A low and clear water, a river full of big trout sipping tiny black things and ready to bolt for cover at the first flash of a line or the first heavy footfall or the first heavy cast: these are the constituents of absorbing and exciting and often wildly frustrating sport. There was a time when, except in a big water and except on some evenings, I fished almost all of every summer at Kilnsey with the August Black. My practice is much more varied now, and even embraces worms, but today, after casting a Yellow Thing hopefully over a couple of trout that were clearly eating something very small, I acknowledged that it was not going to be a day for the easy and obvious delights of a size fourteen dry fly. It was a day for the August Black, dressed small on an eighteen hook, a day for Stewart-style creeping and crawling, for sweat and curses and hard-won gains.

I started at Watersmeet, where the Skirfare joins the Wharfe. The upstream beat is water of infinite charm, with short pools and ripples and glides, all under cover of trees, until the river loses its shyness and comes out into the open and, growing perversely more mature as it progresses towards the source, broadens out into long flats and deep, wide dubs. The lower half of this beat is perhaps my favourite stretch of the whole Kilnsey water. It was here this morning that, in a short and turbulent willow-fringed run, I saw a trout rise and flicked the August Black over him. A moment later my rod was bent.

He was a most beautiful trout, one pound three ounces and perfectly proportioned. Looking at him in the net I thought of pure, swift water and of rich summer feeding; I thought of brown bread and butter, slices of lemon, grand cru chablis and the subtle flavour of pink trout flesh. I went through the same thoughts five minutes later, when I caught a trout that looked like his brother from a rocky glide twenty yards upstream. Again I had seen the faint tokens of his feeding, but he did not come to the first cast or to the tenth. I thought I had put him down, then I tried a throw a foot or so higher and he swirled at the August Black and was on.

These two trout were a great comfort, for they showed me that I could still fish the most demanding of all styles with something like competence. In low water the upstream wet, with small unweighted flies, is at least twice as difficult as the dry fly. But, fished efficiently, it is often many times more effective. In recent years I have grown almost shy of it and have often persisted with dry flies when swarms of smut and scores of sipping rises have been telling me to pin my faith to the August Black. There are days when smutting trout gobble down a bushy dry fly as though they were only smutting under protest and in the absence of more substantial prey. But such days, though delightful when they come, are few and far between. Sometimes something black and dry will catch trout. More often it is the August Black, fished on a greased cast, that deceives them. There are many days when they will look with approval at nothing in your fly-box, because everything in your fly box is much too big.

The challenge of small wet flies is the twofold challenge of accuracy and the strike. You must cast a foot in front of your trout, you must try to see the fall of your fly and you must strike either the rise or any untoward movement of your line or cast. There are days when everything goes wrong and your performance gets steadily worse. Even on good days you cannot hope to get it right with every fish or even with most of them. And, even when your prey seems to have been firmly hooked, the fight that follows is unusually tense. For, whatever the experts tell you, small hooks love to come free. A small hook loves to convince you that it has done its job to perfection and attached itself like a limpet to the jaw of the two-pound trout at present on the end of your line; and then, just as you begin to think that all is well and that the struggle is nearly over, it ends even sooner than you were expecting and it ends with a loose fly and a trailing cast.

I learned this all over again today. For, fishing on and finding nothing doing, I came to the long run beyond the trees. I saw no rises and fished the water in the hope of finding a trout ready to seize my fly. A passing shower spotted the water and cooled my brow. Again and again the line whispered and went out. And then something told me to raise my wrist, the rod bent into a hoop and a great trout was running like a steam-engine for the willow roots downstream. I held him hard and turned him. He thrashed wildly in the open water and ran again. I told myself that he must be firmly hooked and that now he was tiring and that he would surely be mine. I was holding him on a tight line. He was weary and it was only a question of patience and care with the net. The next moment the line was slack and I was very disappointed. I had felt his force and seen his tail and had reckoned him at well over two pounds.

There was a time when the loss of a big fish ruined the day. It still hurts. It still leaves me pulling line through the rod rings and vainly hoping to find that he is still on after all. And there is still the momentary failure to come to terms with what has just happened. But there is no longer the ensuing despair that engulfs the whole day in darkness and taints the taste of Guinness and stays with me until sleep finally takes it away.

I fished on and soon recovered my composure. The river fell quiet and I ate my sandwiches and drank my tea. Colin came along and we chatted for a while. I caught a fish in Black Keld and put it in the bag. I missed one in the run above and found before long that it was five o' clock and time for *The Falcon*. Three fish were not many, but on a day of low water and smutting fish they were enough and there had been a few smaller trout returned. In spite of the great fish that had nearly been mine I was pleased with my day's sport.

After supper the wind got up, but I went to the Skirfare below Hawkswick and found that spinners were dancing in defiance of the rough air. They were large spinners, some sort of false march brown. The August Black came off; on went a Red Spinner and within five minutes I had covered a rise, hard under the bank on the edge of a glassy glide, and I had hooked and landed a trout of one pound fourteen ounces. It was a tense struggle, for he yielded only slowly and I was very keen not to lose two big fish on the same day.

Other trout were less obliging and I think, on reflection, that I should have tried a different fly. But the Red Spinner stayed on and at last brought another trout to net, this one a pounder, on the very edge of darkness. By then I thought that I had earned a bottle or two of Guinness and drove off to *The Falcon*, where I found that two small bottles of Guinness was not enough. I confess that I drank four.

5 July

A blank morning under cloud, spent between Black Keld and the stepping stones. There were fewer trout feeding than yesterday and those that were refused every fly I showed them. I diverted myself, in between bouts of fruitless sport, by walking the banks and finding early signs of autumn in the hanging keys on the sycamores and the bunches of green berries on hawthorns and rowans.

It rained heavily while I was eating lunch and talking with Oliver, my guest for three days. Then the sun came out and the air smelt of nettles and everything seemed green and fresh. I was almost reconciled to a blank day when, exploring above the stepping stones and coming to a favourite glide beneath a high bank, I saw two trout feeding and saw too that a few pale wateries were fluttering off the stream. I decided to try these trout with a small Grey Duster. The first weighed twelve ounces and the second fourteen. They were both beautiful fish.

Moving on I came to a second and much more difficult glide, where fish are almost always feeding and where, unless the water is coloured, I have very seldom caught them. It is a lovely spot; it is a glide, not over gravel, but over the bedrock of the stream. The water slips on its way with barely a ripple and the rock shines yellow and you can see the shapes of trout lifting themselves to pick flies off the surface. Most of the shapes are big.

Late this afternoon the trout were busy as usual. The lowest of them almost took the Grey Duster, but thought better of it at the last moment and went to the willow roots to brood upon his lucky escape. I changed to an August Black. It fell short of the trout I had intended to cover, but he turned and followed it and I saw his mouth open and raised my wrist at the right moment. He was very angry, racing this way and that, shaking his head savagely and putting paid to any thought of more trout from the same glide. He weighed exactly one pound and a half and he pleased me inordinately, for he came from a difficult spot and visible trout are always a particular satisfaction. And suddenly a day of failure had turned into an unexpected success.

The evening was one of the most beautiful I have ever spent by a river. The sky was cloudless, the air was fresh. The water shone white and silver and gold. Above the water danced a shining host of spinners and, as they began to fall, the trout came up to them and made rippling patterns all over the surface of the river. There were many fish feeding, and many of them were big. All of them disdained my flies, my Red Spinners and Houghton Rubies, my spinners with spent wings and my spinners with half the hackle cut away. It was very frustrating, but the beauty of the fading light was more powerful than my sense of failure. I returned to *The Falcon* with a grateful heart.

6 July

Soon after I started this morning, fishing up from Watersmeet, the August Black brought me a bright trout of a pound. There were fish feeding above him and I thought that I was on the verge of great things. A minute later I hooked a second much bigger trout, but he came unstuck after a brief struggle. Then I pricked a trout in a swift run. That was that for the morning.

I sat outside the hut with Oliver and talked with him for almost an hour. Years ago I taught him Latin and brought him once or twice to the Wharfe. We have developed into fishing friends and meet two or three times a year on each other's water. I suppose I have the best of the bargain. I give Oliver the Wharfe. He gives me Foston and the Driffield beck. At lunchtime Oliver had a fine trout of one and a half pounds. It was very pleasant sitting there in the warm and cloudy afternoon, talking about fishing while a gentle breeze stirred the long grasses along the bank.

At last it was time to start again. I hooked a fish in the same spot that had brought me the morning's trout. He felt a firmly-hooked fish, until my line came back to me. And then, exactly where I struggled with the monster on Monday, I fought a trout, a much smaller but still substantial trout, for perhaps a minute before the line went slack. In Spout Dub I turned two fish without making a firm contact. And, in the evening, a quiet grey evening with a less abundant fall of the same ecdyonurid spinners, fishing what seemed an appropriate pattern, I rose and hooked a trout feeding in a thin glide. He was a big fish and a fit fish and again he seemed a well-hooked fish until he was no longer hooked at all.

And that was the end of a frustrating day when fish dropped off the hook for no obvious reason. I have known many days when, whatever fly I have used, I have pricked trout after trout and caught few or none. But they have been pricked trout, touched trout, not hooked and then lost trout. Brief encounters of the former sort are particularly common with wet flies in a coloured water. Never until today have so many apparently firmly hooked fish found themselves suddenly free. It has made me very keen to catch trout tomorrow.

In the afternoon it rained very heavily between three and half past four: a lovely windless downpour, with big, bloated drops falling and splashing heavily on the grey surface of the river, falling and beating noisily on the broad and quivering leaves. The air seemed full of water. It is raining again as I write these notes before sleep. Perhaps tomorrow the river will be up and there will be a peaty water, pleading for an angler to fish wet flies upstream and to fill his bag with spotted trout.

7 July

The river did not colour overnight, but there was certainly an extra inch or two of flowing water this morning and a livelier look to the Wharfe's progress. The day was warm and fresh and the rain had washed away the heavy airs that have hung in the valley all week.

There is not much to say about the day's sport, except that, like most fishing days, it was better than days that do not put a fishing rod in your hand. I fished above the stepping stones and killed a trout on the Grey Duster. I passed on to the rock glide, where I rose a good trout and missed him. I have missed too many fish this week. The fly was clearly wrong and, with other trout, I tried the August Black to no effect. They were smutting trout, but they would not look at an August Black tied on an eighteen hook; it was much too big to deceive them.

Lunch was beneath the sycamores that lean over Knipe Dub. It was leisurely, and in the afternoon I decided on a change of tactics. The trout were smutting, but in that desultory way that rarely brings good sport with the August Black. I restored the Grey Duster and determined to fish it through the rougher runs, looking for rising trout but fishing the water as well. For some time it seemed as though this would bring nothing, but then I spotted a trout feeding in the neck of a rocky pool and sent the Grey Duster over him. He weighed a pound exactly. Moving on I came to a turbulent run with pockets of grey water beneath the cloud. In such a pocket I thought that I had glimpsed the brief dimple of a rising trout. The Grey Duster went out again and a second later the rod was bent. He was a big fish and he was slow to surrender. He dashed from one side of the pool to another. He sulked under rocks and pulled for the roots. More than once I thought that I must lose him, but he stayed for the net and the spring balance told me that he was one pound twelve ounces.

I put down a trout near the outflow of the Kettlewell sewage pipe. Then I turned round and strolled downstream, contented with my afternoon's sport and more or less ready to call it a day. It was half past four and I noticed that already there were spinners dancing low over the water. Passing the rock glide I noticed that, as usual, there were two or three good fish feeding quietly. I could not leave them. I did not believe that, in such smooth water, the Grey Duster would fool them. I did not think it was a day for the August Black. And so I tied on a little spinner. It had a body of red silk ribbed with silver wire. The hook was size sixteen. The hackle was palest ginger. That was all. I cast it onto the glassy surface, just in front of the nearest and lowest trout, and he grabbed it with a savage greed that shocked me into a late strike. His antics put down every other fish in the glide and he weighed six ounces over the pound.

He was the most beautiful fish of the week, with a short head and a deep belly, with red spots, gleaming yellow flanks and a dark, shining back. He was everything a trout should be and I rather think he was a she. I wandered back to the tall sycamores by Knipe Dub and talked with Oliver for a while. He had caught a brace and wanted to fish on for another hour. I left him to it and drove back to *The Falcon* to collect my frozen trout. Then I drove off to Grindleton to collect Merlin.

131

It has been a fine fishing trip to the Wharfe. The weather has been quiet, so that casting a fly has been a delight. The fish have not been easy, but many of them have been willing to consider a well-presented fly. All the trout I have killed have been in the pink of condition and they have all been the owners of perfect fins. The river has been clean and bright. The evenings have been very lovely. Guinness has seemed a just reward at the end of each long day's sport. I am happier to be a fisherman than for ten years past and I think that on Sunday I shall go to the Wenning

9 July

The late morning and early afternoon were spent at High Park, checking the pen and the electric fence. Both seem in good order. The meadow is just as lovely as it was ten days ago, still full of flowers. It is also full of grass and, given kind weather, it will produce a heavy crop of hay. The small pasture beneath and to the right of the house could also become a meadow, so providing more cover for nesting birds and perhaps more profit for me. But it is still too soon to dream of what I can do at High Park. Contracts may be exchanged next week. Today I saw two red squirrels and far too many magpies.

10 July

I went back to my little ditch today, spending four or five hours by the Wenning and wondering why I am so fond of it. Its water does not flow with quite the shining clarity of the Wharfe; there are no stately trees lining the banks and there is not a great trout sipping down flies in every pool. It is an unpretentious little river, flowing in the shadows of twisted alders and dead elms, through rough pastures and through flat meadows that are mown for silage. And it is fence-infested, with the top two or three hundred yards imprisoned between lines of posts and wire. It has been cruelly confined between high banks and sadly changed. It is much slower than the bright river I fished twenty years ago. Much of its former loveliness has been torn out and dumped on the banks.

But perhaps this is, in fact, the reason for my renewed love of the Wenning: that it has been mauled and ravaged, that, scarred but undefeated, it has survived and still looks beautiful and still breeds flies and the trout to eat them. And I go there with easy expectations and come home happy with a brace of eleven inch trout. There is a delightful solitude to be found there, not the high and daunting solitude of the hills, but the softer and more welcoming loneliness of unfrequented fields. I have sat alone on the top of Scottish mountains and felt challenged by the empty spaces all around me. The loneliness of the upper Wenning is much less intense and far more soothing. Swallows and martins share it with me. Trains hoot in the distance. Cows swish their tails and amble down to the water for a drink. It is lowland loneliness and it is delectable.

I got my brace of eleven inch trout today, both to a Grey Duster and within five minutes of each other. There were a few large spur-wings again. The males have orange eyes. But I decided the fish were smutting and tried to tempt them with my smallest August Black. It hooked one and pricked two and could do no more for me. I tried the Grey Duster and very soon the brace was in the bag. Late in the afternoon I saw a fish rise in the pool below the stepping stones and felt certain that he would rise to my fly. He did and, for the Wenning, he was a good trout, but he came unstuck after a few seconds and left me disappointed. He was my last chance of a Wenning trout until August, when I shall come to the Wenning in the evenings, at the end of days devoted to my pheasant poult, and fish the late rise as the blue wings hatch and the spinners fall and the seatrout stir from the pools and begin to move through the summer gloaming.

Since term ended I have fished seven days out of nine and I have enjoyed almost every moment of it. Once or twice I have wondered whether I should be devoting so much time to a mere sport. For the world is full of things that matter more than fishing, and I suppose it is selfish to spend days on end with a rod in my hand and with no thought for anything but the problems and pleasures of angling. I am a self-absorbed bachelor and I spend too much time enjoying myself along riverbanks. My only justification is that I enjoy myself with reverence and with gratitude. At the end of every fishing day, as I take down my rod and stow my tackle in the Land Rover, I thank God for the pleasures of the day and for his great goodness in making trout and trout streams part of his creation. There are perhaps some riverside days that end without this little ritual of thanksgiving, days that end with me renouncing fishing for ever and threatening my rods with imminent fracture or fire. To be honest, there are some days of this sort, but they are rare days and I cannot recall one this season.

13 July

I drove to Scotland today, under a blue sky with floating clouds, past Stirling and Perth and Blair Atholl and then up over Drumochter. It is here, where wild lupins line the wayside and where great purple slopes rise straight from the road, that I feel I have at last reached the Highlands. Then the huge shapes of the Cairngorms come into view and the rolling outline of the Monadliath. It is a revelation I have enjoyed every summer for fifteen years. Today it was as fine as I have seen it and I am very happy to be in Scotland for more than a fortnight. Tomorrow I shall climb a hill.

14 July

I am going to litter this entry with Gaelic names and give the first full day of my Scottish diary a truly Celtic and highland flavour. It will help to establish the right mood.

It was a morning of warm air and high cloud. We went into the Monadliath, parking the car at the end of the road up Glen Banchor, then walking almost back on ourselves across the heather to strike the path that runs up the Allt na Beinne; from there up onto Am Bodach, which means the old man, then over to A'Chailleach and down the side of the hill and across the Allt a Chaorainn and back to the car. It was an easy and a pleasant walk, a good beginning for legs that have spent more time by rivers this summer than they have spent climbing hills.

As soon as we reached the estate track by the Allt na Beinne, a ring ouzel flew chacking from the rocks. A minute later a buzzard was floating over us and mewing his disapproval. Then a raven came by, croaking with slow and deep hatred of sassenachs. It was only a few more paces before a pair of merlins sprang from the heather and raced and tumbled through the sky, chittering with alarm. We watched all this and plodded on and slowly upwards, falling into that thoughtless rhythm of moving feet that is one of the pleasures of walking in the hills. There come periods of more intense and less pleasurable exertion. The steep side of Am Bodach was just such a period: twenty minutes of laboured steps and heaving lungs and the hope that it would not last much longer, leading finally to the exhilaration of the top and the sense of perfect well-being that belongs to high places as a reward for the effort that has been expended in reaching them.

But today my delight in the summit was poisoned by toothache, not the violent sort that makes all other forms of pain seem more like pleasure, rather the dull sort that nags away at you and turns your thoughts to decay and mortality. When we had crossed the beallach, which is what you call a col when you are walking in Scotland and feeling pretentious, and when we had toiled up the long drag to the top of A'Chailleach, I sat there smoking and reflected that I must have sat there at least fifteen times before, listening to the swifts screaming around the cliffs. And it occurred to me, as I acknowledged the steady complaint of carious gums and rotten teeth, that next year would probably find me sitting there with a mouth full of plastic. And I began to wonder if false teeth destroy a man's pleasure in wine. Meanwhile the hills sank into a purple and ochre haze and within five minutes it was raining. It seemed the beginning of a downpour, but within five minutes it had turned dry again and, by the time we had reached the car and pulled off our boots, the sun was trying to shine.

15 July

The morning was passed lazily. We lay late in bed and then lounged around reading newspapers. In the afternoon we climbed two of the most boring hills in Scotland: steep-sided humps with featureless summits to the east of Drumochter. I am a lover of undramatic mountains. I like wide slopes of heather and rounded tops. But these two, A'Bhuidheanach Bheag and Carn Na Caim, had little to commend them. They are nothing but tedious outgrowths from the earth and today it was too cloudy for compensating views.

There were mountain hares running ahead of us. There were the wild pipings of golden plover. There were tame dotterel pleading to be turned into trout flies. Down in the heather there was the blue of butterwort and milkwort, the white of dwarf cornel and the pinks and purples of the moorland orchids. But these sights and colours and sounds belong to all the mountains hereabouts, together with the smell of bog myrtle and of wild thyme. It was good to walk and to sweat with uncomplaining teeth. That was the best thing about today's expedition. I do not think that I shall ever climb A'Bhuidheanach Bheag and Carn Na Caim again. And it is a shameful admission that it was only their status as Monros that drove us up them in the first place.

16 July

A fine walk today: the three summits of Beinn A'Ghlo, the mountain of mist, climbed on a day of high and luminous cloud, beginning by a lochan where a fisherman was drifting in a boat. The initial ascent, to the top of Carn Liath, was steep and very long. My companion Roger, who is very fit as well as being a polymath, bounded ahead of me. Eventually I joined him at the top and lay there, drenched in sweat, heart thumping and blood coursing. But weariness soon drained away and I felt made of health. Then it was on along a high and elegant, a curving and comfortably wide ridge to the next summit and the next. I have forgotten their names, but they were both memorable peaks with wide views of other mountains. The way down was even steeper than the way up. The walk back to our starting point was delightful, with hazy sunbeams finding passage through the clouds and shining on distant heather and distant pines. There were trout rising in the lochan, when we returned to it, but the fisherman had gone. Rabbits beyond number had come out to feed on the edges of the plantations, scurrying away from the Land Rover's approach, racing over the road only inches away from its bone-crushing wheels. More than once I braked hard, for, much as I love shooting and eating rabbits, I can no more run over them, either with casual unconcern or with malevolent purpose, than I could drive down a dog and not feel sick. If Merlin were here, and with this wealth of rabbits all around him, he would be as steady as a rock to their flushing within a couple of days.

17 July

No summits were conquered today. The weather was bright and hot and my legs were aching from yesterday's exertions. I started at Spey Dam and trudged along the Red Burn as far as a rotting bothy about five miles up the Markie valley.

The bottom of the valley is ordinary enough, with a rushing water along its floor and wide sweeps of heather on either side. But when,

137

after three miles or so, the sides of the valley close in and the path leaves the burn and climbs the steep slopes above the water, you come to a place of secret loveliness and you are entranced. You cross the precipitous course of tributary streams, tumbling down into the deep and twisting ravine that is now way below you. Great buttresses and bastions of rock shine pink and red in the sun. Shattered screes slope down steeply to the edge of sheer rock faces. Rowans find giddy purchase in fissures and crevices along the margins of falling water. Even though there are tall crags above you, you feel somehow higher than you felt yesterday on the summit of a high mountain. There is a feeling of hidden elevation, with a sense of discovery and the private joy of penetrating to a secret and special place.

Beyond the bothy there is a high waterfall. Today I left it unvisited and lay in the heather and dozed for half an hour before retracing my steps. Last year I went there. Above me an eagle floated and croaked disapprovingly. I think he must have cursed me, because two hours later I was completely lost, and came off the hill late in the evening into a remote valley with a ruined lodge at its head. At this point my companion (not the polymath) found his bearings - I should never have found them - and, like David Balfour and Alan Breck, we climbed back into the heather as the light died, by winding burns and gleaming lochans, and spent the night in either end of a plastic sleeping-bag. We were woken by the calls of waking grouse and reached the car at seven o' clock in the morning, just in time to ring the mountain rescue and tell them not to come looking for us.

When you go walking in the Monadliath, you will get lost as we did if you think that the old fence along the ridge, which follows the line of the district boundary from Carn Sgulain to Carn Ban and beyond, continues to do so further west. It does not. At some point it feels a sudden urge for the north and bids the district boundary farewell. The ruined lodge at the head of its lonely valley is certainly worth a visit, especially as night draws on. But on the whole I should prefer to visit it by design and without combining my trip with a bivouac on a sodden hillside. I hate any form of camping.

18 July

Today it was the hills to the west of Drumochter. I climbed them last year, with the polymath, on a day of unbroken sunshine and clear light and limitless views. Today's sunshine was hazy. The surrounding mountains were vast shapes rather than sharp outlines against the sky; but we could make out the high snow fields on the flanks of Ben Alder.

They are fine hills, these hills west of Drumochter. They are rounded and graceful, quite unlike the dull protuberances to the east of the road, and they do not deserve the scorn that has been poured on them by men who can see upland beauty only in thrusting peaks and sheer precipices. They are rather like my Howgills, except for the heather that carpets them; and they are higher and lonelier and the valleys that run between them are deeper and more secret. The first of them is called Geal Charn. A'Mharconaich comes next. The last and finest is Beinn Udlamain.

19 July

It was hot and sultry today. We drove to Lagganside, to Luiblea, where a wooden bridge spans the river that connects the two parts of the loch. We crossed this bridge and followed a broad, stony track eastwards towards the hills. We found some purple gentians, and then we ate our sandwiches, and drank tea from our flasks by the shores of Lochan na h'Errba, while a gentle breeze ruffled the water. We then plodded south along the estate track to the end of the lochan and turned east again, up a narrow glen along the course of a steep burn, heading for the ridge that would take us up to the summit of one of the innumerable Scottish mountains called Geal Charn.

I have never walked in so airless a place. There was no breath of wind. A haze had crept between us and the sun, and from the sky there came a grey, glaring light. It was still sunshine of a sort, for we threw thin shadows ahead of us, but all the time it was thickening towards cloud, trapping the warm and humid and motionless air in the narrow valley where we walked. Flies buzzed around us and mobbed our sweating brows. We stopped frequently, splashing water into our faces, and then panted on our way and very slowly we climbed out of the valley and at last reached the wide and stony bhealaich that was our intermediate goal.

The sun had gone by now. There was a wind on the ridge and it felt cold after the sultry calm of our trek up the burn. We watched a deer walking with sure feet across a steep snow field in the corrie beneath the summit of Geal Charn. Then we set off along the ridge and picked our way through a desert of shattered rocks to a tall, domed cairn, where we stood for a while and looked at the grey shapes of the hills around us. Then we hurried down over desolate tracts of broken granite and climbed to the top of a sharp pimple called Creag Pitridh. I confess that, if it had not been classified as a Monro, we should never have bothered with it. It is, I think, the only mountain-top where I have rested and not taken out my pipe. This was partly because Creag Pitridh did not seem to deserve the dignity of tobacco. It was also because by now it was cold and dreary and unwelcoming up in the hills.

We soon left the wind behind us, scrambling down into warm and humid hollows, crossing boggy ground where hordes of midges were dancing in the muggy air and waiting to bite us. Meanwhile the sky darkened, the mountains around us rising dimly into it, purple and ill-defined and infinitely impressive forms. There was a solemn and gloomy calm, a brooding grandeur about it all. As we walked down the track towards the car, we gazed, not at clear shapes and sharp divisions, but at sombre and blurred impressions of landscape. The water in the loch was grey and still.

It was after nine when we got back to Newtonmore, for we never head to the hills until late in the morning. There was time for a bath, then for a glass of gin, with lots of gin in it and not too much tonic; just one gin, export gin, and then two glasses of wine with supper; then one or two whiskies by the fire, while you make plans for tomorrow and savour the feeling of perfect contentment that alcohol spreads through warm and weary limbs after a day in the mountains.

It is the one way to end a day's walking, sitting in a chair with a glass in your hand, and with a bed and a bedroom waiting to receive you when the glass is empty. The thought of a tent and an unwashed body and a sleeping bag is too dreadful for words. And the thought of a bothy, with other unwashed bodies as well as your own, with beards sticking out of sleeping bags and quivering in rhythm to the snores of their owners, with hearty mountain men rising at dawn and singing folk songs as they splash their arm pits in the cold waters of the burn - the thought of a bothy is like thinking of hell on earth.

20 July

One of our party (a television journalist and so a man of hard and conquering determination) has badgered the head keeper of the Ben Alder estate into allowing us to take a Land Rover up the gated track to Culrah, and so we set off thither today and bounced up to Loch Pattack and on to Culrah. We left the Land Rover by the bothy, even as a bearded figure came out of it and stared at us in disapproval of our soft ways. And then we made off for Ben Alder.

Looking at the rocky outline of the sharp spur that runs down from the summit plateau, a spur known as the Long Leachas, I felt distinctly nervous, and thought with affection of the steep but undaunting slopes of the Howgills back at home. I do not like airy ridges. I like them wide and without vertiginous slopes directly beneath your boots. I suppose this pusillanimity is the result of being clean-shaven.

I was very happy when the television journalist suddenly announced that we had trekked too far up the burn and that it would be better now to leave Ben Alder for another day, and to climb the great mounds that rose to the west. And so we scrambled up the steepest and longest slope I have ever tackled and headed south west to Aonach Beg. It was an unwelcoming day, with a lowering sky and a cold wind, and there was little of beauty in the mountains. There was an impressive grimness about them. I did smoke on the summit of Aonach Beg, but it was not for long; then we plodded back, over a hump unsurprisingly called Geal Charn. Then it was down a narrow ridge, which was just tolerable, up to another summit, this one called Carn Dearg, and down through the heather to the bothy, which by this time was beginning to fill up with unwashed bodies and beards. I asked a pair of them about the Long Leachas and they pronounced it a piece of cake. I did not believe a word of it.

As we rumbled down the track to Dalwhinnie, there were droves of beards moving in the opposite direction to congregate in the Culrah bothy. I fell to wondering what could be driving them to spend a ghastly night in each others' company, confined in a dank wooden hut in the middle of sodden moorland. There was a very gaunt beard who seemed in flight from a long sorrow. There was an obviously cheerful beard who looked as though stale sweat and baked beans and a damp sleeping bag were his idea of fun. There were two beards together, and I could not resist the impression that they had found love somewhere among the peat hags and were hoping that the long summer gloaming would find them the only occupants of the Culrah bothy. This was a dishonourable and doubtless false notion. I renounced further speculation upon such matters and spent the remainder of our journey looking at the landscape, at the grey and restless waters of Loch Pattack, at the grey shape of yesterday's Geal Charn rising behind it, at one or two pale patches of blue sky and at faint gleams of sunshine moving over the heather.

The very thought of beards and the Culrah bothy made every sip of tonight's gin doubly sweet.

22 July

The sun shone today and we conquered Meall Cuaich, another hump east of Drumochter, but altogether more worthwhile than the two up which we plodded ten days ago. The way in to Meall Cuaich is very tedious, along a wide stony track with the unsightly pipes of an aqueduct running along the edge of it. But the hill itself is covered with heather and glows in the sunshine and the views from the summit are very fine.

This afternoon I said goodbye to Ned and Maz, my colleagues in Sedbergh, my hosts in Scotland, the best of friends wherever they are. I bade farewell to the polymath and to the television journalist and drove to Oban. I am sitting in a hotel room now, which might as well be in Basingstoke, and tomorrow I sail to Tiree.

23 July

I got out of bed at a quarter to five and the ferry sailed at six o' clock. There was a slowness about it all, slipping out of Oban on the still water, that suited my drowsy mind and eyes. There was a grey sky, a dappled-grey sea, there were the grey-green shapes of mountains coming down to the rocky margins of the water; there was a grey and luminous air. The engines chugged and throbbed and, in the wake of the ferry, the sea was churned to white foam. And white birds and grey birds circled the vessel and it was all very peaceful.

During most of the crossing I sat out on the deck, watching the mountains slide past. For a time I went inside, hoping to doze in a comfortable chair. But there were children squabbling with each other, while tired parents struggled to keep them from blows. And this

143

provoked, not irritation, but that sense of barren and selfish bachelordom that comes over me from time to time. They were my age, most of those parents, and it seemed to me, as I watched them coping patiently with their fractious sons and daughters, that they had achieved more, by bringing children into the world and by loving them, than I shall ever do by writing diaries and teaching Latin and catching fish. I felt old and tired, with nothing young to cling on to, and so I went out on deck and watched the grey sea.

The ferry docked on time. I have settled into my cottage and slept for an hour or two. I have walked with Malcolm and seen fulmars and grey geese. I shall lie late in bed tomorrow, for mass is celebrated nowhere in Tiree, and I shall go fishing in the afternoon.

29 July

I have neglected my diary over the last days, and so it is only now, on a grey and wet and windy evening, with the grey light seeping through my window and with the wind and the wet beating against its grey panes, that I sit down and put together some thoughts about my week on Tiree.

I should hate to live in the Hebrides. The haunting beauty of the name would be no consolation. I should surrender to strong liquor within a few months and drink myself to death within a year or two. The wind would drive me to it, the wind and the rain and the sense of isolation. And when the sun shone and the air turned silver and my island seemed bathed in an infinity of light welling from somewhere beyond the margins of the world, then I should gaze at it with red eyes and with fuddled wits and think sad thoughts about how happy I might have been if only the wind and the rain had not battered my spirit and turned it sour and pickled it in whisky. I should be a gentle drunkard, filled with a great sadness whenever the sun shone.

For, whenever the sun shines, Tiree is a marvel of loveliness, a marvel set in an ocean of light. And the whole island shines with the sun. The lochans shine silver, the meadows shine yellow and gold and green. The sand on the sea-shore is shining white and the sea itself shines silver and blue. The white terns and the gulls are flying and wheeling and floating specks of solid light. There is a sense of limitless space. Then the clouds come and everything turns dull. All that brightness drains away and disappears. Now there are lowering browns and sombre greys. A sodden despair seeps out of the earth and sounds on the air in the shrieking of the gulls. The wind comes too. The menace of the confining sea booms in your ears and Paradise has turned into a prison.

If I lived on Tiree, and even if I managed to avoid the temptations of the whisky bottle, I should never be at peace with myself. The spirit of the place is too unstable, convincing you one minute that the world is beautiful beyond words, insisting the next that life is dark and grim and a long act of endurance. It was the same on Uist five summers ago. Storm and sunshine brought such swings of mood that I never knew where I was with myself. I could never be sure that my heart was telling me the truth, for, whatever it was telling me at a given moment, I knew that it would presently be telling me the exact opposite.

I have found my week on Tiree confusing, but I have enjoyed it nevertheless. I have fished Loch Bhasapoll, where wet flies have been utterly useless, and I have killed nine trout with floaters. They have been trout of extraordinary beauty, with flanks of gold and shining black spots all over their backs. I fished the loch one cloudy afternoon when the wind dropped suddenly. With the stillness came muggy air, and midges came out of the heather in biting swarms, while from the loch came clouds of caenis, which turned into spinners quicker than you could say 'dun' and covered my Barbour and my waders with a film of white.

Terns have screamed above me as I have fished and swans have floated far out on the water. I have heard snipe drumming in July and one morning, while I was casting away, a head popped out of the water and gazed at me inquisitively. I thought for a moment that it was a seal. It was an otter. Then there was one evening of perfect beauty by the loch, when the water rocked silver in a gentle breeze and the banks shone white and purple and yellow and pink with the heather and the flowers and the pure light upon them. I caught a brace of trout and then sat down on a rock and smoked for half an hour.

I have wandered along the edges of meadows, still unmown so far into the summer, and heard corncrakes rasping from their waving shelter of flowers and grass. I have watched hundreds of geese sitting out on the water and, whenever I have squelched my way through boggy ground, snipe have sprung screeching into the air at every third or fourth footfall. There are colonies of fulmars among the rocks. Teal take flight from every reedy pool. Eiders bob on the sea swell and the white shores swarm with scampering flocks of plovers and sanderling. I have walked many miles on the shell-sand, in the dunes, over rocky headlands and through lowland heather where the air is scented with mint. I have resolutely refused to play golf.

One day the sun has shone. The next had been grey and windy. Now the gloom has settled again. I am ready to see Merlin. I am ready for home and for a month tending young pheasants in their pen at High Park. But, before all that, and without fearing that it will prove the undoing of me, I am ready for a dram.

31 July

Yesterday I rumbled down from Scotland in the Land Rover and found that, as expected, I was glad to be home again, glad to be back in England and particularly glad to be back in that little patch of it that I think of as mine. Near Penrith the sky and the earth beneath it turned a livid yellow, then black. Great spots of rain clattered on the bonnet and the windscreen. The clouds were riven by flashes of lightning. It was difficult to distinguish between peals of thunder and the constant roar of the engine. But the storm came to nothing and the landscape turned sullen and brooding again. The Howgills are apt to seem pimples to eyes that have grown used to Scottish mountains. But yesterday evening they were somehow raised in stature by the sultry gloom. They reared up indistinctly into the clouds and the Shap fells exuded a dark menace. But for me they were a welcome sight and I waved at them as I drove past.

The night was stifling. I woke before six and could not get to sleep again. Then I made the mistake of turning on the wireless and was soon so angry that any thought of sleep was a thousand miles away. Alas, it was Sunday; and I chanced upon a revolting programme called *Morning Has Broken*. It was a programme of supposedly Christian music and it made me sick, for it was full of that jaunty cheerfulness and that folksy tunelessness that nowadays passes for worship.

It did not turn my thoughts to God, but rather to wispy beards and saccharine smiles and bodies slightly swaying and arms outstretched in meaningless affirmation of something or other. The relentless merriness of so much modern devotional music is truly appalling. It is cheap music, dealing in cheap and false emotions. It is an insult to God and to the suffering men and women who fill the world with their moans. The expression of Christian joy should be an act of defiance, encompassing sin and pain and death and climbing above them in the glorious mystery of faith. Or it should be serene, penetrating the veil of the senses to a calmer and a deeper truth. Happy-clappy melodies are a denial of the cross. I met them again at mass this morning and they ought to be banned. If I were the pope in Rome, I should declare them a heresy.

147

The air is heavy and still. I hope that God is marshalling his forces to express his displeasure at the contemporary state of church music, although I also hope that I do not get caught in his outburst. I have to drive to Grindleton to collect Merlin this afternoon; thence to Wigglesworth, to pick up thirteen bags of grower pellets. On Wednesday I go for my pheasants.

1 August

I always feel guilty when I pick up Merlin from kennels, though guilt never goes deep enough to prevent me from abandoning him the next time. But he looks so pleased to see me, so grateful that I have at last appeared to reclaim him, that it pulls, in a superficial sort of way, at my heart-strings. The truth is that, being a dog who finds it impossible to deal with humans other than his master and one or two others, it would be impossible to take him away on holiday. He would find unfamiliar places and the strange men inhabiting them a constant agony. He is slightly mad, and it is good that Digby, whom I watched sitting to command and retrieving dummies and generally behaving himself, seems such an uncomplicated creature. I shall write more about him when I have more time.

The smell of dogs is indisputably an unpleasant smell, except, that is, for the smell of one's own. This is a truth that has only just revealed itself to me, for Merlin is lying at my feet as I write and the damp smell of him is a comfort to me, a part of his presence in my life, just like the sound he makes when he is dirty and sets about licking himself clean. It is good to have him by me again, and it was good to have him at High Park this afternoon and to run him through the rushes now and then when I took a break from work.

The formalities are not yet complete, and so the Blessed Virgin has still to take up her quarters in the larches, but there is hope that she will move in next week, and there seem to be no obstacles lurking in the path towards possession. I am waiting more or less patiently and preparing for the coming of my pheasants.

There are owls with young in the wood. I have flashing lights ready to deter them from the pen. The mesh is sound and the electric fence is working and free of trailing strands of grass. The hoppers in the pen are half-full of pellets. The water-butt is full to the brim. Inside the wire there is plenty of cover for the young birds. There are no signs of mink or foxes. I shall set the fen traps on Wednesday. They should, of course, have been lying in ambush for stoats and weasels for months past, but it cannot be so because I cannot be out at High Park every day. For the next month either Austin or I will be there each morning, and so for the next month my fen traps can perform their limited service, along with cage traps for mink and snares for the ravenous fox.

Heaving bags of pellets up Pheasant Hill was very hot and very sweaty work. The sun was hot. The air was heavy with the threat of thunder. Flies were buzzing and biting malevolently. In between bags I sat panting and wondered why I regard freshly stocked trout as questionable objects of sport and yet am happy to shoot reared pheasants. Part of the answer, at least as regards my own pheasants, is that my involvement with their rearing and release is as much a pleasure as the eventual shooting of them. Trying to keep them safe from predators and from disease: watching them grow: sitting in the pen on sunny afternoons as they peck around me: herding them back from the gorse beyond my boundary: siting hoppers, discovering that they have found favour and that the spreading birds are often busy beneath them - in all this there is much pleasure and anxiety and satisfaction. I shall shoot my pheasants this autumn and winter, if there are any left, with no sentimental twinges, and I shall think, when they fall and when Merlin dashes off to gather them, that it is the appropriate culmination of a long process of husbandry, and that the pleasure of it all began way back in August.

The Land Rover has a tyre with an accelerating slow puncture. I must get it mended. I must remember to buy some grit, unless I can find last year's bag, and a can of Renardine, and I must also remember to arm the electric fence with a new and vigorous battery. I have remembered to order a ton of wheat. Tomorrow evening I shall go fishing, for it will be the last evening for a month when I shall be able knock a trout on the head without wondering whether a fox has somehow penetrated my defences and is tearing off pheasants' heads in the pen at High Park.

3 August

I am perhaps prone to run ahead of the season, but I felt today that it was already late summer. I felt it from the rank and yellow and seed-laden grasses, from the pastures made spiky by sprouting this-tles, from roadside banks tufted with untidy ragwort, from verges tall and pink with swaying willow herb and white with twining convolvulus. And the song of a wren rang through the heavy air like a defiant anachronism.

There was thunder forecast, and thunder came, with brief torrents of rain and sudden colour in the beck at High Park. I post-poned the collection of my pheasants last night and I was right to do so. I shall go for them tomorrow and make, on my way from Waddington to Brough, my most anxious journey of the year. For what am I to do if, while carrying its precious burden of 130 pheas-ants, the Land Rover turns spiteful and insists on breaking down in the middle of nowhere?

In between the showers I worked round an empty pen. The elec-tric fence has been given its new battery and some new posts. I spent at least ten minutes testing the malevolence of the charge with blades of grass. The owl-deterring lamps are ready to be turned on. I dug two new tunnels and loaded them with fen traps, sprung and eager to break the necks of marauding weasels and stoats. I found one of the mink traps and reset it. It still needs baiting and there is another one somewhere beyond my knowledge. Perhaps Austin will remember where it has gone to ground.

This afternoon I heaved more bags of pellets up Pheasant Hill and hung some hoppers in the immediate vicinity of the pen. The wheat will arrive soon. I still need grit and I still need Renardine. Most of all I need good fortune in the form of a few days of kind weather. The outlook is good: perhaps a few showers tomorrow, but nothing threatening, and then a weekend of warm sunshine and light winds. Please God may it be so.

4 August

The journey was safely made and now there are 136 pheasant poults in my pen. And for the next month my world becomes much narrower, with my gaze fixed anxiously upon a hundred yards of wire and its immediate surroundings, upon the provision of food and water for a penful of witless young birds, upon keeping them safe and sheltered until their flight feathers have grown again and they can flap out into the wild world beyond the protection of their pen and their electric fence.

I called for them at eleven o'clock and was on my way back by noon. They are eight weeks old and they are big for their age. Some of them already have well-developed tail feathers and they are altogether splendid poults. The reason I have their flight feathers pulled is that my ground is very narrow and the pen is therefore necessarily near my boundaries. If they could fly over the wire as soon as they arrived, I fear that I should lose too many of them to my neighbours. But flightless pheasants are terrifyingly vulnerable. Their pen must be as impregnable as possible. Hence the electric fence.

Austin helped me to carry the four wooden crates up Pheasant Hill, four aching and sweaty trudges, followed by the blessing of tea and sandwiches in the sunshine by the side of the beck. We baited the mink trap (the whereabouts of its partner remain a mystery). We sited and set another fen trap. We splashed Renardine around the edges of the pen and, inevitably, upon ourselves. Then we sat in the sun again and listened to the poults squeaking and chirruping as they began to explore their new home. I watched them sipping water and lifting their heads and swallowing daintily as though treating fine wine with due reverence. I watched them picking at pellets and felt relieved that they still knew how to eat. They should be on poult pellets now, but I give them an extra fortnight of grower pellets, slightly more expensive but more nutritious and steeped in prophylactic chemicals.

I would have sat there longer and Austin's patience would have been sorely tried, but I had agreed to take the crates back to Wigglesworth this evening, whence our keeper would transport them to Waddington on his way home. And so, after checking at least five times that the gate of the pen was secure, and after giving myself little shocks for five minutes, to make certain that the electric fence was working properly, I wrenched myself away and drove off to Wigglesworth, where the birds are almost out of the pens and so far unharassed by the teeth or claws of predators.

I wonder how my birds are now. I wonder if ranks of foxes encircle the pen with gleaming eyes and slavering chops, if an owl is sitting atop each post and glaring with slow malice at the terrified poults, if great badgers are bustling past and wondering whether or not to rend wire before rending flesh, while stoats and weasels sit at a respectful distance and hope there will be some pickings left for them. And perhaps even now a hissing mink is shinning up a tree, about to drop into the pen and prance all round it in a frenzy of slaughter. Only tomorrow will tell.

152

5 August

It is a tense few moments, walking up Pheasant Hill and wondering what I shall find when I reach the edge of the wood and come to the pen. It was sunny this morning and I found a scene of perfect peace: poults scratching in the grass and eating and drinking without a care in the world. I replenished their water and filled their hoppers. I went round the fence and picked off blades of grass, while Merlin sat in the shade of the trees and snapped at flies.

There were two birds out of the pen - they must have come to High Park with their flight feathers intact - and it took all of twenty minutes to get them back in. There was nothing in any of the traps. I heaved a container of water up from the beck and sat and smoked, and then worked the dog through the rough ground above and to the east of the pen. I do not know what I did for so long, but it was already three o' clock when I chugged down the fields and drove away.

6 August

All was well again and again the sun was warm. The swifts have gone. One of the problems of my shoot is that the whole of it is grazed, and so hoppers are exposed to attack from hungry sheep. Last year I tried to protect them with barbed wire and it was no more than a partial success. It stopped the sheep knocking the hoppers down, but it did not stop them pushing under the wire and bumping the hoppers and helping themselves to my grain.

This year the plan is to surround the hoppers with upturned sheep-wire, in the hope that this will allow access to pheasants but deny it to sheep. I enclosed three hoppers today. I shall leave the rest of them until I see whether the sheep-wire is an effective deterrent.

I checked the gate only twice before leaving and, while driving

153

through Kirkby Stephen, I began to wonder if I had turned the electric fence on again.

8 August

My pheasants were all alive yesterday, and they were all alive this morning. But Merlin found a dead red squirrel under the trees. It was a young animal. There was no mark of violence on its body and no evidence of food in its gut. I think it died of starvation and, in my unwillingness to waste the gifts of nature, I shall skin it and use its tail and its fur for trout flies.

The poults have started using the slit-hoppers in the pen. It always surprises me how quickly this happens and it is always a relief, for it means that when at last they leave the pen they will know where to find an easy supply of food. They are growing fast. There are no signs of fox or mink. The traps are all empty. The owls seem to have abandoned the wood and I have neither heard nor seen a sparrowhawk.

This afternoon I spent an hour on the Eden above Scandal Dub. It was warm and completely still and there were fish smutting under the willows. I tried them with a floating fly and put them down. Then I smoked for quarter of an hour and tied on an August Black.

At the top of the Willows the line went suddenly tight and a big fish was lunging for the roots. All I could do was to lower the rod to the horizontal and pull hard against him, trying to forget that the hook was size eighteen and the breaking strain of the point only two pounds. There was no room for delicacy. He had to be kept from the roots; and, by some miracle, the hook stayed in my trout's jaws and my nylon stayed in one piece. He came into the current and hung there bemused. I seized my chance and shot the net under him. He weighed one pound twelve ounces and his flanks were gold. I was sorry that I was going out for supper and could not stay, although the prospect of Hermitage '78 was something of a consolation.

9 August

There was a mature hen pheasant in the pen this morning, looking splendid with her full complement of tail feathers. There was a brood of young birds foraging in the field at the top of the drive, and Merlin flushed another brood of well-grown birds from the edge of the gorse above the weir-gate. I explored the wood thoroughly and startled a tawny owl from a holly tree. Then only a minute or so later I heard the screech of a sparrowhawk and there she was above the trees. As long as she does not start eating my pheasants she is welcome to share my wood with them. I am sure she has had none as yet. But, on two consecutive days last year, I found a dead poult in the pen, each with the mark of a sharp and powerful beak on the back of its head. I think a sparrowhawk had struck and then found that she could not lift her booty from the pen. I was aware of no subsequent trouble.

10 August

My pheasants continue to prosper and the old hen continues to inhabit the pen in which she probably grew up either last summer or the summer before. I shot a crow from behind the Land Rover, a crow sitting in the grass, and I felt proud and unashamed. I am off to Scotland tomorrow, walking a grouse moor on Saturday and returning on Sunday.

Austin will look after things at High Park. He works for the river authority. He has lived in or near Sedbergh all his life. He knows all about the ways of mink and foxes and badgers. He knows about traps and snares and where to set them. He can build fences and lay hedges and he shapes beautiful sticks. He loves hunting and shooting and the creatures that make his sport. He is a true countryman and a true friend and I am not going to tell you any more about him. He will probably never forgive me for the little that I have just told.

155

14 August

Today is the feast of the Assumption of the Blessed Virgin, which helped me to decide that, when she goes to High Park, she shall go there as the Queen of Heaven. My land will be dedicated to Our Lady of the Assumption. Every shoot will be held in her honour, and the names of the drives will acknowledge some of her other titles and attributes and potencies as Our Lady of Perpetual Succour and Our Lady of the Immaculate Conception and Our Lady of Lourdes.

I was in Scotland yesterday, on Cameron Moor above Loch Lomond. The sun shone all day and the heather glowed back at it and Ben Lomond rose calmly into the sky. All day we crossed and recrossed the moor, plunging through man-high jungles of bracken, pushing through deep and woody heather, hoping for grouse. The day turned sweltering and full of buzzing heather flies. White sails dotted the distant loch.

A few coveys showed themselves, and some were in shot, but there were certainly fewer birds than when I was on the moor two years ago. It is not a large moor and it is not really a managed moor. It has not been burned for years and it is grazed by far too many sheep. It is a moor for a day's fun each season, and no one seems to care much whether the bag is four brace or fourteen. Yesterday it was four and a half. I fired one shot at a snipe, which jinked at the wrong moment, and two at a departing grouse which flew on unwounded. I suppose missing these birds was good for my humility, for I cherish the secret conviction that, whatever my shortcomings as a driven shot, I am rather above average with walked-up birds. Failure with three shots may have been good for my humility, but it was not enough to tarnish the pleasures of sunshine and exercise and good company.

Any one who thinks that the only people who shoot grouse are people who make drawling noises and millions of pounds on the stock-exchange should have been on Cameron Moor yesterday, where there was a vet and a lawyer and a doctor and a surgeon and, as well as these,

156

a company of Scottish beaters, the stalwarts of pheasant days later in the year. They were not beating yesterday; they were shooting with the rest of us. And they were not shooting because they thought it the thing to do or because they are rich enough to indulge themselves.

They were carrying their guns and sweating across the moor because they loved the mere hope of a grouse. They swore with perfect good humour and enjoyed themselves enormously. So did we all. The highlight of the day was a hen pheasant, flying fast and high and brought tumbling to earth by the surgeon of the party, who was also an American.

On the way back I got hopelessly lost in Glasgow and began to think that I should never again find myself on familiar roads. But eventually I realised that I was driving north towards the Erskine Bridge and Loch Lomond, and that if I turned round and drove south I should probably be heading in the direction of England. I was right and, once I had left Glasgow behind me and was chugging through the Borders, the evening was so calm and so beautiful, the roads so quiet and the hills such restful shapes, that peace found a way through the noise of the engine, through the dust and the dead flies on my windscreen, and stayed with me all the way to Sedbergh.

During my absence the pheasants at High Park have grown appreciably. Feeding them this afternoon, looking at their sprouting tails and listening to their squeakings and their cluckings, was a pure delight. I need another two weeks of good fortune and then I shall be able to declare this year's release a success; I shall be able to start looking forward to a season of record bags on my little shoot. We may even have a day when the tally registers double figures.

15 August

The meadowsweet is turning brown; rose bay willow herb is grown lank and untidy. The air is full of drifting thistledown and hot afternoons are full of the crackling and snapping sounds of exploding gorse pods. The rowans are laden with reddening berries and high wires bear chattering congregations of swallows. Summer is old. Leaves are dry and tired and already there are yellow and brown leaves among them.

The wind died as I worked around the pen this afternoon; there was a feeling of somnolence. My pheasants, lying in the sun and dusting themselves and stirring to peck at the hoppers, seemed bigger than they were yesterday. Within a week they will be leaving the pen in dozens. I am beginning to scatter wheat and to mix some with their pellets. From now on I shall put only grain in the tray-feeders, and I must remember to take up some more grit with me tomorrow.

There is a pleasant monotony about releasing pheasants when things go well: a daily round of feeding and watering, of chasing back into temporary captivity the two or three poults that have found their way out of the pen, of sitting and watching the young birds and wondering what to do next, of hanging outside hoppers and filling them with wheat, of checking to see if the wild pheasants have begun to frequent those you hung a week ago, of hoping that this quiet employment will continue undisrupted by disease or predation until the release pen is almost empty and the trees are full each evening of pheasants in adult plumage roosting high out of harm's way.

Of course I cannot relax yet. There may still be heavy losses when the birds start flying to their freedom in ever larger numbers. Most mornings there are between four and six on the wrong side of the wire. Very soon it will be twenty or thirty and, when this happens, I shall let them roam and hope for the best. And the fact that there are no signs of mink or of cats or of foxes encourages me to hope that, for once, the best may just occur.

A pleasure of recent days has been frequent sightings of wild birds and of some strong wild broods. There are now two broods on the right of the drive where, a few days ago, there was only one. They are there every morning, pecking through the grass, as I drive down to the house. There are two hens, each with half a dozen poults nearly as big as their mother. There is the brood Merlin flushed from the edge of the gorse a week ago. And this afternoon, when I had fed the birds and hung another hopper and filled it with grain, I worked him through the top fields and he sniffed out two broods of smaller poults. He flushed two rabbits and a hare as well and he chased none of them. I was carrying my gun but, though it was loaded, it remained unshot. I was more interested in the dog. Tomorrow I shall go over the same ground with Merlin and, if he flushes ground game and is steady to the flush, I shall make a bang and hope to kill. I am pleased with my dog and happy with my pheasants and altogether very content with life. And this weekend there will be the delight of fishing at Driffield and at Foston, for it is the weekend of my annual visit to Yorkshire's trout streams.

18 August

At ten o'clock this morning I was closeted with my solicitor. He picked up the 'phone, made contact with Mr. G.'s solicitor, and by some lawyers' rigmarole known as formula A, contracts were exchanged. At the end of this solemn process he put down the 'phone and intoned, 'Now you are secure.' And then he asked me for an enormous cheque. Completion does not take place until 7 September, because he is going on holiday for a fortnight and I shall be away when he returns. The enormous cheque was therefore post-dated. I should quite happily have signed it for twice the amount.

On leaving my lawyer, with thoughts of this evening in mind, I went in search of a bottle of *Bollinger Grande Annee '85*. I found that it had already been drunk and I shall have to settle for a humbler wine.

The Virgin will go to High Park tomorrow. Or perhaps it would be better to wait until the day of completion? Today I went there myself with Austin, who walked Holly, his young labrador, round the pen as a test of her steadiness. She is a splendid creature and Austin is rightly proud of her. I fed pheasants while Austin watered them for me. I looked at blades of grass and told them that they as good as belonged to me. I looked at trailing shoots of bramble and assured them that they would shortly be mine. I gazed at the tall firs and at the graceful larches, at the running water and at the rise and the fall of the land, meadow and pasture and wood, and I told them all that very soon they would have a new owner.

I was very happy indeed and forgave Merlin for chasing a rabbit yesterday. The pheasants too seemed happy enough, and they are taking to wheat more quickly than in previous years. They are flapping their wings more now, jumping off the ground and fluttering into the low branches. There were perhaps eight outside the pen and I decided to leave them there.

We filled the outside hoppers. There are more to be hung but there are enough in service for the time being, and they all seem to be attracting pheasants. The sun shone as we ate our sandwiches, with that golden light that comes late in August. A sparrowhawk came low over the larches and I felt like welcoming him to my land with an amiable invitation to prey on robins and swallows and thrushes to his heart's content. If Austin had not been sitting beside me I should have waved in greeting to the buzzard that flapped over the Douglas Firs; I should have waved in greeting to him and pointed him to the spot where rabbits were thickest on the ground. And if a fox had ambled along and congratulated me on the exchange of contracts, I should have seized my gun from the Land Rover and I should have shot him without a second thought.

The weekend belongs to Driffield. On Monday I must do something about the duck pond over my boundary. And next week, given kind weather, I must fish the Wenning or the Eden on a couple of evenings. As I write my window looks out on a grey sky and fading light, on leaves dripping slowly and flowers drooping sadly in heavy drizzle. I have no champagne; it is overrated anyway. I toyed with the idea of opening a bottle of 1915 Madeira and decided that it needed friends. Claret also wants company and it wants to be drunk with food and not in front of a word-processor. I have gone for a country wine: tannic, rough-edged and characterful. I have gone for a bottle of Madiran and I am only half way through it. The smell of it is strong and earthy and somehow it reminds me of my land.

20 August

Yesterday, after feeding the pheasants and watching them pecking at the hoppers and preening their feathers and chasing each other for half an hour, I took Merlin to Grindleton and was shown how Digby is developing. He is not gun-shy and is now retrieving cold game. He sits promptly to whistle and comes in at once when called. What he lacks as yet is drive. He is a soft dog and he is not as busy and eager as a good spaniel should be. He loses heart quickly and wearies of hunting when scent is poor. His trainer thinks that he should now be put through the rabbit-pen and then delivered into my keeping and taken shooting. He thinks the thrill of gunfire and scurrying game will soon teach him the delights of hunting. He also thinks that, if Digby goes wild and chases what he flushes, it will, in his case, prove an easy fault to cure.

Then it was off to Driffield and a night with Oliver and his parents. Their dining room looks west and, as we took our places at table, the window was aflame with the setting sun. One of the best things about East Yorkshire, apart from the generosity of my hosts, is the wide sky. Less commendable are the vast fields, where E.C. subsidies wave in the breeze, and the pervading smell of poultry manure, which seems to be the preferred dressing for those of the vast fields that have already been harvested.

At ten o' clock this morning Oliver and I were in the clubhouse of the Driffield Anglers. At the moment there is no keeper and we were alone. It must be a dozen years since I first stood there nervously, clutching my guest ticket and asking the keeper if visitors were allowed to fish the nymph. I have been there every summer since, and always the clubhouse, with its stuffed trout and its old rods and its photographs of the different beats, with its wide windows looking down to the shallows and with its air of changeless calm, is a deep delight. It is tempting to sit there longer than you ought, leafing through the season's record and drinking in the peace.

But in little more than quarter of an hour we had managed to drag ourselves away and were busy on Dawson's Dam, the beat immediately above the clubhouse. I left the lower half to Oliver and went above the road bridge, where tall willows line the beck on both banks, concealing the golf course that spreads on either side. It is a shadowed world beneath the willows, a world of green shade and waving weed and sliding water. And poised in the sliding water are the shapes of great trout. There may be a golf course on either side of the beck, you may hear the smack of club on ball and the occasional shout of 'fore', but this has no power against the stronger and exclusive potency of the willows and the sliding water and the poised trout.

I started with a Poult Bloa on the end of my line, for even at half past ten in the morning there were a few blue wings hatching. That dead squirrel at High Park has enabled me to tie Poult Bloas as they should be tied: yellow silk lightly dubbed with fur of the red squirrel, the hackle from under the wing of a young grouse. It may have been the squirrel fur, it may not, but within ten minutes I had covered a fish that was eating something just under the surface of the water. I had lifted my wrist and the line had gone tight and my rod had bent and now my first trout was in the bag. He weighed one pound and a half. He was short and deep as the trout of a chalkstream ought to be.

There was no general movement, but there were some fish stirring and I caught two or three of them, all on the Poult Bloa; they were all just too small to keep. The bigger trout treated my fly with contempt,

162

refusing to stir a fin, or running from it in fright. Around midday the trickle of fly thickened into something more like a hatch and more trout began to feed. I saw a dun or two taken and changed to a dry fly, with the body of a Poult Bloa and a double Cree hackle. It took a fish, which weighed just over the pound and went in the bag, but it frightened others, as did the Yellow Thing and the Imperial. Soon it was time for lunch.

In the afternoon cloud came over and the fly came down more thickly. There were small dark olives as well as blue wings. The fish were clearly busy with the hatching nymph and so the Poult Bloa was reinstated. His charms were now more difficult to resist, although one or two big trout were not impressed and slid away under the banks. Others succumbed and, though several were below the limit or only lightly hooked, by four o'clock my bag concealed four trout, which were as many trout as it was allowed to conceal. None of them was big by Driffield standards. They all weighed between a pound and a pound and a half. I thought of fishing on and returning whatever I might catch. But I knew that this would inevitably bring me a four-pounder, and I could not face the agony of giving him back to the water. I ambled downstream and sat happily in the clubhouse, drinking tea for half an hour. And then at five o'clock I drove off to mass in Hornsea.

I fish chalkstreams too infrequently to pronounce on how they ought to be fished, but I will risk suggesting that too many anglers think of the artificial nymph as something that must sink like a stone. Over the years at Driffield I have had great success with lightly hackled spider flies, and they have caught fish for me on days when a weighted Pheasant Tail sent every trout it covered straight to his lair. Poult Bloa, Partridge and Orange, Dark Pheasant: these and one or two others are the patterns that Driffield trout have swallowed in the false belief that they were living nymphs. They have caught me many more chalk stream trout than have leaded flies, and many more than floating flies. They were, of course, the inspiration for the patterns of Skues. I love the hackled flies of tumbling northern streams. I fish them as an act of piety on smooth waters where white chalk shines through from the bed of the stream. And always it delights me to discover that this piety of mine is prudent as well as pious behaviour.

21 August

The sun was hot today. It was a day for shirt-sleeves, a day at Lowthorpe on the Foston Beck, full of the dust of the harvest and bright with the wings of butterflies. And there were dabchicks splashing and diving along the edges of the stream, there were swans, white swans and young swans in grey, drifting unhurriedly on the current; more than once there was the orange and blue flash of a king-fisher; there were tall clumps of seeding willow herb, there were taller beds of whispering reeds; there was white chalk and pure water and the sound of it spilling over little wooden weirs.

There was one weir-pool in particular, where the beck turned a corner. At the top of the pool a huge willow rose forty or fifty feet, hanging its branches down to the water and brushing the stream, its leaves quivering silver in the breeze. And the bright water of the beck shone in the sunshine and the bright chalk shone through the shining water and shone more brightly because green weed waved beside it in the current, while the weeds rustled drily and feathered seeds floated on the air, while swallows chattered in the sky and finches chimed and unglimpsed birds made little noises in the bankside cover. And it seemed to me that this scene, with its heart of willow and water and weed, was just what a chalkstream scene should be on a sunny day late in August. And just for a time, for twenty minutes in the afternoon, there was flies coming off the water and there were big trout gulping down the flies.

When I first fished at Foston three summers ago, it was little better than a ditch. A succession of dry summers, with unabated abstraction near the source, had almost sucked the life out of it. But last summer, after plentiful winter rains, the beck was full and lovely. And this summer, with its springs still charged from the teeming wetness and the heavy snowfalls of the winter, it is even fuller and far brighter, for the healthy sweep of the current has washed away much of the silt and revealed the shining bed of the stream. And this year, even in August, the weirs are open still.

In the morning there was no movement of trout. There were fish lying on the edges of the weed, but they were not feeding trout and they would look neither at a nymph nor at a floating fly. But, in the afternoon, as I headed upstream to explore fresh water and passed the weir-pool with the willow, I saw two or three big trout rising in the fast water, great golden shapes pushing out of the stream. I realised that the blue wings had come and that there was hope of filling my bag.

I tied on my Cree Hackle, which is my present favourite for trout eating blue winged olive duns; I covered two fish and immediately put them down. I should have paused then and changed my plan of attack, because it was quite clear that there was something wrong with my pattern, but I pressed on foolishly and put the Cree Hackle over a third trout. He took it and was hooked and I was no sooner counting him mine than the hook came free: a sure signal that he had taken my fly with less than complete confidence.

I am ashamed to admit it, but even this did not force a change. I fished the next pool, only slightly less lovely than the one I had just left, and returned two small trout. I passed on to a large pool below the single arch of a low bridge. And here at last, after my fly had been refused by two or three trout that were feeding too greedily to be put down, I looked more carefully at what was happening and decided that the trout were taking hatching nymphs rather than duns. I tied on a Poult Bloa and hooked the first trout I covered. He fought doggedly but stayed for the net and weighed one pound and a half. And then the hatch petered out and left me cursing myself for a careless and a lazy

165

fisher of flies, undeserving of success with chalkstream trout.

I fished on and caught some small fish. But by now the big ones had stopped feeding and no more were killed. Thoughtless persistence with an unsatisfactory pattern had cost me the fulfilling comfort of a heavy bag. It had been a fine day, but there was a sense of failure with good fish, with the rankling conviction that it stemmed from nothing more complex than indolence. My mind's eye dwelt upon the golden trout rising in the shadow of the great willow, and how they would have bent my rod and filled my net and shone in the grass as they lay on the bank, if only I had fished for them with a Poult Bloa and not with a Cree Hackle. If only!

At four o'clock I had to finish. Merlin was waiting for me at Grindleton and I expected heavy traffic on the roads. I am at home now and there has been no call to tell me that my pheasants are all dead. Tomorrow I shall go and tend them and tell them that I am sorry for abandoning them for two whole days. I intended to fish the Wenning on August evenings and I have never been there once. Perhaps I shall find time next week.

24 August

I think the shooting of the duck pond over the fence will be mine. It is not certain, but I have got permission to feed it on the understanding that, given a satisfactory agreement concerning the hay in my meadow, I shall have the rights for the pond this winter and for the field in which it lies.

And so I went to feed my new pond this morning, and four duck took flight from its reedy margins, and all along the muddy edges there were sodden feathers. It is a lovely spot, lying in a deep hollow in the corner of the field, with willows behind it and a steep, scrub-covered bank in front. It is hidden away from its surroundings, as flight ponds ought to be, so that you can retreat to them as the darkness falls and feel that you have left the world behind. I hope for a first flight in the middle of September. I shall feed the pond again tomorrow.

25 August

I tended my birds today with quiet satisfaction, thinking how well they were growing and how the danger of mass slaughter would soon be past. They are strong on the leg now and not so feeble on the wing. More than half of them have left the pen and many of them have long tails. The plumage of the cocks is changing fast. Things have never gone so well. I do not think I have lost a single bird as yet. But perhaps the foxes are playing a joke on me. Perhaps they are waiting until I am certain they are not there, waiting until I stop worrying before descending on my birds and tearing them all to tattered pieces.

It is time that my pheasants were out of the pen. Those already living beyond the wire are growing long elegant tails that seem inches longer every day, whereas my stay-at-home pheasants have big bodies - most of them - and rumps adorned with a thin stubble of stunted feathers. They look deformed; there is a suggestion of pygmy and misshapen ostriches in the way they scuttle around the pen with a bedraggled and embarrassed air, squeaking in protest at the sharp attentions of unfriendly beaks. It is the same every year and every year I feel the same reluctance to force birds from the security of their stronghold with its high wire and its electric fence. It is too much like tempting fate but it will have to be done.

The sheep wire around the hoppers seems to have done the trick, except with one of them where I decided to be economical and used only a single post. As a result the wire is too near the hopper and the sheep can nose through and bang it and then nose through again to gobble up the scattered grain. They are commendably determined creatures and I enjoy my annual struggle with them. This year I am going to win.

I went from my pheasants to the Eden. I have fished it little this year. It is on my way home from High Park, rather than twenty miles away on the other side, like the Wenning. It seemed sense to fish the Eden and I am glad that I went there. One of the season's unfulfilled resolutions has been to pay frequent visits to the Eden between Scandal Dub and Eastfield Bridge and to discover the true state of things there. My last visit, on a windy summer's day more than two months ago, gave me some hope. This evening's visit confirmed my hope. I do not think there is much wrong with the river around Eastfield. The trout are still there.

The water was up and coloured when I came to the river late this afternoon; it was shining brown and red and amber in the windy sunshine. First I wandered a little way up Scandal Beck, but my wet flies brought no trout grabbing at them. Returning to the Eden I fished up from the junction, and suddenly it was evening as it ought to be. The wind had dropped. There were vast oceans of blue sky above me. There were great white clouds sailing through them with inexhaustible patience. There were also trout rising, three or four of them, along the edge of the willows.

I was fishing with Brown Owl on the point and with Simple Simon as the sole dropper. I covered the nearest trout and hooked him but he flopped off. I hooked the next too and he was big; he rushed for the roots and I held him hard and he came into open water and lashed with his tail. I was thinking of the net when the hook came free; and when I had hooked and lost the third of those feeding trout, then at last I thought of Foston and acknowledged that something must be wrong with the flies on my cast.

I looked round but I looked neither long nor hard. For above and on every side of me, and streaming noiselessly upstream with egg sacks extruded so that they looked something like bloated ants, were vast hordes of blue winged olive spinners, all shining in the slanting light. I think it is the silence of these vast spinner swarms that makes them so impressive, so memorable. There may be twenty thousand insects over the water, rising and falling in intricate, endlessly varying patterns that proclaim their urge to couple and then die; or flying upstream, as were this evening's spinners, flying upstream with passion spent and purpose almost fulfilled, driven by one last compulsion to lay eggs, and happy then to float down the water with wings outstretched in death. It is an incandescent spectacle, a great and moving drama, a performance enacted in servile obedience to those primal forces that drive the whole life of nature. Every one of those twenty thousand shining spinners is doomed. Fulfilment brings extinction. And it all happens without a sound.

These thoughts have occurred to me as I write. At the time, looking at the great flight of spinners, I hoped that I had not realised too late what was happening and I knotted on a new spinner pattern: amber silk ribbed with gold wire, two small and very pale cree hackles, spent wings from white fibres of swan herl, a wide-gape sixteen hook. I found a fish feeding under the bank, feeding with a steady determination to make the most of a heavy fall of spinners. Every second or so the sliding water ridged briefly as he pushed out his snout and sucked in another victim. He sucked in my fly too and fell a victim to his own greed. He weighed one and a half pounds.

Falls of spinner are often too short for comfort, especially as the season advances and the air turns cold with the sinking sun. I caught the next fish I covered and, at three quarters of a pound, he was big enough to go in the bag. Then I roamed upstream and pricked a bigger trout before the rise failed and darkness came down over the quiet pools. There was still light in the west and, as I walked back slowly to the Land Rover, I heard the whisper of a line and saw that another angler was searching for peace along the margins of running water. I had found my peace and took it back to Sedbergh with me; and then I moved it to the bar of the *Dalesman*, where I mellowed it with two pints of bitter beer. Then I went home and savoured it with a glass of whisky. And then it was time for bed.

28 August

It is the back-end of summer now, with grey skies and strong winds and restless gatherings of swallows, with laden brambles ready to be plundered and green berries thick upon the sloe.

Yesterday I found the tattered remains of two poults, a mangled wing and a half chewed thigh. Just possibly they were the remnants of a single bird, but the distance between them makes it likely that they once belonged to separate organisms. Both were well away from the pen, over the beck and beyond the gorse, the wing in Well Close and the thigh in the Hag. They might have belonged to wild poults and there is no reason to suspect a fox. There is no sign of a fox - no smell, no droppings - and I think it likely that a fox would have picked up the scent of more than a hundred birds on Pheasant Hill and gone in for carnage on a grander scale. It could be a stoat or a weasel or a cat. It could be buzzards, especially as I seem to have most of the buzzards of Cumbria flapping over my land. It is nothing to panic about; it is part of releasing pheasants. It is when, one sunny morning, we find the neighbourhood of the pen strewn with carcasses, that we releasers of pheasants start wondering whether a single bird will survive into October.

Two seasons ago I came upon such a scene, and I can still remember the seething rage that swelled up in me as I found one corpse and then another, until at last there were fifteen: all uneaten and all unbitten except for the absence of a head. I wanted every fox in England killed. For several mornings I rose early and was by the pen before first light, but the fox did not return until I had decided that he had moved on, and at his second coming he found the birds more widely dispersed and had to be content with five. Last year birds were killed in ones and twos and I think it was done by cats. But the traps we set caught nothing and by the end of August I was a happy keeper.

In another week, if all goes well, I shall be a happy keeper again. If you can keep birds safe into September, you are unlikely thereafter to suffer devastating losses. Thus far, I am ashamed to say, it is Merlin who has been the chief predator. It happened yesterday and it was largely my fault. He had sat by the pen, as usual, with poults scurrying under his nose, gazing at them contemptuously as though he knew they were too young for sport. With my tasks finished, and coming off Pheasant Hill, I foolishly sent him into a patch of gorse. It was a moment of forgetfulness, and a moment later Merlin returned to me with a poult in his mouth. It was alive and uncrushed but it was moribund and I knocked it on the head. And then Merlin behaved disgracefully. He shot off again before I could stop him. He ignored my shouts and my whistles and he seized a second poult. And, knowing that he was beyond the pale, he bit it and he chewed it.

I felt like biting and chewing him. Instead of this I seized him and I shook him and I roared at him in a voice that shook the skies. Merlin rolled on his back and waved his legs in the air. It was a bitter lesson for me, for during the past week I have been working Merlin over my top ground. He has not been perfect, but he has flushed hares and rabbits and a few pheasants and he has remembered not to chase them. I have fired at one hare and at one rabbit and missed them both. They were both fleeting chances, but the truth is that I am a poor shot at ground game. Not that this matters. What matters is that Merlin has behaved himself. He has got better rather than worse. He has become sharper to whistle and less prone to sudden fits of unmanageable excitement. And now he has taken to slaying my pheasant poults.

It does not mean the end of his career as a gun-dog. It means what

171

I have really known for months past, that he will never be entirely dependable, that he will work steadily one day and then go berserk the next. He is four now and, although I can still hope for change, it is too late to expect it. He will work cover with fearless enthusiasm. He will sit at a peg with an unsecured lead around his neck and remain sitting while pheasants tumble around him. But he will run in to retrieve shot game if it falls when he is working, and there will be times when he runs riot and draws me in roaring and red-faced pursuit.

And his mouth will always be suspect, especially when he is retrieving without waiting to be told or when he is helping himself to the pheasants in my gorse. And soon it will be September and time for him to sit with me by duck ponds, time for those scarcely audible whimpers of excitement that announce that he has heard the rhythm of wings somewhere above him in the darkening air. I think the first September duck flight is the best occasion of each shooting year. And now that I have two ponds (you will join me at the one that does not border my land before long), I should be able to shoot them no more frequently than a flight pond ought to be shot, which means not more than once a month. I love flighting so much that, in the past, and with regular access only to one pond, I have sometimes succumbed to the temptation to go there too often with my gun.

29 August

The end of summer is one of the best times of the year. It is very beautiful, for the sun shines with a lustre of gold and the light slants early and brings a moving patchwork of shadow to the land. There are cool mornings and chilly evenings and the midday heat has lost the savage hostility of high summer. Darkness brings a yellow moon. And the best of it is that there is so much to do.

There are still trout to be caught. Duck are in season or so near to

172

it that anticipation no longer breeds impatience. There is hope of partridge as a bonus and a blessing. There are still pheasants to feed and every day brings growing confidence that they will survive to fly on cold winter mornings. I am off to the Wharfe tomorrow for three nights. I return on Friday. I shoot grouse at Hartside on Saturday. On Monday, alas, there is school again.

But there will still be time for a few afternoon's fishing, for a couple of evening flights and, of course, there will be all the pleasures of schoolmastering to enjoy all over again. The worst thing about being a schoolmaster is starting again in September. It comes as a shock. And there is the sadness too of finding gone those of whom you have grown fond. I shall miss last year's Classical upper sixth. They were good company. They were intelligent. They worked hard and all five of them got top grades in both Latin and Greek. But my old friends will still be there: Vergil and Horace and Herodotus and Thucydides. And I shall be able, now and then, to leave them for the afternoon and sit by the beck at High Park, thinking alternately autumnal and proprietorial thoughts.

Austin and Mr. G. will care for my pheasants while I am away in Wharfedale. There are not many left in the pen, no more than forty. I have been opening the gates while I have been there these last few days, so that the birds can wander out, and only closing them when I leave: a sort of compromise between letting unadventurous poults bid farewell to their pen when at last the mood takes them and chasing them all out against their will. There are not more than half a dozen with stubble instead of tails, and even this half dozen will probably look elegant enough by Christmas. I have had worse seasons for feather-pecking.

The sheep, however, are proving tougher opponents than I had supposed. I watched an old ewe this afternoon, going to work on a hopper too near the wire, pushing and thrusting and banging and eating greedily. There are just two hoppers under regular assault. They need more stakes and they shall have them before long.

173

Meanwhile I shall think of my pheasants and hope that they are well, but my thoughts and my hopes will be from a distance. I shall be more closely engaged with trout.

6 September

I am sitting in my study in a stupor of depression. A whole week has passed without an entry in my diary and now there is only time for a few jottings. Four days by a trout stream and a day of sunshine on a Pennine grouse moor deserve better than this. They were all of them good days, worthy of individual celebration beneath the record of their own date. And the whole purpose of keeping a diary is to fill it with fresh and sharp impressions: to remember each day before it is past and not to lump days together and come to them from a distance when the memory of them has already faded. But it will be good to escape into last week for an hour or so, now that today and tomorrow are darkened by the gloom of a new term. It is a dreadful thing, the beginning of the school year. I am happy to be a schoolmaster, but I hate the beginning of a fresh bout of it.

Last Tuesday I was a fisherman, way up the Wharfe at Yockenthwaite, where the river is lovely beyond imagining. Last Tuesday it was at its loveliest, flowing full and clear over the white and yellow rock. And the air was moist and still. Red berries hung on the rowans and the hawthorns. The elders were heavy with purple. It was my first visit to Yockenthwaite since April, for the water has never been there. Seeing the river in such perfect order for a fisherman's flies, I thought it barely possible that I should leave it without a bag full of trout.

It took half a mile of water with no sign of a fish to sow doubts. After a further hour disillusion was more or less complete. By five o' clock I had returned two troutlings and acknowledged that the fish were down. All day black gnats had been thick on the water and all day they had been ignored. Usually, with such a fall of fly, there would have been trout sipping them down in every pool and run. Were they sated with the rich feeding of a week's high water? Was it a day of fast and abstinence for the trout of the Wharfe?

It is difficult to understand why there come days when an abundance of trout-food floats down the river unharassed, but such days do come and they are very poor days for sport with the fly. In the evening, after supper at the *Falcon*, I raced up Cowside Beck and fished the last half hour of daylight. I caught nothing, but the sky was clear and the air was cool and I walked downstream, whispering my prayers and thanking God for the sound and the silver of flowing water as the night falls.

Wednesday was a better fishing day. I spent the morning at Yockenthwaite, where I hooked and lost a sizeable trout. In the afternoon I came downriver to Watersmeet and immediately caught two trout on the Orange Partridge, a stock-fish just over the pound and a wild fish a few ounces smaller but much lovelier. The runs above Watersmeet pool brought nothing but pulls and twitches, until I came to the broad run beyond the trees and found that the blue wings had come with me.

There were not hordes of them, but there were enough to bring half a dozen fish up to eat them in the smooth glide at the bottom of the run. It is a glide where trout are almost unapproachable in low water, but when the river is full and still flowing with a touch of colour, you can wade carefully and hope to catch them. I put on my Cree Hackle and I think I rose four. Three I missed, and they were true rises. The fourth I hooked and he leaped and looked huge and flounced off.

An hour later I was back at the same spot, to see if any trout had started feeding again. I saw a fish rise beneath the willows and, when my Cree Hackle fell over him, he seized it and dived for the roots. But I held him and turned him and in the net he was very beautiful. He weighed one pound eleven ounces. Another fish from Mile House Dub, smaller but just as lovely, made four for the day. Then the drizzle

175

turned to rain and, as I drank Guinness in the bar of the *Falcon*, the rain turned heavy and I feared that it would bring the river up in flood and ruin the next day's sport.

The river did come up, but not in flood. The Wharfe was high and coloured. The Skirfare was clearer. Both looked as though they would fish better in the afternoon. It was a morning for a small water, a morning for Cowside Beck and the lonely valley through which it flows.

I have written elsewhere of the pleasures of Cowside Beck: of the steep sides that enclose it, of the sombre yews that line the high cliffs, of the sense of deep seclusion that comes to the men who fish there. I have also said how rare it is to find conditions right for a day on the beck; for, to fish it upstream, which is the way it must be fished, you need a wind from the east or the north-east, whereas to fish it at all you need a full water but not a spate.

On Wednesday morning the water was full but not in spate, and it was shining twenty different colours; here over a sheet of bedrock it was yellow; there in the middle of a deep pool it flowed with a deep stain, almost purple; elsewhere it was amber and brown. In places it was blue from the clear sky above, or white from the sailing clouds. And, up on Arncliffe moor, the heather was glowing darkly, and, down by the beck, the wind was racing upstream and blowing spray into the air from the broken and foaming water.

To begin with there was no fly. But it was one of those mornings when the fish were willing. Within ten minutes of my starting, in the short run below the Bathing Pool, five of them had risen to my dark pheasant. Three had been landed and a brace, both well over the pound, had been killed. There followed two hours of the best sport that fishing can provide: fishing upstream with wet flies for trout that are not obviously feeding but are on the look-out for food, so that you never know just when the line will dart forwards or slide to one side or pause for a moment in its progress downstream. There was not the hectic activity of that first run. But every cast was full of the hope of a fish, and every five or six or ten minutes the line sent me its message and I raised my wrist and tightened into another trout.

I kept two more, big fish for the beck, and I returned perhaps half a dozen. All were victims of the Dark Pheasant. The fancy fly on the dropper, a Simple Simon, was ignored. Then a few pale wateries started hatching and my flies were refused by rising fish. But a Grey Duster did the business and made my bag five: five trout weighing five and a half pounds from a beck that, for most of each summer, is so shallow, so starved of water that you would swear it could hold no trout longer than your little finger.

It was only two o'clock. I had fished little more than half a mile from the point of my starting. But five trout is enough for a fisher on Cowside Beck, and so I turned round and left the high and lonely places, the deep pools in the shadow of dripping cliffs and the great trout that live there - I left them unvisited and told them I should make amends next season.

I went to the Skirfare at Hawkswick and sat in the sun and fished a little. I wandered down below the bridge and fished a little more. I ate my sandwiches and smoked my pipe and fished again for a while. But the trout were sleeping and, although I tried to rouse them with several changes of fly, they refused to abandon their dreams and so, at five o'clock, well content with the the morning's five trout, I decided to finish and strolled back through Hawkswick to the Land Rover.

I cut off my flies, thinking that, when I had stowed my tackle, there would be time for tea and tobacco before returning to the *Falcon*. But then I discovered that in my bag there no longer was a fly box to receive the Orange Partridge and the Simple Simon that had just been snipped from my cast. I did not panic immediately. I asked myself where last I had changed flies. I drove down to the bridge and strode downriver to the spot where I remembered deciding that the Poult Bloa had been on long enough and that it was time for something else. There was no fly box there.

I crossed the river and retraced the course of my earlier upstream progress, longing every step to see the grey glint of metal in the green grass, or among the white rocks by the edge of the water. Small stones in the fields assumed the shape of a fly box and bred false hopes. Large pebbles down by the river gleamed at me with a lustre of grey and seemed wonderful things and then turned back into trivial fragments of rock. My search became random, as I roamed this way and that along the riverbank, with roving eyes and with the mounting conviction that my favourite fly box had somehow slipped into the river and was now on its way to the sea. And with it were travelling almost all my wet flies.

The thought of my loss tainted the convivial pleasures of the evening. I discovered that losing a fly box is even worse than losing a much-loved hat, for it is more intimately connected with past sport and, anyway, this was my first experience of such bereavement, whereas I lose at least one cap a year and have become hardened to the suffering each loss brings with it.

On Friday, of course, I fished at Hawkswick and spent at least an hour searching places where I had searched for more than an hour the day before. Then I hooked a two-pounder on my dry Cree Hackle and, while he pulled and ran and splashed in the sunlight, my mind was full of him and had no time to brood on the fly box that was no longer in my bag. But when I had netted him and killed him, the dark truth of what had happened yesterday came back to me and set me rummaging in the long grass again for another twenty minutes. There were two or three more chances with big fish, but I was off form and bungled them all. My thoughts were running elsewhere.

It is not just the fly box that has gone. It is the flies that were in it, and many of them were old friends. There were Greenwells tied over ten years ago and still waiting to catch a trout. There were March Browns resting patiently in the compartment where they had rested for six or seven years, ever since, one early April day, I met a hatch of true March Browns on the Eden and tied a few artificials in anticipation of the next one. There were Orange Partridges in my box that had seemed such perfect specimens of their kind that I had never been willing to give trout the barbarous privilege of rending their hackles with sharp teeth. There were flies that had proved themselves in combat, flies with broken strands of herl and tattered feathers and rusty barbs: veterans with proud battle scars, unfit for further service and living in honourable retirement in the place where they had always lived.

And where were they now? They had been swept half way to the North Sea, or they were lying neglected in the wet grass, or they had been drowned in the dark water of one of the river's deepest pools. And next spring, when I take out my boxes and sort through my flies on the evening before my first day's fishing, they will no longer be there to greet me and remind me of the past. It is a heavy loss and it will take me time to come to terms with it.

I finished fishing at four o'clock and went to reclaim Merlin and to take possession of Digby. My new dog celebrated his entry into my life by leaping into the Land Rover, by sitting on the rod that I had carelessly left propped against the front seat and by shattering a cane top that has bent with the weight of innumerable noble trout. It was my fault not Digby's and I cursed myself for a fool. I also consoled myself with the thought that the top piece of my Sharpe's Eighty Three, even before it turned into a springer spaniel's cushion, had already been bent and enfeebled. A replacement would certainly have been needed before long. Then Digby was sick on the floor during the drive home.

There were four days fishing and on Saturday, there was the first

179

day on which I have shot driven grouse in sunshine, and it was a wonderful day, at Hartside in the company of the Rowleys. It was everything a shooting day ought to be. It was a relaxed day, but at the same time it was a serious business and things were done properly. Shooting is a wretched activity when, every time you miss a bird, you wonder whether you will be invited again; it is a disgrace on the rare occasions when it degenerates into the thoughtless indulgence of men who must do something between breakfast and dinner and who decide that they might as well fill the gap by killing things.

The sun was not meant to be shining. The moors were meant to be covered in cloud and soaked with drenching sheets of rain. We took heavy coats with us to the first drive and flung them behind the butts and waited for the birds, straining to see them and marvelling that the sky was blue. Once or twice I thought for a second that a hovering heather fly or a buzzing bee was an approaching grouse, but there was no mistaking them when at last they came.

Waiting in a grouse butt, high on a Pennine moor, surrounded by heather and sunshine and blue sky, is a strange blend of tension and restfulness. It is easy to become drowsy in the warm air, with the flies droning around you; it is easy to decide that the birds will never come and that it is time to light your pipe again. And then of course, just as you reach for your matches, a bird is upon you and you are hopelessly unprepared. It was almost so this morning. I began to expect the beaters over the crest of the hill any moment, with the sound of the keeper's horn to announce the end of a blank drive. I was beginning to think of tobacco when a large pack went through the butts below me on silent wings. A minute later a single bird came low to me and I shot it behind. There was another single bird and, wonder of wonders, I shot it in front. There were two more and they both fell and I could not believe it. I am a poor shot at driven grouse.

Never before, on the few occasions when I have occupied a

grouse butt, have I left it in the knowledge that I have not missed a bird. More than once I have left my position in the line all too grimly aware that every shot I have fired has missed its mark. And so, basking in the sunshine and in the warmth of unexpected competence, it was with deep pleasure that I lay back in the heather, smoking my pipe and chatting and feeling that the rest of the world was at least a thousand miles away.

At the next drive I missed the single bird that came my way, slanting high over the line. Grant Rowley, in the butt below me, brought it crashing to earth. Then it was time for whisky and sandwiches in the shooting hut, before a long pull up a climbing line of butts and a drive that brought another singleton in range of my gun: an easy bird that was shamefully missed.

The reason I miss grouse is that I cannot persuade myself to take them in front. They seem too near my neighbour or too low and, by the time that I decide they are neither, they are already behind me and at long range. But they are a wonderful sight as they skim towards you, lifting and dipping and jinking on cupped wings. And there is a fine quality of defiance in the way they cross the line; it as though they are silently challenging you to shoot them in the sure knowledge that you are not up to it and that they will fly on.

At the last drive I was most certainly not up to it. The birds were flying downhill and they were difficult to see until the last moment. And they were fast and very low and beyond my skill. Give me a high grouse and I may well miss him, but at least I know what I am meant to do. I treat him like a pheasant and raise my gun and swing through him and he falls or continues on his way.

But send a low grouse in my direction, hurtling down the heather towards the butts, and there is a real chance that I shall not see him at all. And, if I do see him, a sort of panic seizes me; I hop from foot to

181

foot and wonder if now is the moment or whether I should wait another second before I pull the trigger. And what do I do when I shoot? Do I point? Do I swing? Do I close my eyes and hope? Do I push out at him? Do I flick my gun from tail to beak? I do none of these. I dither and delay and end up with a despairing volley behind. And, if he is one of a covey, then my indecision and incompetence are multiplied by the number of birds around him and it is pitiful to behold. I am a poor shot of driven grouse.

At the last drive today I fired ten shots and killed one bird. And the day was clouding over and there were the first spots of rain on the wind. There was a huge tea in the Rowley's kitchen, which helped me to forget about the last drive. Then there was a dash to High Park to feed my pheasants and find that a sparrowhawk has started eating them. I shall have to talk about her another day.

6 September

Cloud and heavy showers, a sighing wind, the sad singing of robins: an autumnal and dreary scene at High Park this morning, complementing the depression induced by the thought of the boys' return in the afternoon. Within a week I shall be happy again. I shall have re-accustomed myself to the sound of strident adolescent voices and the rhythm of life in a boarding school. In a week I shall be happy again, but only if a hen sparrowhawk has stopped preying upon my birds round the margins of the pen. I surprised her at it on Saturday evening, and she has struck again, and more than once. She has had four poults now, and there can be no doubt that she will be back for more. The keepers of old would have known what to do. I know what to do but I am not allowed to do it. Mr. G.'s son, James, is home for a few days and I have asked him to lie in wait and frighten my sparrowhawk with loud noises. If this fails I shall leave a radio playing by the pen and find out whether she has the good taste to be repelled by modern popular music. I should have hung lengths of sewelling from the posts that hold up the wire, but I was short of time and left it undone. It has been a successful release and it is annoying to encounter this trouble at a time when I was beginning to think that anxiety belonged to the past.

I shall leave my diary for a few days. When next I make an entry I shall be a contented and committed schoolmaster, and I shall be lumbering round a fives court again with all my old enthusiasm. The sparrowhawk will have flown away. My pheasants will have tails longer than their bodies and I shall be looking forward with impatience to my first attempt to shoot a few of them. I have forgotten to mention that today is the day of completion, that now I am the owner of High Park. I have also forgotten to take the Blessed Virgin to the larches. It will be done before the first shoot. And I must write about Digby soon. He has been with me for nearly a week. I shall write about him when I have time to do him justice.

11 September

Grouse at Dufton yesterday, with wind and cloud and the high becks full. The birds were wilful and unhelpfully bent on self-preservation. Few could be persuaded to fly over the guns. But it was a fine sight to see them rising and curling and racing out of the sides of the drive in contempt of the gesticulating flags of the flankers. Standing behind a wooden butt was very cold, even in brief moments of rushing sunshine. I fired five times - or was it four - and killed one bird. The bag was nine and a half brace.

And so ends my sport with grouse for the season. I have killed six of them with 23 shots. I shall never shoot grouse often enough to become good with them. But I love the few days I get on the moors. I love the sight of grouse on the wing, the cackling sound of them as I wait in my butt. And there is nothing in shooting more exciting than watching a pack of grouse skimming over the heather and wondering, with both hope and trepidation, whether or not they will cross the line where you are waiting for them with your gun.

I went out to High Park this afternoon and filled hoppers. The sparrowhawk seems to have moved on and I was happy to find no more corpses. But the pen was a cheerless sight, with only two poults inside the wire. Less than five weeks ago it was a populous place, full of sound and movement. Now it has fulfilled its purpose for another season. It stands lonely and all but abandoned, strewn with dead leaves and with its last inhabitants wandering round its empty spaces like lost souls in a deserted city.

I have been wanting the pen empty for some time, and, with the gates permanently open now, the birds will wander back again when- ever they are moved to visit their old home. There will be afternoons when I find as many as twenty gathered there in reunion. But today, on a damp afternoon beneath lowering clouds, I found myself almost longing for August days when I sat beneath the trees and watched poults sunning and dusting themselves, dipping their beaks into trays of water and pecking experimentally at the hoppers inside the pen. I turned the electric fence off when I left this afternoon; it will not be turned on again until next August. I fed both my duck ponds and shall flight one of them within a fortnight. Both are being used.

15 September

Digby and I are beginning to get used to each other. He is, as yet, an unadventurous dog. He does not show the zest for hunting that I asso- ciate with spaniels. He potters while Merlin flies, and I wonder whether he will ever develop Merlin's longing for gorse and brambles and the birds that lurk there unavailingly. But, when Digby finds a scent, immediately he speeds up and begins to look more like a springer spaniel. He may just need experience, and he is certainly biddable. It will be my fault if he does not remain so. He sits to the merest pip of a whistle and turns instantly to the recall. He retrieves dummies with more pleasure than many of his kind and is beginning to understand hand signals, and beginning to respond to them even when there is no dummy lying somewhere in the direction where they point.

Merlin has accepted the intrusion of another dog into his life with admirable composure. There is not an ounce of aggression in his nature and I love him for it. The bulk of the work will be his this winter and High Park will remain his kingdom. And I cannot spend ten years calling a dog Digby. I should like to call him Dog; but from now on he shall be Digger.

17 September

In the course of an otherwise uneventful day Merlin was buggered by an ageing golden haired retriever. I am not sure that he enjoyed it, but he ate his supper with his customary relish and I take this as a sign that he is psychologically unscarred.

19 September

A grey stillness lay over the Wenning this afternoon. The air was not heavy; rather it was tired, and the surrounding fields breathed out a message of slow fading and decay. Even the river, though full and clear from a week of rain, seemed somehow to be drained of energy, sliding and murmuring on its sad way beneath the cloud. The wind was no more than a faint stirring of air, too weak even to sigh through the withered grasses. The leaves - a few of them just touched to brown and pale yellow - were too weary to whisper or move. And I, telling myself without conviction that I was not falling victim to a heavy cold, plodded on my way from pool to pool.

I could not help looking back to my first April day on the Wenning and recalling how everything had seemed filled with joyful impatience and prospective vigour. For April longs to be May, and even May looks forward to June. But September, in its still and shrouded mood, looks neither one way nor the other. It sinks into itself and into an enervated contemplation of time and decay and mortality.

In between conventional autumn thoughts, I fished with a slow delight. A few blue wings drifted down the pools, rather more pale wateries. A few trout rose without enthusiasm and at long intervals. Wet flies, even the Poult Bloa, were ignored. But my Cree Hackle caught four, all just takeable and all returned. The Imperial brought me a better fish, a very beautiful fish just under the pound and still, even towards the end of September, in the very pink of condition.

I fished up to the confluence of the becks and fished no further. I have not re-explored them as I promised myself in April. I wandered downstream, thinking, as I have rarely thought on the Wenning this season, of summers and Septembers over twenty years ago and half wishing that I was back in them. I missed a fish beneath the viaduct and remembered once catching a monster there, as a train rumbled over, on the last day of the season.

While I was taking my rod down, the sky was suddenly full of swallows, dark shapes flitting nervously through the grey air and chattering impatiently. They ought to be gone; they are out of place in these quiet and fading days as we drift slowly towards winter. I am very glad that I do not have to join them in Africa.

That will probably be it for the Wenning this year. I have not fished it as often as I intended. Today was my first visit since July. It is difficult to do justice to three trout streams, when there are boys to teach and dogs to train and mountains to climb and pheasants to feed. Next year I must try harder.

22 September

I thought my cold had gone away. Yesterday it came back with a vengeance and brought a touch of 'flu for good measure. I felt all the more wretched because the afternoon was one of perfect autumnal calm; it was everything a late September afternoon should be, with long shadows and golden light lying warmly over the earth. And there was I, with red eyes and heavy limbs and a head that seemed made of catarrh.

I could not do nothing on such an afternoon and so, while starlings chuckled and whistled contentedly in the old apple trees above me, I picked blackberries from the patch of neglected ground next to the dog-hut. The brambles were heavily laden and the berries were juicy and purple-black. There were succulent clusters hanging along every shoot and glowing darkly in the gilded light. I scratched my hands as I reached deep into bushes to plunder the lurking fruit; and the berries stained my fingers the colour of wine. I had soon gathered enough, but then I would glimpse fresh riches hidden away among the leaves. I would add them to my store and then catch sight of more berries, drooping down to the earth or hanging from climbing brambles and almost out of reach. And so it went on until it was time to feed the dogs and then sit in a chair and feel sorry for myself.

I left the pub unvisited and consoled myself with whisky, which is wonderful comfort for a life tainted by a rough throat and a blocked nose and by heavy-headed weariness. It spreads a warm blessing through aching limbs. Its potent vapours explore nasal passages and release them from the choking grip of catarrh. It is pure and powerful and purges corruption with its pungent touch. It is something to look forward to when all other pleasures have been dulled. The only trouble is the temptation to have too much of it. But this was a temptation I managed for once to resist. I was in bed before midnight and asleep a few seconds afterwards. Today I felt restored.

24 September

I was at Yockenthwaite yesterday afternoon, not in the calm sunshine that has blessed the last three days, but in rain and cloud. There was a moaning wind, blowing brown and yellow leaves onto the pools, and the pools themselves stared blankly at the dark sky. The air was dank and the earth was sodden and everything wore a dejected and a weary look. It was not a day to listen to the wistful song of the robin and wallow in the pensive sadness of autumn; it was rather a day when the irresistible message of the season sank into me with every slow step and was felt like a burden. You cannot fish on such days in late September, watching the leaves fall, seeing how the riot of growth along the banks has shrivelled and rotted away to a few gaunt thistles and a few pock-marked butterbur leaves, you cannot listen to the wind or look at the grey water without thinking disturbing thoughts about change and decay and the end of the trout season.

The wind was upstream and, anyway, the stretch below Yockenthwaite is sheltered from its worst excesses. I fished through the dreary landscape and within twenty minutes I had caught a two-pounder. He came from the side of a huge boulder that juts out into the stream. I cast my flies onto the water once or twice, and was just remembering how I had caught a trout there on the last Saturday of the season ten years ago, when I realised that I was into a big fish. It sounds unlikely but it is true. He was short and deep-bellied and weighed exactly two pounds.

The high river has been dour during my few visits this year and it was dour again yesterday. Most seasons bring two or three Yockenthwaite days when the trout feed all day and when, if I wanted, I could go home with twenty or thirty of them. I thought the two-pounder would be the first of a big catch, but he was not. The pools were full of floating leaves. There were no trout rising among them. At last I found a fish feeding on floating gnats on the edge of a run. I changed to a dry fly and rose him and missed him. Then hard against

188

the walled bank in Ash Pool, a pair of trout were swallowing the odd olive that was coming down the stream. I put on my Cree Hackle and felt sure that I should have them both. But they both refused my fly and both went down with the first cast.

I should have changed flies, but I was feeling dispirited and could not be bothered. I decided to fish the water for half an hour and then, if the half hour brought no trout, to finish and go off to the *Falcon*. I did not see another rise, but my fly disappeared in the run below the bridge and a fish of a pound fought hard before he surrendered and made the brace.

The cloud had sunk lower by now. I moved above the bridge in an eschatalogical gloom. It was not yet five in the evening, but already the light had deepened to a dank and lowering brown, and the sky was sagging so wearily that it seemed it must settle in exhaustion over the rough fields. And it was in this premature darkness that I came to a part of the river I have not fished for more than ten years.

The problem with the water above Yockenthwaite Bridge is that the road runs along it, and so every fine summer afternoon brings hordes of tourists with dogs and stones and blaring radios. But yesterday the glowering menace of the evening had driven them early away; even at five o'clock I had the river to myself. I thought how lovely the narrow rockpools were and remembered the features of each of them as I came to them again. I remembered too how, ten and more years ago, I fished and thought like a young man and I realised that I cannot do it any more. I caught another trout, another pounder, and told myself that, next year, I must seize the few quiet days that the season brings to the high river beyond the bridge and fish these inviting road-side pools.

They are very beautiful, for the water is open, with lonely, leaning trees and with climbing fields all around; and there are big trout lurking in the deep holes and dodging the stones that the tourists fling over their heads. It was here that I first fell in love with the top of the Wharfe and, on days of full water, I fished among splashing humans and swimming black labradors and caught trout in spite of them.

I caught no more fish yesterday. I realised that passing cars were groping their way through the evening with the help of headlights and I decided that it was time to finish, plodding down the darkening fields to where my Land Rover was waiting to take me off to Arncliffe.

The *Falcon* was deep in autumn, with darkness outside at supper time, with a fire burning in the bar again. The rain came heavily again overnight and the Wharfe came up with it. This morning I saw how full the river was when I drove to mass in Grassington. And the wind was roaring downstream and the sky still looked full of rain. A young man would have fished, but I did not. I came home and fed my flight pond at Skennerskeugh and took the dogs out.

27 September

Fishing thoughts stirred within me this afternoon, for the cloud cleared and the the sky turned blue and the wind dropped to no more than a faint stirring in the leaves. Rose hips and hawthorn berries glowed in the sunlight. The air trembled with the singing of robins. Wagtails were flocking on the cricket square as I walked home from lunch and a few swallows were dipping low over March Hill fields.

There were the dogs to exercise. If I did go fishing there would be work late into the night, and I am still feeling tired and slow in the aftermath of last week's cold. And there was a sense, as I stood at Yockenthwaite on Saturday evening, taking my rod down, that the time for trouting was past; that next April would be soon enough to go fishing again. And so I left my rivers alone and took the dogs out. I marked some books and read some Herodotus and than I went to Skennerskeugh.

It was not an evening for flighting duck. There was a clear sky and no wind, but I was glad to be out in it, walking down the fields and wondering if there would be any duck on the pond. I sat Merlin a hundred yards from the edge of the water and crept up to it. I had just decided that there were no fowl there when a teal sprang from a corner, and with him rose four or five mallard, quacking in alarm and beating their wings noisily. Thinking of food I went for the mallard and each shot brought one dropping from the sky. Merlin remained where I had left him, gazing at me in an agony of longing, pleading mutely to be given his first retrieve of the season. He had soon brought me my duck and he treated neither of them roughly. I stowed the first mallard of the autumn in my bag and settled down to wait for flight.

I was far too early. I am always too early for flighting duck. But the long wait as the light fades is part of the pleasure of it all. This evening there were midges dancing above the muddy pool in the hollow of the field. From the other side of the wall there were cattle bellowing at me, pushing their heads under the wire along the top and snorting and breathing heavily. They settled down before long and things fell quiet. Crows flapped slowly through the sky, shying away suddenly when they saw me lurking beneath them. A leaf or two floated down from the trees. A wren broke into a brief snatch of song and I sat smoking in the angle of the wall, while Merlin scanned the horizon impatiently. I felt tired and it was peaceful sitting and waiting and not caring too much whether any duck came in.

They did. As the risings and fallings of the field where the pond lies were turning into dark and indistinct shapes, and as the light drained from the middle of the sky and gathered and gleamed along its rim, a pair of teal came low and fast down the pasture towards me, grunting through the shadows. Perhaps they saw me, for they swung wide and Merlin sighed deeply. I should build a butt against the wall. It needs no more than a couple of pallets and a couple of posts. And yet I know that it will never be done; because I like things as they are at Skennerskeugh and I rather feel that flighters of duck should make use of what natural cover is available and not cheat by erecting commodious hiding places where they can sit in unseen comfort and drink champagne while they wait for their prey.

Another teal came, and this one dropped into the pond without the chance of a shot. I clapped him off and missed him as he fled, losing sight of him before I had time to fire with my second barrel. Only a minute or two later the steady rhythm of mallards' wings was beating above me and the dog was hissing in my ear. I saw them, four birds circling high and wide over the pond. Twice they wheeled round. I made mimic mallard noises with my duck-call, and the sound of wings told me that they were now behind me and closer than before. Suddenly one of them was clear against the sky: a dark shape of wide wings and a long neck. I raised my gun and the shape fell to earth. Merlin dashed out and brought it back to me.

It was not yet dark. There was still silver and red along the edges of the sky, while over the fields there lay a suffused greyness. Indisputably it was mallard time. But, with three duck already in the bag, I decided to go and give the birds a chance to flight in and eat my grain undisturbed. It was, of course, a decision inspired by self-interest as much as by compassion, for duck that arrive without a greeting of gunshot and then fill their bellies in peace are duck likely to arrive again the next time the inland fowler feels the urge to sit by his pond.

Even as I stood up and whispered to Merlin that it was all over, there were wings above me again. A single teal flew fast overhead from behind the wall and then turned in the meadow and whistled back again. The gun went up and the teal fell on the edge of the pond. Merlin snorted and went off for him without waiting to be asked.

And now truly it was time to walk back through the fields, pleased with four birds from five shots and a record bag for Skennerskeugh. I could hear the sound of duck above me and I knew where they were heading. There is no better sport in the world than flighting a pond with only a spaniel for company, even a spaniel that loses its head and dashes off in search of teal with no regard for his master's displeasure. Next week it will be the pond at High Park.

1 October

The trout season faded away very quietly yesterday and I spent no part of it by a river. I shall not take out a rod again until the end of March. It has been a fine season and, in a day or so, or in a few weeks, I shall gather statistics of flies and fish and rivers and I shall look back over a spring and summer that have brought great pleasure even though they have not brought sackfuls of trout. I have not fished very well this season. It will be interesting to wonder why.

3 October

To High Park this afternoon. There was a keen wind blowing from the north and the sunshine between the cloud was very pale. The air was cold on my cheek, the earth was sodden from the torrents of rain yesterday. Trees are still chiefly green, but early-turning ashes have faded to a wan yellow; rowans are brown and russet and half bare, though they are still heavily laden with berries. Beneath the hazels the ground is strewn with black and rotting leaves. Birches show flushing tints of orange. Beeches are browning. Oak leaves are withering and hang dry and crumpled on the branch. But alders remain defiantly green, and most of the turning trees are still more green than any other colour.

193

There was a feeling of restless change today, a sense that the year was stirring itself: to strip away the things that belong to summer and to warm times, so that the earth can show forth the spare shapes and the sharp lines that are the essence of the winter landscape.

I slipped and slithered and cursed my way over the sloping fields. All the hoppers are being well used and filling them now is costing me a fortune. I tried, as I carried buckets of grain this way and that, to work out roughly what my pheasants have cost me so far this season, at a time when not one of them has yet been shot. I came up with an approximate figure of seven hundred pounds, and immediately decided to forget about expense. I would rather not know.

Releasing pheasants is a rich man's game and I am not rich. I do it instead of subjecting myself to a revolting foreign holiday beneath a sun so hot that it makes any form of exercise impossible. I do it instead of going to Greece and being bored to stupefaction by the beauty of the Acropolis. I prefer it to travel, to art, to culture. I suppose that I am a philistine as well as a murderer and I do not care.

6 October

Ashes surrender their leaves to the first sharp cold of the year. There was frost on Tuesday night and again on Wednesday. There are carpets of shrivelled but still green leaves under the Sedbergh ashes. There were deep drifts of them along the hedges at High Park this afternoon; and ash keys, which were pale yellow on Monday, have withered and turned brown. Already there are beeches pointing bare branches at the sky.

It was a sombre world beneath the cloud. From a distance my wood seemed to be rusting away in the damp air, and down on the sike, the yellow leaves of the willows were faded and sad. But I was happy

194

in the midst of this decay, for there were pheasants everywhere and hoppers that were filled only on Monday needed filling again.

And the pen was once more inhabited and seemed almost cheerful. There must have been twenty birds there today, all of them cocks. Their tails are growing fast and they should be ready for the first shoot in just over a fortnight. Most of the hens are ready now. There are birds in the brambles above the Douglas Firs; there are birds in the blackthorn thicket by the larches; there are pheasants all along the hedge that climbs above the meadow and there are pheasants peering out of the edges of the gorse. Back in the wood too there are plenty of pheasants and there are more pheasants in the birch scrub over the beck. Wherever I went this afternoon there were pheasants, well-grown pheasants, and the sight of them filled me with the hope that the first shoot will be a success.

Before then, perhaps one day next week, I shall have my version of a boundary day. It is a day just for Merlin and for me. It does not last much longer than a couple of hours, for that is all the time it takes Merlin to hunt out a few clumps of gorse and rushes in the top fields. Then there are bits of cover on Mr. Allinson's land and, this year, there will be the steep bank above the duck pond and the thick hedges along the field-edge. And, if three old cocks rise with streaming tails and if two of them fall to the sound of my shot, then my boundary day will have been a memorable day indeed.

And so to Digger, for it is he who goes to High Park with me at the moment. If allowed away from heel Merlin would certainly peg young birds. I shall risk him on my boundary day, on the edges of the shoot, but he is better kept away from the heart of it for another fortnight.

Digger is still an unenterprising spaniel, but there are signs of progress. As soon as he smells rabbit or pheasant a change comes over

195

him and he is eager to be off on the trail. Once or twice, in the vicinity of the pen, he has darted forwards to pounce on a pheasant, and I have been pleased that a gruff shout or a sharp blast on the whistle has stopped him in his tracks. I think that, if only I am sensible with him, he will develop into a dependable and obedient dog.

He does not like being told to sit and then abandoned; he tends to creep forwards in the direction of his departing master. But even here he is improving and it is a fault that stems from fear and not from wilfulness. It will disappear as his confidence grows. I can sit him now and circle the pen and come back to him and greet him with inordinate praise. Only a week ago he would have been slinking after me before I was half way round.

And a week ago he would not go into the gorse. Today, by contrast, he was longing to lose himself in it; the difficulty was keeping him out. But, because as yet he hunts with insufficient drive, he does get stuck in really thick cover. It has happened once or twice in the woods around Sedbergh. I have tried to coax him into jungles of brambles and at last he has leapt in. But then a minute later I have heard a pathetic whimpering and have had to push in after him and set him free. I suppose this has been bad practice, likely to provoke a permanent fear of dense and tangled places. It seems to be working.

But there are still times when he refuses to leave my side, however ardently I plead with him. And if I whistle him too much he stops trying and gives up altogether. Perhaps, as Brian suggested, he needs giving his head for a time, so that he can learn the joys of the chase before he is reined in again. It is a strategy I am reluctant to employ, frightened that it might achieve its purpose all too effectively and leave me with a second spaniel with a mind too much his own.

No! I shall go on steadily, blowing my whistle less frequently and insisting, when I do blow it, that Digger obeys. I shall take him flighting in a week or two. I may try him in the beating line at Wigglesworth, although I shall have to be very careful that he does not learn far more than is good for him. I must not surrender to impatience. He is only eighteen months old and he will grow up in his own good time. At my service meanwhile there is Merlin, who will hunt all day and anywhere and do what I tell him more often than not. But it would be pleasing to own a spaniel and know that he would never let me down. I am a rank amateur with gun dogs, but I do enjoy my feeble efforts to train them and to keep them steady.

10 October

Yesterday evening I went to Low Park pond, which is what I have named my new flight-pond. It was an evening of complete serenity. The brightness in the sky seemed to be coming straight from Heaven and the sun's slanting transfigured midges into diaphanous specks of dancing light. Just above the horizon a thin moon was hanging unobtrusively, waiting with patience for its moment to shine. Behind me there was a line of yellow willows; there were crab apples too, hung thickly with clusters of reddening fruit; beyond them were Scots pines, tall and dark. I crouched in the rushes and faced the falling line of the field. Dry grasses hung motionless above me. And, while robins whistled and my pheasants shouted in nearby fields as they thought about flapping up to roost, I thought about my father, wondering whether he was dying, and hoping that he was not.

Merlin was beside me, and his unawareness of old age and death was a strange comfort to me. He watched every crow with interest. Every time a pheasant called, his ears pricked up. And at the sound of the first duck he froze into a statue: a statue with its nose pointed at the sky.

The duck came in plenty and they came fast. Some came alone, some in twos and threes, others in parties of half a dozen and more. Against the sky they made every shape that a mallard can make; there were long necks with folded wings; there were wings outstretched and webbed feet thrusting forward; there were wings beating rhythmically across the thin crescent of the moon; there were shapes hanging in the sky and then planing down, or flapping down vertically onto the darkness of the water.

I was in the wrong place. The birds were coming in at the far end of the pond. The shots I fired were hurried and misplaced, and for five of them I dropped only one bird. It was bad shooting, and the fact that my shots were hurried ones at half-glimpsed targets is only a partial excuse. The duck I did shoot fell somewhere in the willows. Merlin had marked the fall and was back with him in less than a minute. It was the best thing about the evening's sport; it was Merlin showing me that, if I choose to do my job incompetently, he at least could still perform his more difficult function with speed and skill.

Next time, in a month, I shall be in the right place, which is in the rushes half way along the pond. And next time, please God, my father will be well again and I shall be able to sit there and think about nothing but duck.

Today he was much better and I went out to High Park with an easier mind. It was an October afternoon so beautiful that it defies description and I shall not insult it with the unworthy attempt. As I drove to feed my pheasants I came across the hunt. In my part of the world you come across the hunt often enough at this time of year.

Land Rovers are the surest sign that the hunt is nearby: Land Rovers, old pick-ups, battered vans and a variety of vehicles with long aerials sprouting from their roofs. And inside them, or standing outside with eyes raised to the hills, is a marvellous collection of Cumbrian faces: sharp-featured, chinny and bony faces on top of wiry bodies and themselves topped with dark, wiry hair: deeply graven faces lined by fifty lambing times and marked by the obvious absence of teeth: great round florid faces shaped by whisky as well as by wind and weather (these faces are normally inside the Land Rovers). There are cheerful and morose faces, eager and inert faces. There are very few bearded faces, though there are some faces disfigured with a moustache, and there are more old than young faces. Nearly all of them are rural faces and I wave at those of them that I know. Always I look to the hills around me, in search of the sight of hunting hounds, and, if I see my friend, Toy Winn, and perhaps Austin with him, I stop for five minutes to ask how things are going and to discover whether the hounds have killed.

I saw the hounds today. They were streaming through the bracken not far from the road and there was a pink coat somewhere near them. I could not hear the music of the hunt, because the engine of my Land Rover drowns all music but its own, and I did not stop because I did not have the time. I did not have the inclination either, and this was because watching hounds would have made me very angry. I should have seen them surging through the bracken, heard their belling and baying ringing round the hills, heard too the learned commentary on the action from the Cumbrian faces around me. And I should have felt very angry indeed: that this great ornament of the rural scene is likely soon to be declared illegal as well as immoral, because men and women who know nothing about foxes think they are appealing creatures with clever faces and bushy tails and think too that the men who hunt them must be very cruel and very nasty and should be made to stop it immediately.

I drove on through the sunshine and went to feed my birds. As I filled hoppers and watched pheasants, now well grown and almost ready for the gun, strutting under the trees, and as I marvelled at the heavy harvest with which rowans and hawthorns are still hung, I began to think once more about fieldsports and the general disapproval in which they are now held. And again I asked myself whether my love of fishing and shooting was a cruel and heartless perversion rather than the blameless recreation which I have always assumed it to be. In February and March I thought much along these lines and felt that I had found some answers. But it is always good to think again and to approach old problems in the hope of finding a new insight. I have to confess that I was never deeply disturbed by the possibility that, at the end of an afternoon's deep reflection by my beck, with pheasants calling around me and dry leaves fluttering down and settling on my cap, I might stand up and declare that my land was now a nature reserve, and then drive home and put away my guns and my fishing rods for good.

I was not truly worried by the thought that fishing, shooting and hunting might after all be wicked pursuits. Rather, as I sat and smoked and briefly watched a red squirrel peering at me from the yellow leaves of an ash tree, I tried yet again to penetrate to the heart of the mystery and to discover why the shooting of birds and the catching and killing of trout, activities that seem monstrous to a growing number of people, seem to me an affirmation of the glory of creation and a very proper form of praise.

I did not rehearse the old arguments in favour of fieldsports. I went straight back to the problem of killing for pleasure, which is what we sportsmen do, and which is also what sticks in the gullets of most of the men and women who think that we are cruel and should know better. For most of the men and women who dislike the idea of hunting and shooting, and perhaps fishing as well, are not aggressive vegetarians or members of sinister organisations prepared to go to any lengths in their promotion of what they believe to be the welfare of animals. Nor are many of them new-age travellers or members of outlandish religious sects; nor are the majority of them political extremists with a hatred of everything that smacks of wealth and privilege; and very few of them, I think, are urban thugs who like a breath of country air and a change of scene for the practice of their thuggery. No! Most of them are decent men and women who cannot imagine how otherwise decent men, and a few women, can take pleasure in knocking pheasants out of the sky or knocking fish on the head or watching a pack of hounds chasing a fox this way and that through the countryside, until finally it is caught and killed and torn to pieces. It is difficult to see how, on the face of it, they have not got a point.

It was, I think, at this stage that I looked at one of my pheasants, a fine cock of the year with a long tail and an arrogant air. I looked at this cock, scratching beneath one of the hoppers - this season, by the way, I seem to have a dozen cocks for every hen - and I asked him why it was that I wanted to shoot him. Then, realising that he lacked the power of speech as surely as he lacked a soul or any potential for good or evil or any moral or spiritual awareness, or any capacity for affection and reflection, realising all this and reminding myself that I could hardly hope for a reply, I asked him the same question all over again and began to answer it myself.

'You are,' I said to him, 'very handsome. You will also, if you are ever shot by me or by one of my friends, and if you are hung by the neck for a time that varies according to the state of the weather and the stage of the season and the differing opinions of men on the subject of hanging birds like you once they are dead, provide me or my friends, or my friends and me together, once you have been plucked and spent some time in a cooking pot, with a delicious meal. You will in fact be so delicious, when at last you come out of the pot, that it would be irreverent not to wash you down with a bottle or two of fine claret.

201

'I want to shoot you,' I continued, 'because I want to eat you. I am sure you have heard all this before, but I think I should go through it again quickly. If I do not shoot you and eat you, some other animal will eat you before very long. I think it will be a pity if your flesh is wasted on the unappreciative palate of a fox, a creature that would never think of uncorking a *cru grand bourgeois exceptionnel* to grace the ritual of your consumption. I also think it would be a pity if you were to die and nothing at all were allowed to eat you. It would be spitting in the face of nature. You are designed, you poor, handsome creature, to provide other, flesh-eating creatures with their sustenance. It is, I am afraid, part of the great scheme of things. And although, unlike you, I am able to shape my relationship to this scheme of things, it would surely be wasteful of me to deny your undeniable purpose within nature's plan by renouncing the pleasure of your roasted or casseroled flesh? I cannot see what you would gain from such a stand-offish attitude on my part. You would in fact be the poorer for it, because you would not be here at all.

'But now,' I added after a few moments' reflection and a few draws on my pipe, 'comes the part that you will find difficult. Indeed it is the part that I myself am only now beginning to understand as I sit here and talk to you. I am, as it happens, rather excited by the sudden insight which our conversation seems to have inspired. I think perhaps a new paragraph will help us both to see things more clearly.

'I want to kill you because I want to eat you. So much is simple. The puzzling part is that, although I want to kill and eat you, I want to turn the killing of you into a challenge. I will not, for example, kill you on the ground, as would a fox or a mink or stoat or a cat. And I shall only enjoy killing you if you will oblige me by flying both fast and high, or by springing from cover at an awkward angle to my waiting gun, under which circumstances I am as likely to miss you as to bring you crashing senseless to the ground.

'You must understand that we human beings are very peculiar animals. All that matters to you is food and drink and shelter and sex. There are some humans whose concerns are similarly confined, but, by general consent, they are poor examples of the species. Most of us, in one way or another, are lovers of beauty. Most of us enjoy the challenge of difficult things. We are nearly all of us, after our own fashion, artists, which means that we not only love beauty; we also, in a thousand different ways, strive to create it ourselves. And this is why, unlike you and the rest of your fellow pheasants, who lead lives of serene and unreflective contentment, disturbed only by brief and instantly forgotten moments of alarm, we humans are by and large such a restless and dissatisfied crew. We are constantly disappointed because we do not do things as beautifully as we should like to, whereas those of us who have lost from their lives the longing to find and to create and to enjoy beauty, live in a state of acknowledged or unrecognised impoverishment and degradation.

'You might well ask what all this has got to do with my intention to shoot you if I ever get the chance, with the fact that in about a fortnight my friends and I will dress up in old-fashioned clothes and take hold of our guns and hope to kill you. It has, believe it or not, got everything to do with it. For it is the longing for beauty that drives us out in pursuit of you: the urge to behold and to create beauty, the desire to make art out of necessity. You will not understand a word of this, for you are untroubled by any artistic impulses, but I am now so excited that I am treating you as a member of my own kind and, if you will only put up with me for a few minutes more, I shall leave you in peace - for the time being, that is - to peck wheat from the hopper that I have so obligingly hung (and so considerately refilled) on the trunk of the ash tree over there.

'When we set out to kill you, my friends and I, we shall be in search of much more than food. We shall be hungry for the beauty of my little valley: the beauty of steep-sided slopes on either side of a splashing beck, the tall beauty of the standing pines and the glowing beauty of the autumn larches, the beauty of the blue sky with its moving clouds and the slow and beautiful movement over the earth of the shadows beneath them. We find, you see, in my little valley, if you will allow a cliche that perhaps trips a little too easily off the tongue, food for the spirit as well as sustenance (in the form of you) for our bodies.

'You will probably hear us coming and you will scuttle off into cover. You may be spending the morning on Blackberry Hill. If so you will probably seek safety in the thick brambles above the larches, or perhaps in the tangle of briars and hawthorns further up the slope. You may leg it over the boundary, in which case you will be out of danger. But, whatever you do, you will not feel the cold grip of fear that clamps human hearts in time of peril. You will respond to events in the instinctive and thoughtless fashion of your race.

'Blackberry Hill, as you are probably not aware, is very beautiful, with the Douglas firs rising from the water, tall and slender and dark against the sky. You may have breakfasted on mast beneath the beeches that run along the boundary fence, in which case it is unlikely that you have ever noticed how their trunks shine grey and silver in winter sunshine. You may have lurked in the blackthorn thicket down by the beck, where a few purple berries are still hanging, without ever admiring the marvellous and delicate intricacy of their prickly maze of dark stems and shoots and branches. Perhaps you roost in the oak tree half-way up the bank, where wrinkled brown leaves still rustle in the breeze. It is a lovely sound, though I doubt whether your ears ever bother to mark its loveliness. But they will not even hear it, or the soft pattering of the larch needles, once my friends and I have come to Blackberry Hill and set our dogs to work.

'It may be my Merlin, working with manic eagerness, who first gets scent of you. If it is my Merlin, you had better get a move on, for he will peg you if you loiter and that would be an undignified end. It may be Austin's Holly, in which case you need not clatter on to the wing with such breathless haste. But, be it Merlin or Holly or Toy's Bracken or Phil's Judy, you will have to make a move sooner or later and it will probably be too late to run; you will have to fly.

'Let us assume that you are the first pheasant to seek safety in the air, without any older and wiser bird to guide your course. If you flutter up the bank and over the fence, you will certainly live to fly again. If you skim low over the beck and glide over the hedge into the gorse beyond, neither of the two guns standing by the water will think that you are worth a bang. If you like you can head for the pen, and that will be safe enough as long as you remember to stay close to the ground.

'Here now is what you should not do. You should not feel a sudden longing for the sky. If you value your life, you must not rise in chortling anger with all the false and soaring pride of Icarus. For then, as you despise the larches beneath you as earth-bound things, and as you fly still higher on fast wings, you are in danger of a sudden fall. For then, with your long tail streaming and your feathers shining in the bright sun, you are very beautiful, and you call out to the men beneath you with the challenge of the difficult. And you are very beautiful too in the moment of extinction; for you throw back your neck in a last proud act of defiance and the sudden interruption of onward motion is dramatic and beautiful in its own way, as too is the plummeting fall which follows that fulfilling moment of stillness far up in the sky.

'But it may be that this is what you want. Even now you may be dreaming of those soaring seconds of mortal danger. You may be yearning for the admiration that will reach up to you from the hearts of my friends; it will reach up to you whether you defy their gunfire and fly over them unharmed or whether the shot finds its mark and you fall dead to earth. For they will admire you as you rise into the sky; they will admire your beauty of form and feather and flight. They will admire the high beauty of your death, which they will create together with you, or they will admire the speed and the height and the curl of you and admit humbly that it was beyond the reach of their skill with a gun. If you crash to earth, then a dog will be sent to collect you and my friends will admire the strong limbs and the keen noses of their hunting partners. And when you are found and brought to hand, they will admire you once again, for all the reasons of their earlier admiration and also for the admiration that is owing to the taste of your flesh. My friends and I, you see, admire you more variously and more deeply than those men and women who only want to look at you. We admire everything about you. We admire you living and dead, and we admire you most of all because you help us to make art, to create beauty out of the necessities of life. Such admiration as ours amounts, in fact, to reverence.

'Yes, I admit it, we shall shoot you, if we can, for pleasure as well as for the pot, but the pleasure we shall derive from killing you has nothing to do with cruelty. There will be no savage delight in the sight of death, no lust for blood, no longing for torn flesh or shrieks of agony. There will be, at the end of it all, a quiet gratitude: for the gifts of nature and for those remembered moments of beauty that will be remembered once again when at last you are cooked and eaten. And I now promise you that, if you fall to my gun and are stowed in my bag and end up on my table, you will be consumed with reverence and that a *cru grand bourgeois* will not be good enough for you. For you have helped me to understand my love of shooting and to see clearly what I always knew in my heart: that it is a good and wholesome thing.

'And I now see more than this: I see that it is a noble thing: an expression of that peculiar urge which is the distinguishing characteristic of my kind: the urge to find and to make beauty in all the activities of life, the deep longing to turn every need into art. Thank you very much and, by the way, I shall not for a moment hesitate to shoot at you if, when next we meet, you are flying fast and high over my head. Take comfort, if you like, from the thought that I shall probably miss.

'Just one last thought before I go, and it is a thought of which you will most certainly approve. For you may, in all my insistence upon the delectable edibility of your flesh, have been suspecting that your mortal enemy, the fox, has somehow got away with it, that I am about to declare him sacrosanct because it so happens that his meat is unappetizing. Not so, my friend. What matters is necessity, and the human impulse to turn it into a thing of beauty. There is the necessity to eat, which is where you come into all this. There is also the need to protect what we intend some day to eat, our chickens and our lambs and our geese and our pheasants, from other creatures who would like to eat them before we are ready for them ourselves.

'This is where the hunt steps on to the scene, for the poetic heart of man has transformed the necessity to kill foxes into the glory of the chase, with twenty couple of hounds streaming through the bracken or over the ploughland, with their wild music ringing through the air, with the sound of the horn and the shouts of the huntsman and with the beauty of the trotting fox admired by all who behold him. The hunt and the pheasant shoot are both of them tributes to the aspiring spirit of man. This country of mine would be a poorer place without them.

'Now fill your belly before you go up to roost, while I go down my little valley with a light heart and drive home and turn my thoughts to my own supper. There are no pheasants in the larder as yet, but I think that, even without one to grace my table, even, in fact, with sausages and mash, I shall uncork a bottle of Poujeaux '85 and drink it in your honour. For you have listened most attentively and helped me to see things more clearly than ever before. I hope the hunt have found and killed. And I fear that I am becoming partial and sentimental, because I rather hope, after all, that when the day comes, you will fly over one of my friends and not over me. Goodbye.'

11 October

I become obsessed with trees in spring and again in autumn. In spring it is shape. In autumn it is, of course, colour. Willows turn ochre, birches flush a much brighter yellow, and orange at the same time. Oaks are hung with shrivelled clumps of brown leaves, but in sunshine they burn with tints of orange and red and yellow. Alders cling stubbornly to dirty green, while the leaves of sycamores crumple and die. Chestnuts deepen to russet and beeches turn a paler brown. But sometimes there are all these colours, and a dozen other shades, to be found on a single tree. And every day there are subtle changes.

The light in the woods around Sedbergh today was yellow, and the air was full of the sound of leaves settling on the strewn earth. The ground cover has yet to die back, but the blackberries have rotted and gone from the brambles. There seem to be few acorns and hazel nuts this year. I do not know about beech-mast, but rowans and briars and hawthorns bear heavy loads of fruit. The first fieldfares and redwings will soon be here to start eating them.

12 October

What I wrote about trees yesterday was drivel. There is no rigid consistency to the autumn colouring of a particular species. I saw horse chestnuts today that were glowing orange in the sun and sycamores that had turned a pale and translucent yellow.

The weather is unsettling in its beauty. All day there is a motionless radiance over the hills, thickening to a haze as the evening draws on, while over it all there spreads a sky of pale and purest blue, which turns white along the horizon as the sun sets. And the sun is so tender and the birds make small contented sounds and the trees stand there in a faint whisper of falling leaves. I cannot, from any previous autumn, recall a week of such peaceful sunshine, of such restful calm. There is none of the impatience of spring; there is no summer heaviness. There is kind air and bright air and peace everywhere.

13 October

My boundary day, on an afternoon unfitted for an imperfect world and its mortal inhabitants. The temperate sun, the slanting light, the soft air, the glowing trees, with the oaks along the Rise proclaiming the glory of God in their orange magnificence; it was all too much for me and more than once I was close to tears. There was a gentle shimmer over the land and dead leaves in the beck shone through the clear water like yellow stars.

It was the most beautiful afternoon I have ever spent out with a gun. I shot one hen and two cocks and I was moved by the splendour of being alive and touched by the dark fear of death. Perhaps it is only because I am so afraid of death that I cling so dearly to faith and call so often for Mary's help and prayers. It is extinction that I fear. Awareness, even in Hell, seems preferable to the loss of it. Doubtless, when I get there, I shall change my tune.

I did not have Merlin with me today. I took Digger instead, feeling that I must find out how he behaves to the flush and the fall of game before I can know what to do next. I started over my boundary in flight-pond field, thinking to creep along the hedge, then to cross quietly to the water and see if there were any duck on it. I did not load and, of course, a cock pheasant sprang from the bottom of the hedge and flew through the bright air with white neck shining and long tail feathers shaking indignantly.

At this point two cartridges went in the gun and were ready when Digger bustled a hen from the rough grass. It flew fast across me and fell to my first shot. It was the first pheasant of another season and Digby sat to shot in exemplary fashion and retrieved adequately. His mouth is as soft as butter, but he does hang on to whatever he has between his jaws; it needs coaxing from him with muttered encouragements and soft growls in his ear. It is the growls that work best.

It was time to sit down and feel happy. I smoked my pipe and stroked my dog and also the lovely feathers of the dead pheasant beside me. Then Digger worked through the patches of rough ground along the edges of the field and along the hedges of Trevor Allinson's land. Then it was up to my top pastures: to Well Close and the Hag. There is an untidy line of birches on the high side of Well Close, a line of birches and the rush-choked remains of a ditch. From the rushes a cock rose and fell to my second barrel, coming down over the fence in the Hag. At once I knew that he was a runner and I also knew that inexperienced dogs should not be encouraged to chase running birds. I had forgotten all about this when I decided to bring Digger rather than Merlin.

But there was nothing to be done. You cannot leave a wounded bird without trying to find and pick and kill it. Digger was sent under the fence and pranced around in the rushes, while I watched him with my heart in my mouth, expecting any moment to see a cock pheasant legging it across the field with a springer spaniel in hot pursuit. But, although we spent at least twenty minutes searching, and in spite of the fact that for once I had marked the fall with something like care, we found, between us, no sign or smell of a wounded pheasant and eventually we gave up.

And so to the top of the Hag and the patches of gorse along the boundary, where three cocks sprang from cover and two curling birds were shot. The third was short-tailed and was left to fly on its way. Digger brought me one of my birds and I gathered the other myself. He sat obediently to shot for both of them, and they both had sharp spurs and long tails that stuck out of my game bag and waved in the sunshine as I walked along, crossing the fields and returning to the Land Rover in the meadow. Digger flushed three more pheasants but I did not raise my gun. I had decided that my bag was heavy enough, that three pheasants was enough for my boundary day.

I was pleased with Digger, but I had marked signs of possible trouble in times to come. Here, it seemed to me, was a dog just beginning to learn the delights of hunting, beginning to relish the smells he met in the bottoms of hedges, in rushy hollows and in patches of gorse; here was a dog keener to work than he had been yesterday, though still slow and half-hearted when compared with a spaniel that really knew his business. But here beyond doubt was progress and much hope for the future. Less encouraging was Digger's sudden reluctance to hear the whistle when engaged with a particularly absorbing smell, his sudden slackness in sitting when bidden and in coming to his master when called. There had been no riot, no wild pursuit, but there had been these moments of hard-hearing, these first signs of wilfulness. There is much work to be done with him and most of it should be undertaken without a gun. And his sitting to shot? I have called it obedience. I am not sure this is true. I suspect it was a reaction of surprise rather than the result of ingrained habit. The test of this will come once he has learned to associate the sound of a gun with the proximity of dead game and his delight in gathering it.

But I was pleased with him. He had done well for a dog on his first excursion with an armed master. We sat together by the Land Rover and I lit my pipe. Last week I talked to a pheasant about art. Today I talked to myself along different lines.

I saw the tall Douglas firs across the beck, rising green and gracefully into the sky. I saw the larches above the weir-gate, just touched with the beginnings of their autumn orange. I saw a couple of pheasants scratching beneath one of my hoppers. I saw a pigeon flying straight and high above me. I saw the three dead birds beside me in the grass and all at once I saw why the sport of shooting is so satisfying and why it breeds such deep delight - it is because it involves men in a complete relationship with nature that owes nothing to false thought or false sentiment, but rather rests on truth.

It shows man as the master of nature in his ability to tame dogs and shape them to his purpose, then to stalk and slay wild creatures and take them for his own. But it must be a restrained and a loving mastery or it will destroy the harvest it hopes to reap; it cannot be the mastery of rape. It acknowledges that as master of nature, man is also her dependent, for he cannot fill his belly except from her storehouse. It shows man as the lover of nature in the delight he drinks from the sound of beating wings and the shining of the sun on bright feathers. It is a love that grows from need but it grows beyond need. It is a possessive and a contemplative love at the same time, and it lifts a gun and kills a pheasant with reverence, in the pious certainty that it is right to do so, that it admires and kills a pheasant for what it is; and it believes that pheasants cut off in their prime are as much a part of nature's plan as wily old pheasants alive and skulking in the bottom of a hedge.

We shoot for sport, we shooters do. It is the glory of our sport that, along with fishing and hunting, it expresses the truth of man's intercourse with the world he inhabits. Or so it seemed to me this afternoon, as I sat on the rising ground above my meadow and looked about me, at the sky and the trees, at the dog dozing contentedly at my feet, at the three dead birds lying in the grass with closed eyes.

The sky turned white as I drove home and shone for a while like mother-of-pearl. It has been a most wonderful day.

15 October

The disturbingly beautiful weather of the last week has turned into wind and drizzle and brown light. I went out to High Park this afternoon with Austin and we filled all the hoppers. The pen is still full of cocks. In the evening we went to Skennerskeugh, although the pond there is almost dry. Perhaps this explains why so few duck came in: three mallard and one teal. I fired two shots and killed a drake mallard and that made our bag for the evening.

18 October

The wind today was from winter. There was a cold blue sky with a sharp cold light. There are bare trees now among the yellow and the orange of the leaves. Rabbits are dying of myxomatosis and the land at High Park is strewn with their corpses. The sky above it is filled with the slow flappings and the peevish mewings of buzzards. I heard a fieldfare this afternoon; I heard him cackling and then I saw him, purple and handsome, rocking on a hawthorn branch and tearing greedily at the red berries. There are old pheasants and young pheasants all over the place. The sight of them filled me with delight and excitement.

22 October

I think that men who disapprove of blood sports must be half-way to hating nature. For they think that mankind should stand aloof from all the other creatures that inhabit the world and that pass their lives killing each other without a second thought. In their hearts they must loathe the fox, for the fox tears off heads without so much as a prick of conscience. And do they make common cause with the rabbit and the hare, and with other innocent eaters of grass and grain, in condemning the barbarities of the sparrowhawk and the peregrine and, yes, the thrush with his carnivorous passion for worms?

I have just written a foolish paragraph and I have enjoyed it. I know what my opponent will say in answer to it and I agree with what he will say. He will say that man, in his ability to think and to choose, is apart from and above all other animals. He will have to say this, or he will have to condemn in the stoat and the weasel what he condemns in man.

213

Both the sportsman and his opponent recognise a profound difference between men and other animals. This is why the hunter believes that it is right for him to hunt. It is also why his opponent affirms that it is wrong for him to do so, because he thinks that what is appropriate behaviour in thoughtless, instinct-driven animals is not so in man, because in man such behaviour is unnecessary, also because man determines action through the exercise of choice and possesses a mind that ponders the morality of his conduct.

My opponent believes that I should stand aloof from nature, admiring at a distance the cunning of the fox, the sly ways of the stoat, the deadly speed of the hawk and the patient stealth of the heron, recognising that to hunt and to kill is for most animals the essential means of existence, condemning in man any attempt to join the great hunt that is the life of nature. Depending on my opponent's particular point of view it may or may not be right for me to rear sheep and send them to the slaughterhouse, but it is certainly wrong for me to pick up a gun and go out to shoot tomorrow's supper or next Sunday's lunch.

I understand this position. It is a reasonable position, unless it slips into sentimental inconsistency and starts investing animals with man-like virtues that they do not possess or, worse still, starts pretending that animals are in some incomprehensible way the moral superiors of men. Such nonsense I regard with contempt.

I start with the same assumption as my reasonable opponent, asserting that man is absolutely different from the rest of sentient creation (with the exception, I suppose, of angels), asserting too that an individual man is precious in a way that an individual pheasant is not. In the workings of nature I see a complete disregard for the individual and a sole concern with the species. This is what nature bothers about, and my reasonable opponent will probably agree with me.

But, as a shooter and fisher, I respond differently from my opponent to the chasm that separates us men from other animals. He thinks we should stand on our side of it and gaze across. I think we should leap the chasm, taking with us our powers of thought and our sense of beauty and our guns and our fishing rods and, yes, our hunting horns. I think we should shoot the pheasant as it flies through the blue sky and the duck as it flights into silent waters under the stars. I think we should catch and kill trout and bless the pure rivers that breed them; I think we should shoot and fish reverently (I keep using this word), revering the pheasant and the trout and the duck for what they are: beautiful, thoughtless, edible things that exist to reproduce their own kind and sustain other creatures in death.

I think this is right because it recognises the truth about nature and the truth about man's dependence on nature. In the last week I have associated fieldsports with both beauty and truth. It follows from this association that they should be a joy for ever, from which I conclude triumphantly that they must never be banned.

In two days there is my first shoot at High Park. Meanwhile autumn runs towards winter with rain and wind, with dark skies and oozing earth and more bare trees every day. Everywhere there are loud flocks of fieldfares and by night redwings whistle through the misty darkness. I shall take both dogs on Monday and use them singly as occasion seems to demand.

24 October

I was nervous this morning as I drove to High Park. I was sure the Land Rover would break down and that I should never get there. I was anxious about the weather, in spite of the sunshine, for the forecast had spoken of heavy showers and even of thunder in the Pennines. But what disturbed me most of all was the possibility that there would be no pheasants for sport, that dogs would work all day long without flushing any game, that all day my friends would stand on the edges of cover and walk the long fields and fight their way through my tangled wood, and that they would never, or very seldom, lift a gun to their shoulders. Not that Phil and Mick and Austin would complain. They are happy to stand and walk and work their dogs the whole day long, all in the hope of a pheasant or a rabbit or a hare. I knew that they would enjoy themselves if not a single bird rose within shot. So should I on somebody else's shoot. But on your own shoot, with guests invited, you are eager to show them some game. Perhaps it is a form of pride.

The larches were dropping a silent rain of needles onto my cap as I waited for Austin and his dog - he had Meg with him rather than Holly - to start working the clumps of cover on Blackberry Hill. I remembered that once again I had forgotten to bring my wooden image of the Virgin with me, and so, as I stood there and waited for the first pheasant to flush, I solemnly gave my land into her keeping, praying that every one who came there would leave enriched. It was just then that I heard the sound of wings and, a moment later, a single shot rang out.

More birds flushed. Some flew wisely over the boundary. Others skimmed low and prudently down to the beck and then glided into the gorse. One or two rose into the sky before crossing the guns and were greeted with shot. Three flew past me, fast and wide, and I missed with my single shot at the fastest and the widest of them. At the end of it there were no pheasants to pick and I confess that I was disappointed.

We walked through my faraway to the eastern boundary. Phil and I climbed up through the trees and waited, while Mick and Austin walked back through the wood to their position at its western end. The intention was that they would push birds on to the open land above the trees, where Phil and I would flush them as we worked our way towards the pen; or pheasants might cross into the gorse, where we should catch up with them in the afternoon.

A single shot told Phil and me that our friends were in position and so we set off and tried to control our dogs. Merlin was in one of his amenable moods. I waved him into clumps of brambles and he dived in and stopped to whistle and came back to me when I called him. He even flushed a rabbit and refrained from chasing it (there was no chance of a shot). We came all along the high ground above the wood, working every patch of cover, but no pheasants sprang and sped over the waiting guns. Not at least until we neared the pen. There is dense cover here, and I knew from the wild eagerness with which Merlin leapt into it that he had scented game. Briefly the air was full of birds, and there were more running ahead into the patches of gorse on the top of Pheasant Hill.

There were shots now and Merlin forgot himself and raced madly down the line of the fence. I followed him, shouting, and he returned soon enough. He flushed a hen from the gorse and it fell to my shot and he rushed to collect it. It was the first pheasant of the day and the last of the drive. You are not meant to drive birds away from your pen. Little shoots like mine cannot do only what you are meant to do. I chase pheasants away from home in the morning and spend the afternoon trying to chase them back.

It was into the steep bank of gorse now, which is Merlin's greatest joy. The way he worked it today was also a joy to his master. It is true that he lost his head in a flurry of birds around the pen. I forgive him this moment of weakness, for in the gorse he was both bold and strong. He hunted tirelessly; he came back to my call and stood there, with lolling tongue and panting breath, waiting to be told where to go next. I had placed my guests against the beck and was working Merlin up the choked and tangled ditch that comes down from my northern boundary, hoping to drive birds back over their heads and to deal myself with any that rose and flew out of the sides.

217

I love watching Merlin at work in a jungle of gorse. I love the bustling sound of him as he thrusts through cover that you would swear was impenetrable. I love the sight of waving and shaking bushes, which indicates where he is busy and where you can expect a bird. I love to call him and watch the waving and the shaking move towards me as he answers my call.

He had not been busy for more than a minute when an old cock sprang up ahead of him and clattered away in defiance of my two shots. Then to one side a hen rose steeply and I missed her as well. A second hen rose and sped away and this one I shot. Several birds flushed wide of gunshot, but a cock went high over Phil and fell down dead. It was time for lunch now, pies and sandwiches, tea and a glass of port for those who wanted it. I was one of those who did, for the sun was almost warm as we sat down by the weir-gate, and the larches across the beck were bright. We had seen birds and we had sent many into the places where we would be going after our food. There was hope that we might redeem our poor performance of the morning. Port seemed a good idea.

I shall not describe the afternoon manoeuvres in detail. We finished the main bank of gorse, from which both Mick and Austin shot fine, high cocks. Several birds flushed and one or two were missed; more glided low with the wind and were left to fly on. Digger's turn came. He was confused by the presence of other people and other dogs and he would not move far from my side, but when I shot a hare in the Hag, and when he had retrieved it, he became more confident and began to quarter his ground with something like enthusiasm. The hedge along the Rise produced a last hen for me and made the bag for the day six pheasants and one hare.

The truth is that we shot badly. I fired eleven shots and killed three pheasants and the hare. My friends let off their guns almost as often as I did. Ten pheasants would have been a respectable performance. Half

218

a dozen was poor. But it was enjoyable in the sun and the dogs were a pleasure. And all day I felt a secret joy in the thought that I was shooting with friends on my own land. I looked at the Rise and knew that it must be planted, with oaks and ashes and hazels and rowans. I looked at the line of old birches, straggling along the fence between Well Close and the Hag. My mind's eye saw another fence, running parallel to the present one, and a long strip of conifers full of red squirrels and pheasants. I saw the gorse thinned out and burnt back and with wide swathes cut through it. I saw the little rides that will be made in Brogdens to let the light in and make it easier to drive. Oh there is so much to do and it will all be a delight and in ten years High Park will be the best small shoot in Cumbria.

We shot badly today. Next time we shall shoot well, and I shall not shoot birds that do not have long tails. For I must be honest with my diary; I must admit that one of the birds I shot today should have been left to fly again. It was the hen from the hedge; it was a poor bird with stunted tail feathers and I was not proud of myself as I stuffed it into my game bag. It was a fleeting chance and a passable shot, but even as I pulled the trigger I knew that it was not a worthy pheasant. And I know too that anywhere else the trigger would not have been pulled.

But at High Park I am too keen to make a bag, too eager to reach that point of the season when a fair percentage of birds has been shot and all the effort of August and September seems justified by a good harvest of birds. High Park is not a driven shoot. It produces some high birds but you cannot expect them all to be thirty or even twenty yards up in the sky. And there is challenge and beauty in crossing birds and climbing birds and in birds that spring from rough places when you are least expecting them. There is all the difference in sport between birds such as this and an immature bird shot merely because it has risen in front of your gun.

I was wrong to shoot that hen from the hedge. I have erred similarly once or twice before at High Park and it must not happen again. It does not matter to a pheasant whether it is shot with or without a tail; it matters enormously to the men who shoot them, for we must bring our sense of beauty and decency to fieldsports or they become unworthy activities. To shoot a chortling pheasant with a streaming tail is a fine thing; to kill a bird with a sad apology for a tail is a shabby and shameful act: not for a fox or for a weasel, but for a man. It is wrong for men to shoot pheasants with short tails; it is to start the harvest before the harvest is ripe. It is wrong and it is foolish and I am forty four and ought to know better. I do know better and from now on I shall act better and not be carried away by the urge to add just one more bird to the season's total, which at present stands, for High Park, at nine pheasants, one duck and one hare.

25 October

I went out to feed my pheasants this afternoon, in damp air and watery sunshine. The beck was full and clear and there were pheasants feeding quietly beneath the larches and the firs. There were little clumps of feathers in the fields, reminders of where yesterday's victims had fallen to the earth. It was very peaceful after the excitement of a shoot. It was a pleasure to heave buckets of grain from hopper to hopper, to sit and smoke and drink tea while a buzzard circled high and unhurriedly, while robins sang sadly and flocks of fieldfares flew noisily through the pale sky.

The Blessed Virgin has taken my land under her protection. I fixed her image to one of the larches today. And then I knelt and prayed the Hail Mary very slowly. It was for my aunt that I prayed it, for it was her bequest that made it possible for me to buy the larches and the land that goes with them. I shall say the Hail Mary whenever I fill the hopper that hangs in the larches beneath the image of God's mother.

28 October

Two days with nothing in particular to do, and it has been very enjoyable. I have taken the dogs out and observed how Digger is beginning to learn about the excitements of cover. I have shaken him once or twice, to remind him that questing stops just as soon as my whistle blows. I have smoked beneath trees while heavy showers beat upon the coloured remains of their leaves. In the sunshine between the downpours I have marvelled at the shining clarity of the light. And I have cleared out the back of the Land Rover in readiness for our first syndicate shoot at Wigglesworth tomorrow. It is now almost fit to receive humans as well as dogs.

Today, for some reason, I felt oppressed. I took the dogs to the woods and should have been delighted by the way Digger bounded into cover and then bounded out again in prompt response to the sound of my whistle. I was delighted, of course, but it was a superficial sort of delight and it had no power to displace or soften a deeper gloom. It was as though the sodden decay beneath the trees had infected me and would allow thought only along sorrowful lines. There are times when I wonder whether God has burdened me with an artistic temperament. Perhaps I should try my hand at poetry and heavy drinking.

Anyway the melancholy fit, having fallen, lifted in the afternoon. I was to have gone ferreting with Austin, but Austin is nursing a bad back and so I took the dogs out again and went off to feed one of my flight ponds. And the sky cleared and the sun came out and it was so beautiful that it would have been an impiety to feel other than grateful to be alive. There was the soft drifting of grey and white clouds, with slow patterns of shadow moving over the hills. There was faded grass and slanting light and a glowing harmony of colour from the trees. The Rawthey was full and shining darkly and, as I drove up the valley and looked, as usual, at the flowing water rather than at the road, I saw a huge scarlet salmon heave itself out of one of the river's little pools.

In the field where my duck pond lurks there was a charm of gold-finches making tinkling sounds among the dead thistle stalks; and there was the yellow flash of their wings as they flew away from me. Tupping time is beginning and already some of the sheep have painted rumps; and some farmers have better taste than others in their choice of colour.

The pond at Skennerskeugh, all but dry a fortnight past, was full again and feather-strewn and muddied from the recent paddling of fowl. I began to think of a flight in another ten days or so, and some-time next week I could shoot Low Park pond for the second time. Life was suddenly rich again and, as I drove back to Sedbergh, the silver light streaming over the Howgills was confirmation of the glory of existence. Thoughts of poetry and self-indulgence, which are somehow inextricable, were driven away by delight in the active life and the per-ception that a hangover would ruin it all. I would rather wake up, burst-ing with health, and step out to shoot a dozen pheasants than write a deathless and despairing sonnet with a splitting headache. It will be three whiskies tonight, not a bottleful.

I think my justification of fieldsports runs as follows. I also think that, in a page or two, my diary will have had enough of it, and so I shall keep it as short as possible:

a) It is very obvious that animals such as rabbits, birds such as pheasants, and fish such as trout are meant to live for a while and then to die. Enough of them are meant to live long enough to breed and ensure the survival of the species.

b) The death of rabbit or a pheasant or a trout is not a loss; it is a fruitful natural process, for it provides the weasel, the fox, the heron and man (to list just a few of the beneficiaries) with their means of life.

c) Men are different from other animals. Individual men matter in a way that individual animals do not. As men we should not transfer our very proper concern for individual men onto individual members of other species. Animals show no such concern for each other - except under the compulsion of instinct - and nature teaches us, over and over again and in a thousand different ways, that the individual animal does not matter.

d) To deny the edibility of a rabbit, a pheasant or a trout is a waste of nature, a denial of nature, a rejection of nature.

e) Part of the purpose of a rabbit, a pheasant or a trout is to sustain the lives of other creatures. It is right and proper for man to take part in the feast. In fact, refusing to do so devalues the part occupied by the rabbit, the pheasant and the trout in the scheme of things.

f) By hunting the rabbit, the pheasant and the trout, man acknowledges his (partial) mastery of nature, and his simultaneous dependence on nature. He also acknowledges the way nature is and at the same time celebrates her bountiful provision of his means of existence.

g) But man, when he enters the predatory processes of nature, must do so as a man, taking with him his moral and aesthetic awareness and his sense of reverence. He must impose his own standards on his hunting conduct, otherwise he will degrade himself.

h) Sports such as shooting and fishing are really tributes to the human spirit, for they show how man seeks to find and create beauty even while providing for his basic needs.

i) Fox-hunting is, in similar fashion, the transformation of need (the need to control foxes) into a stirring and beautiful ritual.

j) To shoot and to fish and to eat flesh and to hunt foxes are not

223

barbarous acts but a celebration of nature and of man's unique place in nature. Long may men continue to hunt and to shoot and to fish.

29 October

Down in the hollows of the land it is still autumn but, up on the slopes and ridges of the fields, the trees stand bare in the shapes of winter: rounded sycamore and airy beech and graceful ash.

It was our first shoot at Wigglesworth today and it was very pleasant. There was all the pleasure of meeting my fellow guns again, and of meeting beaters I last met in January, and dogs that I have been meeting at Wigglesworth for the last seven years. There was the slight tension of the draw, working out what number four at the first drive would mean down in the beck bottoms in the afternoon. There was all the pleasure of re-encountering the familiar, and there was the interest of wondering how the new season's little innovations will affect the progress of our sport over the next three months.

Of course you should never expect too much from the first pheasant shoot of the season. Birds rarely fly with real enthusiasm and so guns spend most of the day in a flutter of indecision, wondering whether or not to shoot at the pheasants flying over them and deciding most of the time that they will let them go. And because of this we almost always shoot badly, for it is already too late when at last we tell ourselves that the pheasant over the firs is high enough to be greeted with gunshot. He is past us before we have mounted properly and we miss him a yard behind.

Today was no exception. It was still and dank and misty. The pheasants were mostly unwilling to face the guns. They flew a yard or two into the sky and then turned round and flew back where they had come from. And the few that decided to fly on generally flew between rather than above us and were left to learn how to fly with less prudence and at a greater height.

In the poor quality of the shooting, too, today was no exception to most first days, and I was no exception to the performance of the guns around me. I fired thirteen shots and killed two pheasants and a woodcock. They are not very satisfactory, these first days, but they are necessary to stir the birds up. I think that we were perhaps a week too soon with our shoot today. My pheasants, at High Park, are much further on than these Wigglesworth birds.

But Merlin enjoyed himself well enough. I gave him a retrieve or two and he raced around looking for lost birds and managed to find most of them. He has developed into a fine peg-dog. I put a lead around his neck but I no longer tie him down.

31 October

Yesterday I fed the pheasants at High Park. Today I shot there again with Austin and Toy Winn. Toy lives in Sedbergh and he has retired. He knows more about foxes and fox-hunting than anyone I have ever come across. He is a man of firm views, especially concerning fox-hunting and foxes. He keeps ferrets. He has seven dogs, a horse, about sixty canaries and a glass eye. He is what is known as a character.

Strictly speaking we were too soon after our first shoot, especially so early in the season when the birds are only just ready for sport. But it was not greed that drove us to High Park with our guns. It was rather the fact that half-term ends tomorrow and so today was my last chance for a full day among my own pheasants until December comes along and brings the Christmas holidays.

It has been a fine day's shooting and I had most of it and shot well. It was a windy day with great sodden clouds sweeping through the sky and with brief bursts of heavy rain. But there was more sunshine than rainfall, pale yellow sunshine lying on wet grass and rotting drifts of black leaves, on faded and tangled briars and on brown and crumpled rushes.

To begin with I hunted the hedges of the flight-pond field. There were no lurking pheasants, but down by the water Digger - it was his turn first today - flushed something from the edge of the willows. I heard the sound behind me and turned to see a drake mallard heading down the field and already at long range. It fell to my shot and Digger waited until I told him to collect it. As yet he marks badly. He had seen the duck fall but he searched in every spot but the right one, until at last he stumbled upon his retrieve and brought it in to me.

Blackberry Hill was a disaster. Digger suddenly surrendered to the excitements of the hunt and became stone-deaf to both voice and whistle. I saw him occasionally in the middle of a bramble bush. I even managed to grab him once or twice and I shook him and shouted at him. Then he dashed off again and left me brooding on the ruin of another gun dog. There were only two or three pheasants flushed and none of them inspired a shot. Digger pegged one up against the fence, a cock bird which I knocked on the head gloomily, cursing myself for a fool and the worst of dog-trainers.

At least I had enough sense to return Digger to the Land Rover, bringing Merlin into the field more than an hour sooner than I had intended. And at least I now know that Digger is not ready for the temptations of heavy cover. It will be hedge bottoms and ditches and open fields for him this season, not banks of tangled briars and brambles where I cannot follow him when he does wrong. It is good, I suppose, that Digger has at last realised that he is a springer spaniel, but I cannot help wishing that the revelation had come to him more gradually. It was so sudden that he was unable to cope with it.

Merlin and Toy's Bracken worked the meadow end of the gorse

together. There was nothing there except for a rabbit or two, one of which offered me a fleeting chance and ran on unharmed. I was beginning to feel despondent, beginning to fear that the day would pass with few pheasants seen and few or none shot. The hedge along the Rise soon changed my mood.

In the past we have always worked it from east to west, heading away from the pen. We have done it this way because this was the way we did it first and I have never thought to do it any other way. But today a sudden inspiration came to me. Perhaps it was the wind in my face that told me I should drive my pheasants back home with its assistance. It may have been the wind. It was a very good idea.

Austin and Toy walked along either side of the hedge, while their dogs sniffed and pushed through the cover. I kept about ten yards ahead of them all, advancing with gun at the ready along the bottom of the Rise. Three birds came out of the hedge, three cocks; they all came fast over me and they all fell to the first barrel. They were three good shots. Merlin bounded out to collect the fallen and I was suddenly happy. The day was no longer a failure.

I brought out the port again at lunch and poured it into flask tops. And then I spent the afternoon trying to put birds over Toy and Austin, but for the most part I could flush them only for my own gun. I shot two hens from the top ground above the wood and Merlin pegged his first bird of the season. I missed two from the long ditch that climbs up from the beck. I did put one over Toy here and he shot it gracefully. It was a high bird and it flung back its neck and fell to earth. Another bird rocketed over my guests from the patches of gorse on the north side of the wood. It was too fast and too high for them.

And that was it for the day and, except that I failed to provide much sport for Toy and Austin, it was a good day. And I know that Austin and Toy are happy just to be out with their dogs and are not too bothered about letting off their guns every other minute. The bag was eight pheasants and a mallard, which is about right for High Park, although it would have been better if two of the pheasants had not been pegged by my dogs. I always tell myself that pegged birds make up for ungathered birds. Anyway they go in the game book, and how they got in the bag is honestly recorded.

Sporting days are made by moments. One bird often makes the day: a cock pheasant flying high in the sunlight and crumpling to the sound of your shot: a mallard far above you in the twilight, folding its wings and falling to earth with a thump. Today was made by five minutes along the Rise, by the three cocks that came over me with fast wings and by the three shots that rang out to kill them. And I remember how the earth was so sodden that, as each bird fell, it raised a spray of water into the damp air. Half term is over now and I shall leave my pheasants unharassed for at least a fortnight.

5 November

I went to High Park this afternoon, an afternoon that was the quintessence of November, with near mist and heavy, damp air, with trees dripping slowly onto musty drifts of dead leaves, with fieldfares in the hawthorns and robins singing quietly in the wet woods. The beck was full and brown and I got wet feet crossing it. The slopes of the land were sodden and treacherous and I went up and down them with much slipping and slithering and cursing. Now is the time of year when I wonder why, in dry and early September, it seemed a good idea to hang hoppers way beyond the reach of the Land Rover and ten minutes sliding toil from the bins by the weir-gate. But they are there now, and popular with my pheasants, and I must continue to fill them. Perhaps a fortnight today will be the day for my next shoot.

This evening I waited for duck by Low Park pond. I sat on a bucket beneath a hawthorn, with a screen of reeds in front of me. The dark came early but few mallard came with it. I had expected many

228

more and had told myself that I must not shoot more than half a dozen. In the event I fired three shots and Merlin gathered two drakes for me. It was disappointing, but it was peaceful sitting beneath the hawthorn, waiting and smoking as the grey evening deepened to night. The problem, I fancy, with Low Park pond is that I cannot feed it often enough. I shall wait at least a month, I shall feed it at least twice a week and then on the two successive nights before my next vigil under the hawthorn.

I left the pond before full darkness. It was back to Sedbergh and the house bonfire, where I lit some fireworks with childish delight and said a prayer for the repose of Guy Fawkes' soul. Then there was beer in the pub and a whisky in my chair and then it was time for bed.

13 November

A week of diligent schoolmastering without an entry in the diary, a week of incessant rain. I went to High Park on Tuesday and fed my pheasants in the rain. Every afternoon the dogs have run briefly through the dripping woods around Sedbergh. From my classroom I have watched sheets of rain sweeping over the land and drenching the already saturated earth. I have gone to bed with rain beating relentlessly upon the window and woken to another wet morning. In every field of the valley there are standing pools of water; every day the water encroaches a few more inches upon the land. Rivers are brimful and ready to burst.

It has rained all today, and there has been rain of every sort: at times a white mist of drizzle, at other times grey curtains of rain sweeping and curling in the wind. There have been times when the wind has dropped, there have been places sheltered from the wind; at such times and in such places the rain has fallen in a steady and vertical downpour. At High Park the meadow is full of pools and there are streams gushing down the Rise. Every ditch is flooded or flowing and the bare earth beneath every hopper has turned into a swamp. Every step is an ooze or a squelch, every second step a slide or a slither. I lost my footing in the sike and sat down in the stream. But I was already so wet that it made no difference.

I enjoyed myself this afternoon in spite of the rain. For some reason I was feeling unusually vigorous. And there were pheasants in plenty wherever I went, springing from the hedge and flying away with strong wings and long tails, feeding under the hoppers that hang among the firs and the larches, scurrying away from me as I approached the pen. It was this that delighted me, and also the grim beauty of the sodden and faded scene around me, for, as the light thickened, a sort of lowering grandeur gathered beneath the cloud, with the green of the sloping gorse and the climbing purple of the birches deepening towards night. And the bare trees, swaying against the sky and creaking in the wind, seemed full of a sturdy and intricate vitality.

Winter trees, especially birches and beeches, make patterns with their branches that are infinitely varied and beautiful. Just look at a dead tree, at a blasted oak or an eaten elm, and see how it points a few broken fingers at the sky, and how the symmetry of the living tree has been shattered into gaunt and twisted and unrelated shapes. Then turn your eyes to healthy branches, admire their mazing complexity and the deeper sense of order in it all, and acknowledge the life and vigour that wave against the grey background of a winter sky.

15 November

It rained most of yesterday as well, but the cloud broke up with the darkness and the rising moon and, when I took the dogs out at ten o'clock, the sky was full of windy silver and torn clouds and racing shadows. And there was the sound of heaving and creaking branches, with the swaying outline of bare trees. It is time for winter weather, for cold skies and frozen ground and great red suns sinking beneath the hard earth. There was the first hint of it today. There was an edge to the wind, there was a rawness on the air and there was a sting to the lashing showers that raced out of the north and caught me as I ran the dogs and fed the pond at Skennerskeugh. I felt young today. Yesterday I felt about 94.

17 November

Out to High Park to work Digger around the margins of the shoot, a sort of second boundary day, with a warm wind and sagging clouds, with damp air but nothing that could be called rain.

One or two pheasants ran away from us, but we flushed nothing that flew, except for a woodcock which took flight from the rushes of the Hag and fell to my second barrel. Just occasionally you come upon them in the open and are surprised by their ghostly rising and silent flight. They are made to haunt shadowed places, to flit and to jink between trunks and branches. They are very beautiful and they gaze at you in death with reproachful eyes.

Digger was better today, but there is still a tendency for him to lose concentration or to forget the whistle when he is roused by scent. He is much keener to work now. I think today's sort of excursion is what he needs this season, days with just the occasional thrilling moment as a taste of future delights, days when he is unlikely to lose his head completely, training days with no more than a minute or two of the real thing.

231

19 November

High Park again, this time with Austin and Simon Knowles in serious pursuit of pheasants. I have not time to record it properly, for tomorrow I have a fives championship to run, and the weather is so damp and so warm that I fear the courts will sweat and be unusable. And I shall have to apologise to friends who have come all the way from London, saying that play is impossible and that they might as well get in their cars and drive all the way home again. You accept, with cricket, that rain might wreck all your pleasure. But, in the case of a game played on a covered court, it seems inappropriate that the weather should be able to interfere and spoil things. At the moment the walls are dry - I shall go and look at them again in half an hour - but the floors are slippery with condensation. Unless it turns colder overnight my championship will have to be abandoned. It is only its second year and, if it is called off tomorrow, I do not suppose it will ever happen again.

This afternoon, at any rate, was a success. The sky blessed us with fleeting patches of blue; pheasants flew with purpose and, even from Blackberry Hill, some of them flew where they were meant to fly, which is high over the beck and over the hedge and into the gorse. Simon was waiting for them and shot two from three, while I shot the one bird that came to me as I stood at a new spot towards and below the pen. It was a fast hen, crossing and rising, and I was pleased to see it fall. Simon's birds were both cocks. One of them had the sharp dark spurs of an old bird, but the younger bird, with paler and much shorter and still blunt spurs, had tail feathers every inch as long. Cock pheasants are resplendent creatures; but I think I prefer the subtler beauties of the hen; a well-grown hen pheasant is a picture of subdued elegance.

Simon is a good shot, as boys often are. Old men are often the best of all, port-soaked, arthritic old men with huge bellies and five days a week to go shooting. They look as though a barn-door would be beyond their competence, and then, with a marvellous economy of movement, they raise their guns at a high pheasant and a moment later there is a dead pheasant lying on the earth.

There were eight pheasants shot today, eight pheasants and a rabbit. Simon had most of the shooting, though Austin killed a fast cock from the Rise. Merlin helped himself to a pheasant in the gorse, but he brought in a runner of mine when I was sure it would never be found.

Shot and ungathered game is a trouble to the true shooter's conscience. It does not stop him going shooting, but he hates to leave wounded birds in his coverts at the end of the afternoon. There were two occasions today when I thought we should search in vain. There was my runner in the wood, for Merlin came back to me twice with nothing in his mouth; and then suddenly a change came over him; he began to hunt with a new purpose; he hurtled down the wood and very soon he was back with my bird.

Half an hour earlier we had given up on a pheasant that had collapsed from the sky like a dead bird. Simon had shot it and it fell on the edge of the beck. Merlin and Austin's Meg sniffed along the banks and plunged into the water and disappeared into the blackthorn thicket, but they did not come back with a bird. We wandered downstream in the hope that it had fallen in the water and would be found lodged against a rock or resting in an eddy or caught between lying branches. But there was no sign and, though we ran the dogs all over Blackberry Hill, they returned with nothing to show for it.

I called off the search and we moved on, but there was that feeling of dissatisfaction that always comes to me with a lost bird. And I have to confess that I feel it the more at High Park, where the bag is counted in twos and threes rather than in twenties and thirties. It is, of course, the wrong way of looking at it, but it is there nevertheless.

At the end of the day we came back to the beck and tried again for a few minutes with no success. But then, as we walked down the edge of the water and passed the Douglas firs, in a slack eddy against the far bank, I spotted a brown shape that looked like a floating bird. Merlin splashed round wildly and swam straight past it. But, a few seconds later, he swam straight into it and brought it to hand. It was a deeply satisfying moment. It made the day complete.

I am well pleased with the progress of the season at High Park. The bag stands at 25 pheasants, four duck and one each of rabbit, hare and woodcock. In a fortnight or three weeks I shall allow myself the pleasure of shooting my best ground with only my dog for company. Meanwhile I have just been to look at the fives courts. The floors are damp and gleaming. A misty warm drizzle has set in. Unless the weather changes, unless the sky clears and the wind springs up and the morning brings brightness and cooler air, my competition is doomed and will, by ten o'clock tomorrow, be as dead as the four pheasants hanging in my bathroom.

21 November

When I got out of bed yesterday, I felt hungover and like crying. I shaved in a sullen gloom; I climbed into the Land Rover and drove resentfully to the courts, scowling at the mist hanging low over the fells, staring hopelessly through the grey drizzle that hung and drifted on the warm air. I was reconciled to the impossibility of playing fives and to the unpleasant duty of telling those who had come so far that there was nothing to keep them in Sedbergh and that they might as well go home.

I am still convinced that it was a miracle. It must have been Our Lady of the Larches; for the courts, though damp, were just playable and, by lunchtime, the cloud had cleared and the air had sharpened and all four courts were completely dry. Fives was played in high good humour and, by some, to a high standard. Everyone seemed to enjoy himself and insisted that he would be back next year. And, although I have not emerged as the Winchester Fives Northern Doubles champion, I have once again realised that I love the game. I love the obscurity of it; I love the spirit in which it is played; I relish the satisfaction of my occasional good shots and the taste of beer at the end of a day full of friendship and vigorous activity. Yesterday I loved it all twice as much as usual because I had been convinced that it would not happen.

There were pheasants everywhere at High Park this afternoon, and there was mild sunshine from wide lakes of blue sky, lying almost diffidently on the land, gleaming on the smooth trunks of bare trees. I just managed to fill the hoppers before darkness came down. It will be a whole week before I can fill them again.

27 November

Friends for supper last night. I managed to put edible food in front of them, the last trout from September and the first pheasants of another winter. I drank the correct amount of alcohol: two sherries (dry oloroso), one glass of Sancerre (too light to follow such full-flavoured sherry and not suitable for trout anyway), three glasses of Cotes du Rhone Villages '89 (very good indeed but a little too young) and two glasses of whisky (the Dalwhinnie, nothing wrong with it). It is a lot for a single evening but it is a permissible indulgence from time to time; spread out over four or five hours it does not end in drunkenness, nor does it bring a hangover and self-hatred the next morning. I do not feel that it is a sin.

I went flighting this evening and never fired a shot. Skennerskeugh has been disappointing this season. I have fed it often enough, but the fowl have not come with the darkness. It was pleasant sitting by the wall with Merlin tense and expectant beside me. The sky had cleared and the sunset was red-rimmed. A few mallard hurried past, but none came in. I heard the sound of high and distant wings, but never the near rhythm of duck circling round and down to the grey water below me. On the very edge of darkness a teal whirred in behind me and departed unseen. Then I trudged back through the fields and made my way home.

1 December

Brushing my teeth this morning I realised that so many of them are now so loose that I cannot hope to chew meat with them for much longer. Perhaps, when they have all fallen out of my gums, or been torn from them by my dentist, I should disdain plastic imitations and confront the world, and my pupils, with a proud but toothless mouth, glorying in decrepitude. And it would serve as an admonition to careless youth, warning them that, if they neglect their toothbrushes and their dental floss, they may well, within three decades, look little different from their Latin master.

But today I was untroubled by the rattling proof of decay. There was a pied and dappled sky and a soft silver light coming out of it, gleaming on the greenish and the greyish trunks of the trees and lying very gently over the fields. The air was cool and kind. As soon as I had breathed in the first tonic lungful of it, I knew that I was in a rare good humour. It has lasted throughout the day.

All morning I felt unusually well disposed towards the boys who sat in front of me. It seemed a privilege to be teaching them and they seemed untypically attentive to my efforts at instruction. At lunchtime Austin picked me up and we drove up Dentdale to a friend's farm. On the way we lost the silver sunshine and came into a greyer world, with misty hills and heavier light. But the shape of bare trees was still a deep delight to a man who, in spite of looming toothlessness, was full of gratitude for the gift of life and the prospect of spending the next little part of it with a dog and a few friends and the hope of a duck or two.

It felt raw when we started walking the top fields in search of snipe. There is a pond up on the boundary; it is a reed-fringed pond and it is on the wrong side of the wall. But a shot in the air puts on the wing whatever is resting there and sometimes in the past they have come over us. Sometimes it has been snipe - I remember a wisp of at least a hundred some years past - more often it has been mallard, and it was mallard today, just two of them, and they flew straight over me. They were high, fast birds and I was so surprised to see the first of them fall that I forgot to fire at the second.

Then we walked a long rushy pasture for snipe and there were none there. But a hare sprang up in front of me. I shot it dead and knew immediately who would cook it for me and when it would be eaten. It will be eaten next Friday, to celebrate the end of term, and we shall drink Chateauneuf du Pape between mouthfuls.

We walked another field or two, but the air was thickening to fog and the light was fading fast. It was time to head off to my friend's flight pond and the intimate dampness of its rushy hollow, there to wait quietly until the edge of darkness brought the sound of wings and brief shapes of duck above us in the sky.

I love the slow minutes before flight, lying there as the crows flap past and shout at each other, wondering to myself how many birds will come in and whether there will be teal among the mallard, and how well or how badly I shall shoot, listening to the little noises of the wind in the rushes, to the sighing of Merlin beside me and to the chacking of fieldfares as they hurry past, dipping and rising through the dim light. And then the scraping of invisible snipe begins, and then the first duck decide that the moment has come.

Mallard flighted first tonight, whistling in low between us and settling without a shot. But something disturbed them and they took flight. I missed a fleeting chance. But immediately there was another bird high above me; for once I remembered to move my finger onto the second trigger. I also pulled the trigger at the right moment and there was a dark shape tumbling through the sky with a spaniel whimpering and whining in his impatience to retrieve. Merlin makes no noise at a peg. He sits there with perfect composure and waits for the drive to end.

By a duck pond he is different. The beating of wings calls forth heavy breathing. The splash of settling duck turns it to a breathy whistle and to urgent gasps. He greets the thump of a fallen bird with every suppressed and excited sound he can muster. Thank God he never barks and, as long as there is a lead round his neck, he never moves until I remove it and whisper my command. And duck-flighting will never be the same again, when Merlin is no longer there to deliver his commentary on the progress of the evening's sport. I know that gun dogs are not meant to make a sound, but Merlin's noises have become part of the pleasure of sitting by a pond and waiting for duck.

The light this evening was as bad as it could be. It was thick and misty and the murk was soon impenetrable. Teal came and went in packs of unguessed number. I never saw one of them, but I heard the rush and whisper of their wings and then the splash of water as they settled on the pond. It was very frustrating, for there were many duck coming in and there was the wild piping of wigeon somewhere up there in the sky. Just before we finished I saw a form above me, a mallard-like form, and shot in desperate haste. But the form seemed to fly on and Merlin found nothing except for the duck I knew was dead. There were few shots from my friends and we collected only three mallard. On Saturday I am at Wigglesworth for a syndicate day.

3 December

There was a wild and racing sky this morning, and the hurrying clouds looked laden with wetness. There were torn, dark clouds; swelling over the horizon there were thick blocks and banks of paler cloud that looked wetter still. The wind was loud in the bare trees. The fir plantings heaved and roared and the rain was relentless. I almost wished that I was not shooting.

We did the duck pond first, with the guns lining the wall and the beaters trying to drive fowl over us from the other side. Half a dozen mallard rose and swept away on the swift air. And then the sky was suddenly full of wind-tossed duck, soaring and then stooping involuntarily, diving down the sky and then flaring up again. They were mostly teal, with a few wigeon among them. There were many shots, many of them at birds out of range. Three teal and a wigeon fell and my barrels remained clean.

The first pheasant drive was Pipers, a small planting of spruce and fir on a rise of the land. Sometimes it produces birds in quantity. Today it produced a single hen, flying defiantly over the gun next to me and missed by him with both barrels. I had expected a good show of birds, for on so wet a morning I had expected pheasants to be in the woods, whence the dogs would bustle them into the sky. Perhaps they were so soaked that they refused to fly, but the beaters reported that there had seemed to be few birds in the wood.

We moved to Bradley Moor, a thick and untidy wood on the edge of the shoot. Foxes like it just as much as do pheasants. It is also our best woodcock covert, though none showed today. By now the rain was torrential, driving into my face and my glasses. There was no longer any variety or pattern to the sky; it was a single sheet of grey, pouring water onto the earth. Even Merlin, with streaming ears and dripping nose, looked disconsolate. The guns on either side of me looked thoroughly miserable.

239

But there was no shortage of pheasants. The wind was howling down the wood; birds rose ahead of the beaters and rushed with the wind. They were not very high but they were very fast indeed. Only one came my way and I was glad to see him fall. Then it was on to Hammerton, one of our main woods. It seemed likely that there would be the two Hammerton drives, followed by lunch in the *Plough* and cancellation of the afternoon's sport.

There is a ride down the middle of the wood; the more open half is driven uphill in the hope that birds will rise and turn and fly high over the ride to the temporary safety of the cover beyond. Often this plan works. Today it worked as well as I have ever known it work: not in the quantity of birds that flew, although there were pheasants for all the four guns in the ride, but in their height and speed, in the challenge of their flight and the crumpling beauty of their fall.

Sometimes it happens that difficult birds inspire good shooting from average guns. It was so today. Two cocks rushed over me; both of them threw back their heads and crashed down through the trees. I watched the gun above me kill three or four birds in quick succession, and more pheasants were falling to unseen shooters further up the ride. They rose right at the top of the wood; they climbed onto the wind, then turned on it and came shouting down the sky. It was a wonderful sight and, somewhere in the middle of it, the rain stopped. At the end of the drive, as I followed Merlin into the field below the wood in search of some fallen birds, I noticed a pale ribbon of blue on the edge of the sky, a ribbon which soon widened and spread out of the west, ousting the grey clouds and pouring racing silver light down onto the wet fields and onto the white limestone outcrops of the surrounding hills.

I had a poor peg for the second Hammerton drive: number three on the outside of the wood. It is the back guns in the ride that get the best of the shooting here. One moderate bird came my way and I missed him handsomely. And then it was time for lunch, with no gloomy thoughts of abandoned sport, but with the bright prospect of sunshine in the afternoon and the best drives still to come.

Lunch for me on a shooting day at Wigglesworth is two bottles of Guinness and a bowl of soup. One of the beaters began to mock all my talk of the quality of the morning's sport. There were no high birds at Wigglesworth, he said; if I wanted to see pheasants that deserved to be called high, I should go with him to some of the places where he had beaten or shot and I would never again talk of high birds at Wigglesworth. He was speaking to provoke me, in a friendly sort of way. He was speaking to prick my false pride in two or three good shots. He did not provoke me, for he was speaking the plain truth.

I have missed pheasants in Northumberland that were ten yards higher than this morning's birds at Hammerton. I missed them and had no idea how to hit them, or why one or two of them fell out of the sky above my gun. They were birds on the very edge of range, specialist birds calling for specialist shooters who spend day after day tackling the highest of driven pheasants.

By the standards of the best shoots, Hammerton pheasants are not exceptionally high. Down by the beck the afternoon drives produce birds that would excite admiration anywhere. But Hammerton birds are about 25 yards off the ground, which makes them, with a strong wind up their tails, worthy targets for the generality of pheasant shooters. And I am convinced that the most selective of shots would not have disdained to raise his gun at the pheasants that rose from the top of the wood this morning and caught the wind and streamed chortling over the ride. And I have seen my disparaging beater miss pheasant after pheasant at some of our lesser Wigglesworth drives. Anyway Wigglesworth pheasants are quite difficult enough for me.

Most autumns there appear in the newspapers articles by journalists who know nothing about country sports and yet think it appropriate to write about pheasant shooting as the season for shooting pheasants gets under way. They dwell on the rearing of thousands and thousands of birds for slaughter by rich men in tweed suits, and the usual implication is that only a fool could want to waste his time waving a gun at hordes of obese pheasants that do not want to fly, and that only a much bigger fool, having once raised his gun, could fail to hit and kill them.

Such articles irritate me, because I think writers should take the trouble to learn a little about the subjects on which they write; and they also irritate me because they make ignorant fun of a sport that I enjoy. Shooting pheasants is a skill. It is by no means the most difficult skill in the world. Playing the violin, for example, is an altogether more demanding accomplishment. But it is still true to say that the pleasure of shooting pheasants derives in part from the fact that they are very easy to miss. I should have liked one of those condescending journalists to be standing next to me in the line today. I should have watched him miss everything that came his way and I should have roared with delight and demanded an immediate palinode.

He would certainly have missed the birds that I did *not* miss during the first drive of the afternoon, for these were high birds by the highest standards. I was number five, down in the beck bottom by the edge of the water. Beyond the road, which you are facing as you stand at number five peg and wait for the sound of the horn, a covert climbs a steep slope to the old pen that gives the drive its name. The beaters work across and up. The pheasants run ahead of them until at last they take to the wing and catch the wind. They flap their wings once or twice and then glide high over the road, heading towards the wood that rises on the far side of the beck.

For the guns down in the beck it is everything a pheasant drive should be. The birds are almost invariably high and there is little

242

time to see them and they are often very fast. If you are down by the beck at Old Pen Drive, you will not hit pheasants unless you are on form. There have been times when bird after bird has flapped or glided over me and I have greeted every one of them with two hurried, incompetent and despairing bangs. And then I have climbed the slippery bank to the road, wondering whether I shall ever manage to hit a pheasant again.

There are steep slopes on either side of you as you stand waiting down by the beck. It is a sheltered spot and today there were midges dancing above the water. I took my coat off and looked at the tree tops waving far above me, and they told me, with their swaying and their creaking, that the wind had not abated and that the pheasants would be fast. Down by the beck I always wait for the first birds with just a hint of nervousness. There have been times in past seasons when I have prayed that none will come anywhere near me.

This afternoon I caught the sound of the horn through the splashing of the beck and thought that in four or five minutes I could expect pheasants above me. I considered lighting my pipe again but, even before I could feel for my matches, a cock was floating silently above me. I swept my gun through the sky and he fell dead in the dense firs behind me. A hen followed and she fell too. I missed a cock, I killed two crossing hens, I was way behind a third cock and, when the horn boomed out its command for shooting to stop, I felt very pleased with myself. Merlin was sent to retrieve the slain and was soon back with them. We climbed onto the road with our birds and I tried to grin modestly, thinking to myself that it is the silence and the suddenness of the birds that makes shooting down by the beck so exciting and that makes it so rewarding when they fall.

We did the New Pen Drive next and the wind sent the birds over the far end of the line. I was number seven and shot once only, and unsuccessfully, at a hen crossing behind me. The Point was left for next week and we finished with the Plough Drive, where I found myself in the ride. I fired three times and killed three pheasants. They were not very high birds but they were fast and fleeting chances and I was pleased rather than ashamed at having shot them. I was also pleased that in the course of the day I had fired fifteen shots and killed ten pheasants.

Austin beats at Wigglesworth and he drove me home. We talked of the day's sport and of our dogs and of this and that. Then I lay in the bath, and blessed the headmaster (may he live until he is a hundred) for allowing me to miss Saturday morning school. I will not need his permission next Saturday. The end of term is only six days away. Next Saturday I shall shoot at Wigglesworth as a free man. And I rather think that my diary will not, in its record of subsequent Wigglesworth days, need to record my feats with a gun at every drive. I shot well today and I have written at such length out of conceit, so that my diary will know how fine a shooter is writing it. It will make less tedious reading when its author shoots badly.

6 December

On Sunday I went to Scarborough to play fives, returning to Sedbergh two minutes before the pub closed. Yesterday I spent the day in bed, feeling old and lonely and ill. It was not 'flu that laid me on my back. It was some ill humour of the body that came and soon went. Friends dealt with my dogs. I locked the door and dozed fitfully while the radio droned in my inattentive ear. I rose at four o'clock and gazed at my face in the bathroom mirror and was disgusted by what I saw, so lined and drawn and haggard was the image returning my stare. Then I drank tea and wrote some reports and felt much better.

8 December

After an absence of ten days I dashed out to High Park this afternoon. Most of the hoppers were empty. There was only time to fill them half full, for there was a staff meeting at four. But the end of term is now so near that I can put up with any form of inanity. In less than two days it will all be over for a month, and the many pleasures of winter days will be there for me to enjoy without anything to get in the way.

10 December

I was late to bed, after sherry and Chateauneuf du Pape (wonderful but too young) and a glass or two of the Famous Grouse. These, and the hare I shot last week, gave fitting recognition to the end of term. I was tired at seven this morning, but there was no feeling of shame and excess to poison the thought of freedom and the prospect of a day's shooting. I was a happy man.

I should have been happier still if the weather had been more kind. It was raining, of course, and there was that sullen and unrelenting look to the sky that told me it was going to rain all day long. It was barely light when I set off at eight o'clock: just a gloomy greyness seeping out of the cloud. I drove to Wigglesworth along half-flooded roads and past fields full of lakes.

At Wigglesworth itself I was greeted by a frenzy of rain, lashing against the windscreen and bouncing off the bonnet of the Land Rover. Guns and beaters were sitting grimly in their vehicles, refusing to move. We knew that we should have to start eventually, but we hoped that it need not happen just yet. And I hoped against hope that the rain would stop and that I should be granted a day's shooting under the sun, under a pale winter sun with a keen wind blowing and with bright air between the bare branches, and without the necessity of wearing leggings or waterproof over-trousers.

245

The waterproofs went on, of course, and at last we set off. The rain stopped at Pipers, but only maliciously, to inspire false hope. For the wind rose and turned into a gale and roared exultantly in the bending firs, and, at Bradley Moor, the rain came in again with a lashing ferocity and was almost unbearable. I turned my back on it, and on any pheasants that might come my way, and the sound of the horn rang out like a deliverance, calling me back to the shelter of my Land Rover.

And then the rain did stop, just as it did last Saturday. The rain stopped and the wind howled on. It grabbed pheasants and hurled them through the sky; it made them its playthings; it juggled with them; it tossed them high and then flung them almost to the earth. It was too wild a wind to distribute birds evenly over the line, but if you were lucky enough to be in the right place, you had pheasants above and around you that were hugging the ground one moment and soaring out of range the next, that came and went again before you had thought of lifting your gun. They were wonderful to watch and they were wildly unpredictable. I missed two birds on the corner at Hammerton. They swept round the edge of the wood, rising and curling, and a third was so quick that I never even fired at it. All three of them were snatched from the wild air by the gun two pegs below me.

All day the wind raged. It was one of those days when the wind is so passionate, so assertive that it seems the sole force of nature. It was a megalomaniac wind, driven to frenzy by the sound and the speed and the strength of itself. It was a raving wind. On the second drive of the afternoon four pheasants came rushing helplessly past me. They were low birds but they were as sporting as pheasants three or four times their height. They were past me as soon as I had seen them and, as I fired at them behind, they rose and dipped and rocked from side to side. I was very happy to see two of them fall.

SUDDEN RUSH

Last week we left the Point, a long finger of trees that follows the beck away from the main body of the plantation, with a group of old pines rising above the water at its far end. The guns line the field on the low side of the wood, with one of us on the Point itself, another round the corner and a third left as a back gun where the drive begins. The wind today was howling down from the Point. The old pines were roaring and the tangled covert was full of pheasants. They rose and hurtled down the middle of the wood. I remember one flapping its wings and climbing almost vertically through the sky, higher, I think, than any pheasant I have ever seen, until it acknowledged the horizontal rush of the wind and sped off, far, far above us, like a purposeful and contemptuous leaf.

Most of the pheasants swept down the wood to trouble the back gun. But some broke from the Point, flying low beneath the wind until they turned and came down the line, rising and curling all the time, high and fast and very difficult birds. Two such came to me. The first was a hen, crossing back into the wood. She seemed more an embodiment of the wind than a flying bird; or she was its emblem or its familiar or its highest of high priestesses. She came over me and I raised my gun. A wilder gust caught her, as though to sweep her to safety beyond the puny reach of the weapons of earthbound men. But that wild gust inspired a wild response from my barrels. They swung after their prey in desperate pursuit. They discharged their load of shot and, a hundred yards away from me, a hen pheasant crashed to the earth.

She was the highest and fastest bird I have ever shot. I could not believe that she had fallen and, at the end of the drive, I was not happy until I was quite certain that she had been gathered. I know why I managed to kill her; it was her sudden acceleration as she came over me. What should have saved her worked her downfall, for it made me swing. I gave her no conscious lead - I never give birds lead - but that fatal burst of speed forced me to swing with her through the sky and so I shot her dead. Seconds afterwards a cock flew high over me and flew on. I missed him because he was flying at an even pace and my swing never accelerated to catch up with him. If he had made a sudden rush then I might have shot him as well. From now on I must imagine that every high pheasant to which I raise my gun decides to fly faster just as I decide to pull the trigger. And then I shall never miss one again and I shall grow bored with shooting and join the RSPB. I should join it anyway.

The last drive was the Plough. I shot four more pheasants and drove home in a good mood. It was the wind that made today's sport, the wind and its transforming influence on the flight of pheasants.

11 December

To High Park to fill hoppers left only half full on Friday. I have now used 83 bags of corn and there is no sign as yet that the hoppers are being emptied less quickly. I am shooting my ground with Phil and Austin tomorrow. I should like to kill ten pheasants, but I think we shall be lucky if we get half that number.

12 December

We did not get half way to ten. We got three pheasants and a wood-cock, but the day was fine and we enjoyed ourselves. The poor bag was partly the result of indifferent shooting, but we have also reached that interesting stage of the season when pheasants have developed a degree of cunning and have learned that it is wise to scuttle off at the first sign of man or dog. There are still plenty of birds at High Park. But they are no longer easy to flush. They much prefer running along ditches, or back and forth between patches of gorse, to taking flight and thus exposing themselves to the danger of gunshot.

I spent long parts of the day wondering to myself why it is so much more difficult to write about shooting than fishing. I never grow weary of writing up days that had been spent by rivers. Even blank days seem filled with incident. And it is not because I love shooting much less than fishing that I find it correspondingly less easy to remember a day spent shooting at High Park or at Wigglesworth with an enlivening interest. If forced to a choice between the two sports, I know that I should abandon my guns and cling on to my fishing rods, but the life that followed would feel impoverished; even riverside pleasures would be clouded by the sad knowledge that there were no pheasants waiting to bring delight in their own season.

Perhaps there is more obvious variety in a fishing day: and the flies that, together with the trout, make up the stuff of our sport, are a topic of endless fascination. And a river, I suppose, possesses more personality than a pheasant covert. There are, as part of the essence of a fishing day, periods of repose, which breed thoughts and impressions that rise above their sporting context. Men with guns are less inclined to rumination. And the quickening spring sun, the ripening summer sun and the lingering autumn sun shine upon fishing days, and the river flows through them on its way from source to sea. There is, about fishing, a variety of mood, a pattern of alternate activity and contemplation, a symbolic suggestiveness that does not belong to shooting. Men sit by rivers and think of mortality. Put them on the edge of a wood and give them a shotgun and you will find that for a time they renounce profound reflection upon the human condition.

The woodcock today was mine, the woodcock and a hen pheasant. Phil and Austin had a pheasant apiece.

14 December

I took Digger round the edges of my shoot this afternoon. There was pale sunshine beneath a blue sky and there was a light breeze. He flushed a cock from flight-pond field and I shot it. He brought it to me from the gorse bush where it had fallen. A second cock rose from a patch of rushes in the Hag. This one I missed.

We finished the day at Skennerskeugh. Two duck came in and I killed one of them. Digger rushed out to collect it but refused to take it in his mouth. He will need practice at retrieving fowl. I remember that Merlin was just the same with his first mallard or two, but cold birds soon set him right and now he is as happy with duck as he is with pheasants. I am not worried by Digger's present aversion for dead ducks; it is a sign of youth and inexperience. Indeed I was pleased by his performance today. He seems to be learning that my whistle means stop or turn round and come back, even when his head is full of the excitements of scent.

To continue with my thoughts of two days ago, there are few great shooting books. There are not as many great fishing books as is sometimes thought, but there are perhaps half a dozen that, quite apart from curiosity value and specialist or historical interest, possess a permanent literary worth. Plunket Greene has written one, so has Lord Grey, and so have Negley Farson and John Waller Hills. Arthur Ransome has left us a collection of articles that are a constant delight and, long before any of these writers, Isaac Walton wrote a book which a few of us still read.

Other fishers, if they read my list of great fishing authors, will turn purple with rage because I have forgotten to praise their favourite author as far and away the greatest of all. But how many shooting books, how many shooting writers, have aspired beyond the practical, the episodic, the entertaining? There is Jefferies and there is T.H. White, although shooting is never their central theme.

250

I am not sure there is anyone else. I read shooting books, but this is because I am interested in shooting. There are fishing books that give delight to those who have never held a fishing rod in their hands. Fishing becomes symbol and metaphor in a way that shooting does not; it grows out of itself and becomes a standard of values, an approach to living, a pilgrimage in search of peace. There is some magic in fishing, some alchemy that can touch the written record of it and make it live.

18 December

On Friday I shot at Troutsdale near Scarborough. It was a day of winter sunshine and high birds, indisputably high birds and fast ones too. They were a fine sight, breaking from cover and soaring over the guns. Often there were two shots and a pheasant still flying on its way. Less frequently a bird shuddered in the sky and then fell to earth. They were very beautiful in both flight and fall.

I shot badly in the morning, but things went better in the afternoon and I finished with six pheasants for 28 cartridges. Given the challenge of the birds it was almost a respectable performance, and what pleased me was that I managed to improve. Even a few years ago a poor beginning to a day's shooting invariably meant that I hit nothing all day and went home sunk in gloom. The bag for the day was 61 pheasants, seven mallard and a rabbit. Merlin had a lean time of things, for his birds had generally been picked before he started looking for them. A black labrador coming into season provided a welcome diversion from the tedium of under-employment.

Yesterday was another Wigglesworth day and I shall make short work of it. I shall record a few facts and figures and leave it at that. The bag was 53 and one teal. The birds flew well and again I shot below my best. In the morning I fired five cartridges to no effect. Merlin found a runner abandoned by the gun who had shot it. In the afternoon eight shots of mine killed five birds and once again I was relieved that a poor start did not inspire complete incompetence.

There is no driven shooting for me now until after Christmas. I shall harry the pheasants of High Park one day this week and I may go flighting. But I shall concentrate on my dogs and drink a contemplative pleasure from the sight of the winter landscape. It will be a quiet week, full of quiet delights and, at some stage of it, I shall fulfil a promise that was made at the beginning of October and draw some conclusions from the course of this season's fishing. They may be hard to find at such a distance.

20 December

A very gentle winter's day. There was frost overnight, not the sort that takes a hard grip on the earth: the sort rather that brushes the fields white and then dissolves in the morning sunshine. It had gone long before noon, when I reached High Park and trudged happily up the wet fields. It was a bright day, with thin sunshine lying over the earth in watery greens and yellows. It was a day to look at the gleaming brown bark of hazels and the softer brown of beckside willows, a day to admire the dark flush of bare hawthorns and leafless birches and the deep, tough green of holly in the hedges, scattered with red berries, deepened by the contrast of the grey and warty trunk.

I was very contented, tramping up the steep banks with buckets of corn, upending an emptied bucket and sitting on it for a few mouthfuls of tobacco, watching my pheasants scuttling away or strutting slowly beneath the trees like posturing ballet dancers. I decided to shoot them with Austin on Thursday. I said the Hail Mary before her image in the larches. I fed Low Park Pond, where the film of ice over the water was so thin that it was pierced by the impact of scattered grain. There were many duck feathers along the margins of the pond.

252

Everything I saw filled me with a profound sense of gratitude. Each breathing in of air was a restoration of the spirit; it was like inhaling grace. The shouting of jackdaws and the whistling of starlings were both a delight, as too the silent, unhurried departure of a heron from the pond. There are flashes of water in the meadow and there were duck feathers around their edges. Here too I scattered corn, for if the water holds there may be the chance of an evening mallard in a week or so.

I looked at the larches and the dark firs and blessed the memory of the man who planted them. I looked closely at branches along the hedge and saw the new buds there, waiting for the spring. I thought how lovely the black catkins of birches and alders were in the gentle light. Everything was lovely, everything beneath the pale sky and the floating grey clouds. Tomorrow I shall be 45 and I do not give a fig. They come to me in my middle age, these days, these moments when simply to be alive is a sufficient blessing, when the thought that death is smiling to himself and biding his time loses any power to disturb my peace.

21 December

There was a hard frost last night, not just a transient decoration but a biting frost that still has the earth in its grip. There is nothing but blue in the sky, a deep and intense blue; only along the horizon is it softened and blended with silver. Crows and magpies are busy around the feet of cattle. The air is sharp and Digger's breath steamed as I ran him through the woods round Cartmel an hour ago.

Under the trees there was the constant dripping of rime melting in the canopy. Where the sun reached through the branches to the woodland floor, rotting timber exhaled plumes of white vapour. There was no sound of birds, only the dripping of water and the crunch of my feet and the crashing of the dog through the matted undergrowth.

Digger will face any cover now and he is beginning to work with speed and determination. There is not Merlin's strength in the way he pushes through thick cover, there is not the same contempt for whatever tries to bar his progress. There is a frantic, prancing eagerness, with a wild look to his eyes and the corners of his mouth. He still gets stuck from time to time.

It was Digger's turn this morning, Merlin's this afternoon. He drove and thrust and burrowed his way through the undergrowth. There was nothing for him to flush but he did not seem to care. Shadows came early to the woods. Mist rose and curled off the dark water of the beck and cold began to creep out of the earth.

The sun has set now, with no crimson display. It went down in a sky the colour of ice and, as I sit processing words (it used to be called writing) by the fire, there is a grey and silver half-light lingering over the bay. It is freezing fast and the pheasants of High Park will be glad of the hoppers that I have so generously hung for them all over my land. I have a feeling that tomorrow will be a good day with the gun.

22 December

The frost bit deeper last night and the hoar was very thick this morning and grey in the sharp air. Gateways, so recently squelching mires, are now rutted and hard. The flashes I fed the other day are gleaming sheets of ice and I did not bother to look at Low Park Pond.

Toy, James and Austin were with me and we did Blackberry Hill first. I stood below the pen, admiring the frosted and shadowed scene and the windless calm of it all, waiting for the first pheasants to break. But none flew. A rabbit came loping up the bank. I shot once and thought that I had missed and told myself that I had never been any good with ground game. But Toy's Bracken picked it at the end of the drive and this cheered me up. The lack of pheasants had been a disappointment.

254

A WHISKY DAY

I thought that it must be the sun, that my birds had flapped down from roost, taken their breakfast at my hoppers and then decided that it was just the morning for a long walk. I think that I was probably right. I think my pheasants went exploring today, along hedges and ditches, and that, by the time we started shooting, most of them were already off my ground. There was a bird here and there. I missed a long crosser that came over the wood from the vicinity of the pen. Austin had a bird from the rough ground above the wood. Merlin flushed a cock from the gorse and I shot it. As it took to the wing for the last time it shone in the sun.

It was warm down by the weir-gate, as we ate our sandwiches. There was no breath of wind and we were facing the sun. The dogs lay steaming and panting at our feet and I persuaded everyone that, even though we were warm at the moment, the day around us was cold enough for a generous dram. It was not port weather. Rather it was a whisky day, for the frost was still thick out of the sun on Blackberry Hill and the ground was still hard. One of the pleasures of my shoot is that we take lunch under the sky, sitting with our backs to the hedge and with the beck making noises not twenty yards away. It is much better, except in a downpour, than going indoors and eating too much and feeling almost unwilling to start again.

After the first whisky there were no refills. I am a masterful shooting host and we set to work again. But though we worked our dogs through Brogdens and through the rest of the gorse, we did not put up a single pheasant until Merlin dived into a solitary bush on the edge of the wood. No sooner had he plunged in than a cock flew out, then faltered and flinched with the impact of Toy's shot. I saw him fall, but it had been way back in the wood and I knew that he would be a strong runner and thought that we should get after him.

Merlin set off. Bracken and Meg set off, all three questing with eager haste. Once or twice I thought that Merlin had found the line, for

255

his nose went down and his tail began flapping more wildly. But soon he was back, standing and gazing at me with nothing in his mouth. Suddenly Bracken charged off and was lost to sight and returned with a winged cock pheasant. I was delighted and Toy was delighted and even Bracken looked inordinately pleased with himself. It is such incidents that make a shooting day.

There was still enough light for the Hag, and James shot a hare. Only a few seconds later a cock took flight and rose steeply. Toy's shot rang out and it fell like a stone. It was a beautiful sight: the pheasant climbing up the sky and transfigured by the sun, and then that split second second of stillness and the sudden fall. And the sound of the shot boomed and echoed through the afternoon. It made four pheasants, a hare and a rabbit for the day and I found that I had enjoyed myself in spite of the scarcity of birds. As I drove home strokes and brushes and thin banks of western cloud flushed pink, while the rim of the sky shone with a light that was white and blue and silver at the same time, a light welling up from behind the frozen hills and unwilling to die.

This evening I checked my records for High Park, expecting to discover that, at this stage of the season last year, perhaps half a dozen more birds had been shot. In fact I found that last year I shot with James on my birthday and that between us we killed six pheasants, making 34 for the season. After today's sport this season's bag stands at 33 pheasants, and this season there have also been four mallard, two woodcock, two hares and two rabbits. Last year we shot nothing but pheasants, not even a bunny. We may still get fifty this season. All that is needed is a day or two when we find the birds at home. But if no pheasant is shot between now and the end of January, it will all have been worthwhile and I shall do it all again next year.

24 December

This morning the earth was wrapped in a warm, wet mist as though brooding a mystery. It seemed a miserable day from the wrong side of a window, but almost all days are better once you are out in them, and today was no exception. The air at High Park was mild and grey, the breeze was damp and gentle, the fields were soft beneath a melting crust of frost. But only the edges of the flight pond were water rather than ice.

In honour of the season I knelt before the Virgin of the Larches and intoned the *Memorare*, and then I pottered round doling out Christmas rations for my pheasants. I saw very few of them: one or two near the pen, two or three in the wood, odd ones here and there. I should have liked to see many more, but I remember last year thinking that they had walked out on me and then finding a week later that they had thought better of it and returned to their old haunts.

Digger went feeding with me. I had thought we might hunt a few hedges and work a few rushy fields but we did not. We went home for Christmas instead. The pheasants of High Park need peace and quiet for a few days, and next week is a busy time with the gun. There is a duck flight on Boxing Day; on Thursday an afternoon walking fields and another evening by a duck pond. On Friday I may have an hour on the edges of High Park and Saturday brings driven sport at Wigglesworth. I may take Digger there and see what he makes of it.

25 December

Mass at Flookburgh. The priest had protruding teeth and a voice like an asthmatic owl. The carols were dirges rather than celebrations. But it did not matter. After breakfast I took Digger to the woods. He flushed a rabbit and was inclined to chase it, but the whistle stopped him and I was very pleased. The morning was damp and I was seized all at once by an intense longing for spring days: not for the warm sort, rather for the chilly and vigorous sort when the buds have yet to unfold and the wind blows with a message of change.

I went out with the dogs again in the afternoon, with ragged clouds in the sky and shadows chasing each other over the fields. The becks were full and grey, the land soft and muddy. The last influence of frost has melted away. For a few seconds a wren sang very quietly.

26 December

There are few days that have nothing to recommend them, but this, I think, was one. I can remember a worse Boxing Day, about six years ago, when it rained with unremitting malevolence and I tramped squelching fields in search of snipe with Austin and a few friends. Eventually we acknowledged that there was no pleasure in it and went home. There have been some fine Boxing Days since then. Last year was such a one, spent at High Park with Austin and our dogs. The bag was seven pheasants, all cocks and all shot by Austin or pegged by Merlin. I missed one bird, right at the end of the day, and it did not matter because Austin killed it for me. And all day the sun shone. There have been other fine Boxing Days, hunting our dogs in rough places and shooting the occasional pheasant or duck, beating coverts and flushing birds for others to shoot, gulping down the winter air gratefully and thanking God for the blessings of an active day under the sky.

Today was a rare Boxing Day in that I was not out shooting before dusk. The wind was roaring, the clouds were racing and the rain lashed my face. It was the sort of weather on which true wildfowlers dote. But I am not a true wildfowler with a passion for wind and stormy weather and coastal gutters in which to enjoy them. Tonight was one of the few nights when I would rather not have been sitting by a pond waiting for

258

duck to flight. I could see almost nothing, because my glasses misted over and ran with water however diligently I kept wiping them. Duck came in, perhaps twenty of them, but I was aware of none over me and Merlin did not whistle or whine once. I sat there with the rain pelting down and the wind was so loud in the pines behind me that I feared for my safety and felt ashamed of my fear.

The sound of gunfire failed for once to excite me. I thought of spring and the first trout of the year and began wishing my time away, most of all the next hour. Torches flashed at last and flight was over. I almost ran across the fields to the Land Rover, thankful that the misery of it all was now in the past. Now it is time for conviviality. Tomorrow's sport has been cancelled and I think that I am glad.

28 December

A spate of birthdays: mine a week ago, then God's, and yesterday my father's eightieth birthday, duly celebrated with champagne and the presence of his family. I felt less festive than I ought to have felt. I could not help looking at him and thinking how old and worn he seemed; I could not help thinking how unlikely it was that he would be sitting in his chair a year later and celebrating his 81st birthday; nor could I resist telling myself that his children, of whom I am the youngest, will soon themselves be weak and feeble creatures on the edge of eternity.

Meanwhile nothing but wind and rain. I, who usually love winter, am already sick of it and praying for it to end. Cold weather brings colour to cheeks and the touch of cold air invigorates. We stamp our feet and rub our hands and stride out cheerfully over the hard earth. And the coming of darkness welcomes us back to warmth, where there is food and firelight and where whisky stirs memories of seasons past, while in the world beyond the window stars shine brightly in the frosty night.

This endless wetness saps strength and lowers spirits and makes me think of death. The shooting still has more than a month to run, but I am wanting spring and the sense of renewal that belongs to it. There have been times in the past when I should have liked winter to be prolonged indefinitely, when I should gladly have postponed spring for at least six months. But now one dreary day succeeds another, breeding weariness and depression. There is not the bracing challenge of hard weather, but the interminable moaning of the wind, the ceaseless beating of the rain and the endless tedium of grey skies. For the first time in my life I feel that it might be sensible to flee for a few days to a place where the sun shines.

30 December

To High Park today with Merlin and my gun. The wind blew hard and the rain fell heavily. I shot the one pheasant at which I fired, but birds were unwilling to flush and when Merlin pegged his second I called it a day. One is permissible, but two, I decided, was one too many, although it was not altogether Merlin's fault. I was watching on both occasions and Merlin's victims were pheasants that refused to move. They just squatted and waited for him to pick them up. And, as I crept up Blackberry Hill with the dog at heel, before a shot had been fired or a pheasant pegged, I saw at least half a dozen birds scuttling under the fence to safety. Mine is not a driven shoot, but I shall have to stop the top corner of Blackberry Hill or there will be few birds shot from it in January.

I thought of names as I drove home. Blackberry Hill will not do. It sounds like an outer London suburb. Pheasant Hill might survive as Pheasant Hill, but the two sides of Brogdens need separate names to distinguish them and the several banks of gorse deserve more precise and memorable recognition of their individuality. I shall review the whole question of names and settle it before the end of the season.

31 December

Snow came this morning at Wigglesworth and transformed everything but my shooting. One of the things I like best about snow is the contrast it makes with flowing water, for between the mantled white banks streams run almost black; and there is also the silence of snow and its quiet gathering on the green needles of fir and pine. And falling snow blurs the distinction between earth and sky; it is as though the two are coming together, as though the clouds are fluttering down in tiny particles, painting the air and the land their own colour and spreading over the grass a white carpet of cloud. And the white patches of panting spaniels seem yellow against the startling purity of fresh snow. And snow is the emblem of winter and the ornament of winter sports; to be out in it is at the same time a novelty and a delight.

To be honest there was not very much of it today. It fell heavily during the first drive and stuck to my coat and my gloves as well as to the grass. Thereafter there were only a few flurries and the fields lost their cover of whiteness and turned pale grey and very slippery.

I shot badly today and shall turn my incompetence to account by making it the basis of a lecture on the relative difficulty of the various sorts of driven pheasant. It is always the duffer who is addicted to theorising and who thinks that his friends are impatient to benefit from the results of his analysis. Good golfers play golf; bad golfers investigate the mysteries of grip and swing and then hurry to the nearest clubhouse to spread the good tidings of their revolutionary insights.

Now most shooters think of high pheasants as the most difficult birds to kill. This is only true of high pheasants that are very high indeed, or of highish pheasants that present the shooter with challenges other than that of their distance from the ground. Most high pheasants are between twenty and thirty yards high and such a bird, flying straight towards a waiting gun, should present few problems. I shot such a bird today and I knew, even as I raised my gun, that he would fall. It looks impressive and elegant when this happens and, at the end of the drive, you are always complimented by the guns who were next to you. But in truth it is not very difficult. No, the bird crossing wide and fast (whatever its height), the bird crossing and curling as it flies, the bird dropping down the air as it speeds towards you: these and the genuinely high birds more than 35 yards above you are the difficult birds to bring to earth.

There was a stand today where I fired at four birds and missed the lot of them. I was in a field at the bottom of a steep bank, beyond which I could see the waving treetops of the plantation where the beaters were busy with their dogs. To my left, and on a level with me, was a second cover, into which most of the flushed birds would fly, but I could expect a few to break from the top corner of the high planting and fly straight and fast over me. On several days in the past I have enjoyed myself at this stand, missing some birds but killing others in the approved fashion as they flew purposefully over my head.

Today the four birds that came my way were nearer the ground than I have seen them here before. They did not rise on the wind and soar; they slipped under the wind and seemed almost like grouse as they flew towards me. Of course they were not as low as driven grouse; they were probably fifteen yards up when they went past, but they were dropping throughout their approach; they seemed to be diving towards me and I was mesmerised by them. It was impossible to judge their line or their speed or to swing with their flight.

Two of them came right over me; two turned into fast and dipping crossers; I fired two despairing shots at all four of them and none of them fell. They were much more difficult than the high bird that I had shot at the previous drive. They inspired indecision; they demanded calculation. I think the straight birds should have been taken early, whereas I dithered and then shot behind, for the approach of these dropping birds is deceptive in its speed; they are on you and over you before you have realised that they are gone. I think that, with the crossing birds, I should have waited and watched and then punched my barrels through their line and pulled the trigger. But the problem was that it was only the last second of their advance that told me whether they were straight or crossing birds.

Today I fired sixteen cartridges and killed three pheasants. Those I missed were not all artful and deceiving birds. The truth is that at the moment I am off form, and that form is one of the great mysteries of sport. Perhaps on Monday my form will have returned and every pheasant to which I raise my gun will fall dead. And perhaps on Monday there will be a sharp frost and a blue sky and the taste of sloe gin will be welcome as it only truly is when the breath of those who drink it steams on the cold air.

3 January

On New Year's Eve I was asleep by ten o'clock. It is the only night of the year when I go to bed before midnight. I am a convivial man and I doubtless drink more than I should. I certainly drink twice as much as government guidelines recommend. But so, doubtless, do the advisors who draw up their ridiculous guidelines. I find all this talk of units of alcohol depressing beyond words. It suggests that there is no beauty waiting to be discovered in a bottle of wine, that a pint of beer contains no pleasure except for the mild narcosis that is just one of its gifts, that the warming glow of the whisky you have just drunk is somehow equivalent to a bottle of *grand cru* red burgundy or half a gallon of draught Bass. It angers me that a glass of fine claret, a creation of soil and sun and grape and the loving skill of man, should be lumped together with an alcoholically commensurate amount of Babycham or cherry brandy and regarded with unaesthetic suspicion as a unit of consumption. It also angers me that you are only allowed three of them.

I am a convivial man, but New Year's Eve is too much for me. On New Year's Eve drunkenness turns into a form of secular piety. On New Year's Eve I turn into a misanthropist.

Lying in bed this morning at eight o'clock I thanked God that the New Year was past and that it was a shooting day, a back-end day among my pheasants at High Park. There is great delight in these back-end days, with wily birds that prefer almost anything to flight and yet fly strongly if only they can be persuaded onto the wing. There is also the special flavour that attends things drawing to a close. Gathering blackberries as the summer fades around you, autumn trout fishing as the leaves fall: such activities derive a particular and related pleasure from the air of ending that accompanies them. And so it is with January pheasants. You know that it will soon be over and that you will have to wait more than half a year before you can hunt your dogs through the gorse and the brambles again.

As I lay in bed and savoured the prospect of a back-end day, I heard on the radio that the Shap road and the road over Hartside were both closed because of ice. And so I set off for Brough in good time and drove slowly on my way. There was snow from Saturday's falls lying hard and frozen on the roads, but the journey to High Park was safely made and for once I was there before Austin and Toy. It was a cold morning and I found that I had rediscovered my taste for winter. There were barred clouds with streaks of blue between them and a pale light slanting down from the sky. The ground was hard as iron and standing water had turned into treacherous sheets of grey ice. There was snow in all the fields, a thin cover of white with tufts of yellow grass and brown rushes sticking out of it. Two of my neighbours had seized the opportunity offered by frozen ground and were mucking their fields, so that the heavy smell of rotting manure drifted on the cold breeze and, with its message of moist and warm and fertile decay, seemed out of spirit with the pure, chilly air and with the frozen, unreceptive earth. Toy and Austin turned up and James came out to join us with his cousin, Christopher.

It was a day for the naming of places and it was a good day's sport. We did Blackberry Hill first and I stood on the far side of the larches, hating the name, while Austin crept up to the top of the fence in the hope of stopping birds running over the boundary, while Toy worked Bracken from the firs and across the steep slope. I stood there and thought of calling it Our Lady's and knew that it could not be so. When Austin judged the time right he came down the bank. Birds were trapped between his dog and Toy's and they were forced to take flight. Two broke for the gorse. One or two flew high over the firs. A hen came to me and it was shot. And, as Merlin dashed off to pick it, Blackberry Hill became Beck Bank. It is a good name, a plain and descriptive name. Our Lady will approve.

Toy had not brought his gun. He wanted only to be out with his dog. Austin and he now went beyond the pen and worked their dogs back towards us. As we stood waiting, the sky cleared and the sun shone more brightly. The snow turned a purer and more brilliant white and the birches on Pheasant Hill glowed purple. I decided that Pheasant Hill would serve very well. It is Mr. G.'s name and it will be his gift to my land. The place where we were standing, James and Christopher and I, lined up along the beck between the slopes of Pheasant Hill and the rising bank of gorse behind us: this suddenly became Beck Bottom, and Beck Bottom it will remain. I was working all this out when a hen broke fast over the tall trees in front of me and collapsed into the gorse behind.

It was to the gorse we went next. Apart from my dead bird, no pheasants came out of it. But the ditch turned into the Gutter and the meadow gorse became Whinbank. They are not great names, they are not names full of music or poetry. They are simple and serviceable names. In time I shall come to love them. I have called the hedge above my meadow several names. It has been the meadow-hedge, the hedge above the meadow, the hedge along the rise. Now, together with the rough slope beneath it, it is just the Rise. Two cock pheasants broke from the Rise this morning; one was shot by Austin, the other by Christopher.

The sun stayed out for lunch by the weir-gate and Austin brought out the port. Toy borrowed my matches and set fire to a gorse bush on Whinbank, just to prove how easy it is and to show me how to set about thinning out my cover once the season is past. It was good sitting there and talking, while the sun shone and the snow shone and the bare brown larches quivered in the breeze. And the dogs sat at our feet, pleading mutely for morsels of food. All three were rewarded for their morning's work. Merlin was so happy that he rolled and rubbed himself in the snow.

The afternoon began very quietly. Above Brogdens, running along my southern boundary from its eastern limit to the pen, is a strip of rough open land, choked with rushes and brambles. Sometimes there are pheasants lurking there. This afternoon there were none, and I could not decide whether this narrow strip, empty of birds today, should be called the Top Ground or the South Side. I may already have called it the top ground in this diary. I have certainly thought of it as such. But South Side seemed briefly attractive, until suddenly it seemed more appropriate for a district of New York. And it *is* my top ground, high above the meadow and the wood and the pen, high and wild and neglected. I took away the definite article; two small letters became capitals and Top Ground was duly given its name.

There followed half an hour when I forgot all about names. For

Austin reported that there were pheasants skulking in the wood on the north side of the beck. He and Christopher and James positioned themselves as standing guns, while Toy and I trekked off to the eastern boundary, in the hope of flushing birds back over our friends. Toy worked Bracken through the hazels and birches that climb up from the beck. Merlin plunged in and out of the wide patches of gorse that grow on the edges of the trees. Two or three birds broke back over the gunless Toy. Two more, long crossers, came just in range of my barrels, but neither of them fell. Four or five went down the beck, fast and high, but none of them were killed. Then Merlin bustled a hen from the far end of the gorse and my shot brought it down. A cock flushed the next moment and James killed it. Merlin had the cock within a minute and we went searching for my hen.

Meg and Merlin and Bracken hunted the wooded slope, rushing down to the water and leaping over the beck, nosing excitedly in every hole and matted hollow and in every heap of rotting branches. But they hunted in vain and I began to feel despondent. Christopher said that my bird had come down near an ivy-choked birch and, even as he spoke, he struck the tree and a hen pheasant came tumbling out of it. Its wing was broken but it dashed off uphill and the dogs dashed off in disordered pursuit. We waited for one of them to return with a hen pheasant, but they all came back with empty mouths. So now we put them into the gorse and shouted 'High lost' and wondered where on earth my bird had gone. For it had trailed one wing as it fled; very clearly it could not fly, and it was puzzling that, with a clear sight of their prey, our dogs, all three of them with good noses, had failed to find.

Austin suggested that it was tucked up somewhere in the top of a gorse bush, as far from the ground and from questing dogs as possible. I decided to give Merlin one last chance and motioned him back into cover. Very soon there was the sound of him engaged with a pheasant, a sound of grunts and fluttering wings and excited snorts. It is a sound that I usually greet with irritation, for usually it is telling me that my dog has pegged another bird. But on this occasion it was a sound of hope. There was some anxiety as I called Merlin back to me and waited, for he might emerge with an unshot cock between his jaws. But I need not have worried. It was a hen, a hen with a broken wing and, except for the removal of its tail feathers, Merlin had not damaged it. There was much patting and praising, for such moments, when a long search, almost abandoned, at last brings its prize, when resignation turns into sudden elation - such moments make you almost glad that you did not kill your bird cleanly in the first place.

The last half hour had taught me much. I had learned how to deal with what I have always called the Patches, the less extensive stands of gorse east of Whinbank and the Gutter. I had learned that it needed a dog working forward down in the trees below them, while a second dog, this one a spaniel, hunted the patches themselves. This way there could be no escape for pheasants; if they fled from the gorse they would meet Bracken (or Meg or Holly), whereas if they ran up into its shelter, they would encounter my Merlin and take flight from his unfriendly attentions.

It might be wise to put a gun on the eastern boundary for birds that break back. It wants clearings in the trees so that guns can be positioned along the line of the beck. It wants a name and it already has one. The patches of gorse and the wooded slope beneath them running down to the beck are now grouped together and known as North Bank. By next season a ride will have been cut through the trees on North Bank, so that Toy, or whoever is down there, can work his dog and carry his gun and not find his progress impeded by fallen timber and leaning branches and the tangled confusion of years of neglect. And this, together with the clearings for standing guns, will make North Bank one of the prime features of my little shoot.

We left North Bank now, with Brogdens rising to the south of the beck, with Top Ground above it. We walked though Beck Bottom, with Pheasant Hill to our left and the Gutter on our right. It was past Whinbank and through the weir gate; it was down the meadow, with the Rise and Beck Bank on either side, then up to the farmyard and the end of another day at High Park. Six pheasants made 42 since my boundary day in October, which made 50 by the end of January seem an attainable target; and already, as happens on back-end days, my mind was beginning to look beyond the end of this season and to look forward to the beginning of the next.

As I drove home in the last light, Mallerstang Edge and Wild Boar Fell, both deep in snow, turned blue. They seemed pale ghosts of mountains rather than substantial things of rough earth and hard rock. And even as I gazed at them they faded into the darkness and were lost to view. Merlin was snoring loudly in the back of the Land Rover.

4 January

Last night the wind turned westerly and today the snow has gone away. We are back to drab and faded colours, to damp air and creaking, bending trees. I went in the woods with Digger and Merlin and listened for birds. Occasionally a tit squeaked somewhere in the branches, but there was nothing else except for a few thin notes from a robin. Dunnocks are said to sing all year. I have not heard one for months. But they will soon be singing songs again and soon mistle thrushes will be shouting from high branches and telling us, when winter still seems to have months to run, that the spring of the year is drawing on fast. In ten weeks I shall be fishing for trout again.

But a few sharp days have changed my view of the season. I am happy with winter and am no longer looking forward to putting my gun away. I enjoyed yesterday so much that I should like to feel there were three or four such days waiting for me and my friends in the next few weeks. But term is near and now there will only be time for a few snatched visits on full afternoons; and then it will be time for hedging and fencing, and time to start trapping crows.

6 January

I went to High park this afternoon, filled a few hoppers and wandered round my fields and woods, wondering how they will look in another ten years. I followed the beck up to my eastern boundary, stooping low under leaning branches and clambering over fallen trees. It should not be too difficult to clear a path along the bottom of North Bank and there are several spots where felling only a few birches or hazels will create a clearing for a gun to stand next season and test his skill against pheasants crossing high from Brogdens or flying fast down the line of the sike. I should explain that my beck is really a sike. Maps call it Powbrand Sike and I must start calling it the sike myself. It is a Scottish word, apparently, deriving from old Icelandic, and somehow it sets my beck apart from other small streams that are not called sikes.

Brogdens, together with North Bank, should be enclosed to keep the sheep out; then they should be opened up to the light, in order that grass and flowers, briars and brambles might spring up between the trees, to welcome pheasants and to look lovely under the sun. At present this is a dream beyond my pocket, but some day it will come true. Meanwhile I have less ambitious plans and they are plans that I can afford.

Austin will thin the gorse for me in February and cut rides through it and make it easier to drive. Then he will fence off the Rise and it will be planted this year or the next. This year too will bring the new fence below the line of the boundary between Well Close and the Hag. I can see, in years to come, a dark line of firs rising against my northern horizon, with pheasants shouting there beneath the trees, while oaks and ashes wave their young branches on the slopes of the Rise, while birds build nests and lay eggs and feed fledglings in the thick cover of a well-laid hedge.

The joy of having my own patch of Cumbria is only now becoming clear to me. At first there was the simple pride of possession, the joy of looking at things and telling them that they belonged to me. I have stroked birch-bark this summer because it is my bark; I have stretched myself out in the grass and felt the earth warmer beneath me because it is my earth. This season the shooting of every pheasant at High Park has been a delight to me: because they have flushed from my land, my rushes, my trees. I have loved welcoming friends to what is now truly my shoot. And I loved yesterday's naming, feeling that these names of mine somehow stamped my possession more firmly upon my land. But now there come the deeper pleasures of ownership, pleasures of planting and cherishing and renewal and creation.

I make my ambitions and my motivation sound grander than they really are. I want to plant a few trees, to clear some unproductive cover, to foster a little growth. I want to leave some memorials of my ownership behind me. It will be very expensive and every pound of it will have been well spent.

6 January

I felt it today for the first time: the feeling that the season has turned, that winter is at last in retreat. It came to me from the bright sunshine and the shimmer of it and the way it lay so tenderly over the fields; it came from the longer and the stronger light and the damp warmth of noon; it came from snowdrops pushing up through the soft earth and from the fresh green of their shoots, from closed but yellow catkins clustering along the brown branches of hazels in the hedge. O! there will be frost and snow yet and there will be torrents of rain. But, when the sun shines, it will shine from now on with a power to stir and with new promise and with a message of change.

7 January

A dank and grey day at Wigglesworth, with drooping clouds and drifting mist and ceaseless drizzle. I enjoyed myself enormously, for I shot well and, as my diary knows, I savour back-end days in pursuit of pheasants. They have an atmosphere all of their own. The birds fly well, even in calm and damp conditions such as we saw today. There are many fewer pheasants than there were a month ago, and so you cannot make a hash of things with the first five that come over you and then redeem yourself with the next half dozen.

You must take your chances or your rewards will be small. And already the guns are beginning to talk about next season: whether they will be in or out of the shoot, whether such-and-such a wood is worth what the farmer demands for it, whether kale should be planted on this bank or that, who on earth is going to help the keeper with the poults in July. And the beaters are beginning to look forward to their chance of killing a bird or two, beginning to ask us to go easy and to save a few pheasants for the day when it will be their turn to shoot. Some of the dogs have grown steadier in the course of the season, more have become headstrong and disobedient, one or two of them are perhaps coming to the end of their active service in the coverts and will not be seen again next year. There is the sense of a campaign drawing to a close, the feeling that, all things considered, it has gone pretty well, and already there are plans to make it go even better the next time.

By lunch time I had fired one unproductive shot. But I had stood by the wall above the duck pond and, gazing into its chinks and

272

crevices, I had seen the rusty cap and the mildewed remains of an ancient paper cartridge. I had wondered who had fired it and whether he was still alive, whether he had been poaching with his dog as the night fell or crouching there in the grey light of a January morning as his companions drove the pond. I tried to draw the old cartridge from its sanctuary, but the paper came away silently and the cap fell further into the secret cavities of the wall. There must be tons and tons of metal, attached to paper or to plastic cartridges, lodged in holes and little chambers near the top of dry-stone walls. They are always near the top, because we can never be bothered to bend down to dispose of our used cartridges. And there are too many shooters who cannot be bothered to bend down to pick them from the ground.

I spent the first pheasant drive watching drops form and fall from the tip of a hazel branch. A few rabbits lolloped ahead of the beaters and Merlin whimpered once or twice in his longing to be after them. It was at Bradley Moor that I fired my one shot. I raised my gun a second time there, but soon lowered it and watched the slow and silent wing-beats of a disgruntled brown owl. At lunch the bag was seven pheasants and a woodcock. We talked about next season and whether it would be reasonable to ask one of our farmers not to fell trees on a pheasant day. It is one of the little excitements of shooting at Wigglesworth that you are never quite sure that the woods you leave one Saturday will still be there the next. The heart has been cut from Hammerton in the last month. There is a muddy wilderness where lately there were tall trees, and the pen stands open to the sky. It is, I suppose, unprincipled of its owner to take rent for a pheasant covert and then to set about destroying it half-way through the season.

The woods above the beck were all there in the afternoon. The birds flew well, but where a week ago twenty pheasants flushed, now it was five or six. I fired eleven cartridges and shot six birds and was confirmed in my opinion that straightforward high birds, birds between twenty and thirty yards high, birds right over your head or just slightly to one side, are not difficult birds to kill. The day's bag was 31 pheasants, one woodcock and one guinea-fowl. There are two shoots left, with the beaters' day between them. We should end up with about 45 per cent of the number released, while at High Park I am edging towards 50 pheasants and 40 per cent of the young birds put to wood in August. It would be good to shoot 50 and equal last year's bag. It would be better to shoot 51 and establish a record. But what does it matter? We have had richly rewarding days at High Park, and I have enjoyed feeding my pheasants just as much as shooting them.

10 January

Yesterday was the first day of term. It found me less depressed than such days often find me. All day it blew a gale and all day long the rain poured down, so that my classroom seemed a warm and comfortable place. And my fourth-form Greek set could still decline third declension nouns, which heartened me. And the dogs behaved in the woods and the beer at the end of the evening was very good indeed.

12 January

There were two herons standing in a field as I drove on my way to High Park this afternoon. They were like old men in grey coats, sad old men with hunched backs and heads sunk into their shoulders; and they faced away from each other as though they had nothing to say, as though to avoid the embarrassment of silence. They just stood there looking cold and aimless and lonely. Round the next corner there was a kestrel hovering with purposeful vigilance.

Broken Wing

It had been a cold morning and bright, but the sky was already greying by noon and the air began to soften even as I walked up the fields to Beck Bank. It was completely still. The sunshine had turned hazy. The sun itself was a blurred and pearly opalescence half-way down the sky. Shadows were pale and indistinct. It was a very quiet afternoon and I was very happy to have no company but Merlin and to have two hours to myself to hunt with him for January pheasants.

Beck Bank, Top Ground, North Bank, the Gutter, Whinbank and the Rise. We made a circuit of my land and I began to wonder if there are perhaps too many banks on it. But already my names are too dear to me for any change to be seriously considered. Merlin hunted with relish and I shot with incompetence.

There were more pheasants than I had expected. I missed one on Beck Bank, although Merlin found a pricked bird from a previous shoot. I missed another on Top Ground, a cock that rose in fury from a patch of brambles and clattered away over the wood. Deprived of his retrieve Merlin sat where he had flushed the bird and gazed at me with contempt.

I shot a hen, yes, I shot one, from the gorse on North Bank, but then a straight bird was too quick for me and, in the Gutter, I shot over a fast and dipping cock. Seven shots and one dead bird: a wretched performance, breeding a sense of failure which tainted the pleasure of standing in a field with a gun under my arm and a springer spaniel not far from my side.

From Whinbank, glory be, I hit a cock pheasant, although he survived my first barrel and ran strongly as soon as he had fallen. It was Merlin's bird really, for he coursed it all the way from Beck Bottom to the top of Pheasant Hill; then he lost it for a while, but refused to abandon the hunt, and raced this way and that and suddenly pounced in the brambles as I was plodding up the hill behind him. He had pounced on a cock with a broken wing. I hit another bird on the

Rise, although I missed yet another one first. And this bird too was a runner. When Merlin had brought it to me I fell to wondering why, even when I managed to connect with a pheasant, I could not kill it clean.

The answer, of course, at least part of the answer, is that walking-up always produces a fair number of wounded birds, because most of them are shot going away and at angles which make it unlikely that any pellets will strike the head. But today there was a jerkiness in my mounting and a slowness to my swing that was as much to blame. And late-season birds do not loiter on the wing, so that they are often approaching the limits of range when the rough shooter pulls his trigger. Merlin at any rate was the hero of the after-noon, making up for some of his master's shortcomings and loving every minute of it. I sat on the Rise with him and stroked his head and my thoughts turned from my present inability to shoot pheasants dead to more general thoughts on shooting and the difficulties of writing effectively about it.

I think it is the solitariness of angling that makes it such rich matter for authors. I know we go fishing with friends, but essentially we fish alone, with our own thoughts and our own company. And so fishing is a lonely communion with nature, and the sounds of it are a very gentle incantation: the ceaseless murmur of running water, the endless rhythm of the whispering line, the repeated cries of riverside birds. It is a communion with nature; it represents a whole aspect of man's relationship with his world; and so those who read fishing books are instinctively responsive to this implicit theme and entranced by the sounds that so softly reinforce it. And the single figure of the fisherman brings a coherence and a unity to a fishing day, and to the account of it, that the presence of other figures on the bank could only destroy. It is his experience; they are all his thoughts; it is his slow intercourse with the river that absorbs us and holds us bound.

Now today I was shooting alone. More often I shoot in company, when the presence of my friends, though a delight to me, robs my sport of the evocative quality of loneliness. And a shooting day is full of loud noises, with men shouting at dogs and laughing with each other, with cries of 'Over' and 'Back' and 'High lost'; and at the heart of it there is the savage bark of gunshot and the shattering of nature's stillness, which is not how I feel it when I am out shooting, but it is inevitably how it sounds on the page when I sit down and try to write about a day's sport. And shooting is full of sudden and impulsive movement. There are dogs pushing through cover, there are birds beating the air with swift wings and plummeting through the sky. There is the violent motion of guns. I go shooting in search both of excitement and of peace. This is also why I go fishing. But, whereas in writing of fishing it is not difficult to convey how excitement breeds the deeper gift of peace, in my accounts of shooting days the excitement and the rush and the bustle of it all somehow get in the way of the peace and push it from the page.

And there is a sense too in which a shooting day, even a solitary shooting day, is more episodic than a day spent with rod and line. For through every fishing day there runs a river and it flows through all of it and binds the beginning of it to its end. And, if this is no more than a cheap trick of words, there is a fuller and deeper sense in which the differing moods and emotions of a fisherman are more cohesive, more complementary than those of the shooter. I am becoming unbearably pretentious, but I am launched into this topic now and I am determined to pursue it to its end.

The events, the moods and the emotions of a day spent fishing flow like running water, with the same succession from unruffled calm, from the smooth and the unhurried, to the fast, the broken, the turbulent. There is the same succession and there is the same connection. An angler casts his flies; he searches the water in tranquil hope, with a quiet pleasure in the practice of his art. A trout rises and his mood flows faster. He covers the rise and the trout takes his fly. He turns his wrist and the trout is hooked and, while he plays it, while it pulls and runs and splashes and leaps, his blood rushes with it and that tranquil hope of his has become a more urgent thing. But, even as the trout tires and is drawn gently over the net, his mind is reaching calmer waters, his hope subsides to stillness and his heart finds peace. There is a continuity about it all, a sequence, a rhythm, and it runs on through the day, as his feelings flow into each other and are blended one with another and together produce the balance that is the fisherman's peace.

But the episodes of a shooting day, by contrast, bring jagged and unreconciled emotions. The moments of fulfilment are sharp stabs in the sky. There are troughs and valleys between them, there are steep slopes and precipices and sudden falls. And I am being carried away by my own vapid eloquence and it is time that I reined myself in. There is an abruptness in the act of shooting a pheasant or a rabbit or a grouse that sets the act apart from the events and feelings on either side of it. It is a noise, it is an instant, it is an image flashing through the mind. It stands out and it is separate. It is a moment rather than a process. There is discontinuity rather than connection. There is not the emotional (or the aesthetic) consistency that binds together the experiences of a fishing day in so satisfying a unity.

I have lost myself in abstractions. Here are a few concluding thoughts. In fishing, peace belongs to the course of the day; in shooting it comes at the end of the day. Shooting is a more primitive pleasure than fishing, in that it seeks split seconds of satisfaction, whereas the fisherman, in the casting of his fly, in the deceiving of his trout, in the playing and taming of it, seeks a sequence and structure of pleasure that is more complex, more refined and more profound. A caveman would have loved a day's shooting; he would have thought how much better his loud, new weapon was than the darts and the arrows and the axes upon which he had previously been forced to rely. I think he might have taken some convincing that it would not do to shoot pheasants on the ground. But he would have enjoyed himself enormously and, at the end of the day, he would have filled the walls of his cave with images of matched Purdeys and exploding cartridges. Take him next day to the Test or to the Itchen, or to the banks of my Wenning or my Wharfe, teach him the first principles of flyfishing and the first elements of its delight, and he would find the whole experience a crashing bore.

I love the simple pleasures of shooting. I do not think them more suspect than the pleasures of fishing because they are more primitive, and with them come all sorts of ancillary delights that enlarge their appeal to the human spirit. Up on the Rise I found peace of a sort as I sat there with Merlin. It would have been a surer peace if it had not taken me eleven cartridges to put three pheasants in my bag. I thought of one more day at High Park before the ending of January. I smoked for a time under the cloud, and then I went home.

14 January

I bade farewell to another tooth this morning and celebrated by driving to Wigglesworth for the afternoon. On the way I explored the modified contours of my lower gum, searching with my tongue through the deep hollow where there was no longer a tooth, and along the sharp and freshly exposed edge of its bereaved neighbour. I kept grinning at myself in the mirror, to confirm that the new gap towards the back of my mouth was decently inconspicuous. I could see it, but only just, and when I reached Wigglesworth and ran with Merlin up to my fellow guns, already on their way to the first of the afternoon drives, I smiled at them without embarrassment.

I fired one shot in the course of the four drives that followed, at a hen that came slanting fast to my left while I was standing as number five at Crosses. She crumpled and fell. It was a good shot and I was undistressed by the blank drives that surrounded it. Back-end days on small shoots are days of occasional chances. It was a pleasure anyway to watch the few birds that flushed, climbing steeply out of cover and hurtling over other guns; it was a pleasure to see one or two of them throw back their necks and fall; it was a pleasure to watch more of them fly on. Soaking sheets of drizzle blew on the wind. The bag was nineteen pheasants and one guinea fowl.

15 January

I went to fill the hoppers at High Park this afternoon. Those on the Rise were all but empty, but grain is going less quickly now. Digger brought me a dead hen from the gutter. Both its legs were broken and I fancy it was Thursday's bird from North Bank, the one I thought I had missed clean. But it had certainly been shot and it brings the season's total to 47. I shall probably reach 50 after all, although I should prefer to reach it without further reliance on birds that I have wounded without realising it and find only days later when they are too spoilt for the table.

A great skein of grey geese came over, filling the sky with their clamorous calls. I fed Low Park Pond and should like to shoot it once more before the end of the season. I have done less flighting than usual this season, less flighting and more pheasant shooting. And, by the way, the fact that most of the best shooting literature is concerned with wildfowling and coastal marshes and unfrequented ponds, confirms my theory that the solitary figure of the sportsman is a central element in successful writing on shooting and fishing. Once the sportsman becomes part of a crowd, his power has gone out of him.

17 January

Wet snow last night; it settled after a time, but this morning it had gone from all but the hilltops, which were pale grey like the sky above them. The wind has been keen and it has risen throughout the day and is now roaring in the trees. I heard a song thrush singing very quietly this morning and it took me back to the beginnings of this diary almost a year ago.

I shall miss my diary when it is over, though it is well that it is coming to an end. It takes up too much time. If I were a man of leisure, then I should record my life, every year of it, in similar fashion. But, as it is, I have rushed other duties in order to give time to my diary and, even so, I have given it less time than it has needed.

If I were a man of leisure, then every year I could concentrate on a different area of my life. This year has been devoted to sport; next year would concentrate on the life of the soul, and the next year on my professional life, which would bore even me, although I should enjoy being rude about one or two of my colleagues. But I am forgetting that, if I were a man of leisure, I should not be a schoolmaster. The professional bit would have to be in the form of a memoir. But there will be no diary next year, except for the facts and figures and occasional comments that go in my game books. From the first of February I shall turn back into a model schoolmaster, and it will be good to spend more time with books.

19 January

I was to have gone to High Park yesterday with Austin and Toy, but the weather forecast was so foul that we have postponed our last day shooting together until next Tuesday. The morning turned out bright and cold. Rushing up to school I heard a mistle thrush singing loudly and was cheered by the sound.

By noon the rain had come and the wind came with it and the hills turned white. It was a savage, a tearing and a rending wind; to be out in it was thrilling and frightening at the same time. Today the woods were strewn with fallen timber, and there were not only branches on the floor; there were whole trees, and there were shattered trunks pointing jaggedly at the sky and there were gaping holes in the earth where deep roots had surrendered their long association with the soil.

Between rain and sleet the sun came out this afternoon and the air was suddenly mild, the light pale yellow and soft. In the yard sparrows began to gossip. The trees around the house were full of noisy starlings and the cooing of collared doves throbbed monotonously from the churchyard. In the garden the first snowdrops are hanging white above the dark and sodden earth.

19 January

Beaters' day at Wigglesworth. There were few pheasants but the few there were flew high and fast and the beaters shot well. They are often better at shooting pheasants than the men over whom they send them throughout the season. There were only ten pheasants shot, but that was a good proportion of the birds that crossed the line. Merlin loved every minute of it and I enjoyed watching him thrusting into tangled piles of brash and forcing birds onto the wing. Digger had his turn in the afternoon. He worked hard and he flushed pheasants without chasing them. He even managed a messy but serviceable retrieve. Next season he will be a good gundog.

This evening I had the great good fortune to drink part of a bottle of Chateau Palmer '70. To be truthful there were two bottles and the evening ended with malt whisky (just one of them). I do not mention this merely to boast about drinking expensive wine, or to remind my diary that I possess an experienced and educated palate. I mention it in the context of shooting and fishing and my earlier ravings about their relative pleasures. For the Chateau Palmer and the Mortlach produced more than pleasant sensations in my mouth and my nostrils.

They produced a metaphor. To be exact they produced two of them and here they are. Fishing is fine claret, with structure and complexity and elusive nuances of delight. Shooting is malt whisky, more sudden and assertive in its pleasure, less subtle, more startling and with a lingering aftertaste that is commendable but certainly less fine.

I have been concerned recently that my diary is becoming pretentious. I can see now that my concern was wholly justified.

22 January

Out to High Park to fill hoppers. Only those on the Rise were empty and it is chiefly crows now that are emptying them. I saw only three or four pheasants. Doubtless more departed over my boundaries as I walked up the meadow. I shall try to shoot a bird or two with Toy and Austin on Tuesday afternoon, and perhaps on the following Tuesday by myself. Then all but four or five hoppers will come down and my thoughts will turn from shooting pheasants to preserving them, to mending the Larsen trap, to finding or buying or making a funnel trap. It will be time, in short, to declare war on crows and magpies.

24 January

At the end of morning school I grabbed my gun, bundled Merlin into the Land Rover, leapt in myself and felt that it was barely worth it: rushing to High Park with no food in my belly and two bananas in my pocket, with the prospect of one or two shots or none at all and with a heap of work awaiting my return to Sedbergh. It was raining as well.

But the rain stopped. Ragged patches of blue appeared in the sky and the rooks were busy around last year's nests in the middle of Kirkby Stephen. There was vigour in the raw air at High Park and, roused by it, a mistle thrush began to shout somewhere up the fields. Merlin was keen to be hunting and kept snorting in his eagerness. Holly and Bracken were prancing expectantly, and suddenly I knew that I was going to enjoy myself and that it was most certainly worth it, that it was more than worth it, was in fact essential for both sanity and contentment.

We did Top Ground first, or rather I waited in Beck Bottom while Austin and Toy worked their dogs towards me. I ate my bananas and then smoked my pipe and sniffed the air happily, looking at the hazels and at the catkins hanging from them. Right at the end the dogs flushed a cock from the brambles above the pen. I touched it and Austin killed it. Without his shot it would have kept flying.

I did not kill a bird in the course of the afternoon. I fired at four of them and none fell. But today I was strangely unconcerned by my incompetence; I would rather have hit the birds I missed, but I was not angry with myself as I usually am when shooting badly. Perhaps it was the approach of the season's end and a determination, however incompetently I shot, to enjoy what might be my last outing in pursuit of pheasants for eight long months.

And it was lovely this afternoon, with floating grey clouds and the beck shining brown and with the smooth trunks of hazel and the silver trunks of birch gleaming in the pale light. Pheasants flushed with a sudden clatter of alarm and rushed away on strong wings. And though I shot nothing, Austin and Toy had five pheasants between them and I was pleased with the relative abundance of birds so late in the season. There was the pleasure too of watching Merlin course a runner and then pounce on his prey and bring it proudly to hand.

It was Austin's bird, a cock from the Gutter, and it was more than a runner; it was a runner that could flap its wings and flutter from the ground. And it knew just when a flap or two was needed, so that a brief flutter would lift it beyond the reach of Merlin's closing jaws. It had fallen just over the beck and he chased it all the way up Pheasant Hill. Then it turned into Brogdens and came running and hopping and half flying down the wood, with Merlin in hot pursuit and beside himself with delight. Over the beck it came, with a skip and a jump, and Merlin, scorning such daintiness, plunged after it and caught it at last. And then he brought it to me and lay happily at my feet in panting and weary fulfilment.

Today's five birds make 52 for the season. And 52 for the season, for those interested in such figures, makes exactly 40 per cent, which in my opinion is a good return for a narrow strip of land nowhere more than a few hundred yards wide. I may just be able to escape for an hour next Tuesday, to seek a last pheasant or two and a record into the bargain. But I shall not be too bothered if it turns out that I cannot shoot again before the season ends. And next season, with thinned gorse and the beginnings of new cover, with patches of kale and all the experience that comes from longer acquaintance with the same ground, I shall be very disappointed if I cannot improve on 40 per cent. Next summer I shall probably lose 50 birds on their first night in the pen.

It was still full daylight when we came down the fields just after four o'clock. The rooks were still flapping round their rookery as I drove through Kirkby Stephen, assuring myself that it was right for me to shoot hens throughout the season and not to declare them inviolable in January. It is a wet and a cold spot, High Park, and it will always be infested with crows, for, however vigorously I campaign against them, they will flap over my boundaries from neighbouring farms and plunder my nests. I shall do what I can to protect sitting hens, but it will not amount to very much. Mr. G. will check the Larsen trap for me. I shall try to decoy crows to their destruction on a few afternoons in February. I am looking for a funnel trap. And in April I must check my land for nesting corvids. Last year there were none.

31 January

I had hoped to shoot at Skennerskeugh yesterday, but frost came and froze standing water. I had hoped to shoot there, or at Low Park Pond, this evening; but in place of the frost has come rain, torrents of it all day long, so that now every field is a lake and every road a river or at least a stream. And where yesterday the Rawthey and the Lune flowed with a murmur and a ripple between their banks, now there is a wild surge of roaring water. But the forecast is better for tomorrow and I shall spend the afternoon at High Park.

1 February

There are no special reflections for this final entry in my diary, no grand conclusions. At half past four this afternoon I was sitting by the weir gate. There was no longing for fresh insights into the nature of the sportsman's peace. I knew that I felt it and that it was no illusion and that it was good. I sat back and smoked my pipe and enjoyed it.

It was very calm there and the sky was grey. The larches were still. There were three pheasants in my bag, two hens and a resplendent cock. Merlin was lying quietly by my side.

Recommended reading from Merlin Unwin Books

PRIVATE THOUGHTS FROM A SMALL SHOOT
Laurence Catlow

The perfect book for the shooting enthusiast. Catlow's writing is lively, topical and full of practical advice. His new shooting diary records his year as pheasant rearer, gamekeeper, forester, dog-handler and all-round shooting enthusiast. He has robust views on: the right to roam, the nanny state, game cookery, friendship, disobedient dogs and beloved hats. Magical evenings duck flighting, expeditions rabbit shooting, vermin control - all familiar activities to those who run small shoots. This is Catlow at his most intelligent, funny and thought-provoking best.

Hb £17.99

Delightfully illustrated, imparting a wealth of knowledge. - Sporting Gun

---

ONCE A FLYFISHER
Laurence Catlow

An articulate and fascinating book for the thinking angler. Catlow's flyfishing diary has at its heart a quest: to unravel the mystery and the endless fascination of fishing. Wood engravings by Chris Wormell

Hb £17.99

'Witty, illuminating and moving.' - Daily Telegraph

AN ANGLER FOR ALL SEASONS

The Best of H.T. Sheringham

This author is considered by many to be one of the finest fishing writers of the twentieth century. This is a collection of his very best angling essays, written over a period of some 30 years. With equal gusto, he pursues carp, tench, chub, pike, roach, salmon and trout.

Hb £16.95

His manner is wise and humorous, his style delicious in its elegance and wit - Financial Times

---

A HISTORY OF FLYFISHING

Conrad Voss Bark

With a delightful blend of wit and erudition Conrad Voss Bark tells the story of flyfishing, from the Macedonian 'plumes' of 200BC to the hairwing streamers of today. He reviews the sport's great protagonists: Juliana Berners, Robert Venables, Isaak Walton, Charles Cotton, Alfred Ronalds, George Kelson, Skues and Halford, Theodore Gordon, and many more. **£16** Hb **£12.95** Pb

An enchanting and learned book - The Field

THE DRY FLY

Conrad Voss Bark

Conrad Voss Bark traces the development of the dry fly throughout the twentieth century. With his usual lively and incisive style, he brings an important aspect of angling history to life, recording the contribution of men like Halford, Harding, Skues, Lunn, Marinaro, Wulff, Goddard, Clarke, Patterson and Jorgensen. From the Adams and the Bi-visible to the Funneldun and the Upside-down Fly, this is the story of man's quest to tie ever more ingenious flies.

Hb £20

The Secret Carp
Chris Yates

Chris Yates' acclaimed true story of the events of a single day and night beside an English carp lake in high summer. It is, as *The Independent*'s critic wrote, "one of the few books which manages to capture the real joy of fishing in such a way that even the non-angler is seduced". Yates' prose whispers adventure and there are moments of great drama as monster carp disturb the tranquil world of the angler.

Unquestionably the read of the year, indeed of many years. It is a potential classic - The Times   Hb **£17.99**   Tape cassette **£14.99**

The Shooting Man's Bedside Book
Compiled by 'BB'

A brilliant collection of shooting essays from some of the great writers of the past: W.H.Hudson, Richard Jefferies, Peter Scott, J.G. Tregarthen and Gilbert White. Illustrated and compiled by 'BB'.

This book will surely fire the imagination of another generation - Duff Hart-Davis   **£18.95** Hb

Fishing up the Moon
Harry Parsons

Where have the days of heroic fishing adventures gone? Fine writing, epic struggles with giant fish, crushing disappointments - all set against the searing, steamy and turbulent backdrops of Guyana, Kenya, Papua New Guinea and many other exotic locations. Not since Hemingway and Zane Grey have we heard such ripping fishing yarns. Here are tales of Lukanini from the swamps of Guyana, 1000lb Black Marlin off the Great Barrier Reef, and the story of catching the largest Tiger Shark ever recorded, off Kenya.

£17.99 Hb

TROUT & SALMON FLIES OF IRELAND
Peter O'Reilly

A comprehensive guide to the best contemporary fishing flies for Irish waters. Includes trout, salmon and seatrout flies for rivers and loughs. Dry flies, emergers, wet flies, salmon hairwings, etc. This book, in its third printing, includes invaluable tips and advice from many of the flies' inventors. It is a must for all anglers in Ireland. With 26 colour plates illustrating hundreds of the best Irish flies. **£20** Hb

THE FAR FROM COMPLEAT ANGLER
Tom Fort

Tom Fort, fishing correspondent for the *Financial Times*, travels to some exotic far-flung locations in search of trout, salmon, even dourado. He has fun with eels on the Test and takes his rods to Eastern Europe and Brazil. This is a wonderful collection of fishing travels, interspersed with some profound thoughts about the sport of fishing and written by a man with a sharp eye for the absurd and the funny.

£16.99

Few can match his effortless essay style. This book levers fishing writing out of a rut - The Field

All these books are available from bookshops or by direct mail, next-day despatch, from Merlin Unwin Books, Palmers House, 7 Corve Street, Ludlow, Shropshire SY8 1DB, UK.

Credit card orders on:
Tel 01584 877456
Fax 01584 877457

Or you can buy books via our website (www.countrybooksdirect.com) using our secure charging method.